POSITIVIST
REPUBLIC

POSITIVIST REPUBLIC

*Auguste Comte
and the Reconstruction
of American Liberalism,
1865–1920*

GILLIS J. HARP

THE PENNSYLVANIA STATE UNIVERSITY PRESS
University Park, Pennsylvania

Library of Congress Cataloging-in-Publication Data

Harp, Gillis J.
    Positivist republic : Auguste Comte and the reconstruction of
American liberalism, 1865–1920 / Gillis J. Harp.
        p.   cm.
    Includes bibliographical references (p.   ) and index.
    ISBN 0-271-01041-X
    1. United States—Intellectual life—1865–1920.   2. Liberalism
—United States—History—19th century.   3. Liberalism—United
States—History—20th century.   4. Positivism.   5. Comte, Auguste,
1798–1857—Influence.   I. Title.
    E169.1.H2725   1995
    973.8—dc20   93-30385
                                                                                              CIP

Published by The Pennsylvania State University Press,
University Park, PA 16802-1003

It is the policy of The Pennsylvania State University Press to use acid-free paper
for the first printing of all clothbound books. Publications on uncoated stock
satisfy the minimum requirements of American National Standard for Information Sciences—Permanence of Paper for Printed Library Materials, ANSI
Z39.48–1984.

For my parents

". . . although the virtues are reckoned by some people to be genuine and honourable when they are related only to themselves and are sought for no other end, even then they are puffed up and proud, and so are to be accounted vices rather than virtues. For just as it is not something derived from the physical body itself that gives life to that body, but something above it, so it is not something that comes from man, but something above man, that makes his life blessed."

—Augustine, *City of God,*
Book 19, chapter 25

CONTENTS

ACKNOWLEDGMENTS

I have benefited enormously from the kind assistance of numerous scholars in researching and writing this book. This study began as a seminar paper on Lester Frank Ward for Dorothy Ross at the University of Virginia. I remember vividly how impressed I was then as a graduate student with Ross's erudition and insight. Years later, I remain a keen admirer of her work, especially after reading her magisterial *Origins of American Social Science*. Dorothy Ross offered cogent criticism of earlier drafts of this book and whatever is valuable in the present volume is probably the product of her salutary influence. Robert D. Cross also contributed substantially to the initial stages of this project with characteristic good humor and common sense.

Charles Cashdollar, R. Jeffrey Lustig, and Thomas Bender all read the entire manuscript, made countless helpful suggestions, and were instrumental in helping me not "lose sight of the forest for the trees." Several other colleagues have furnished constructive criticism on individual chapters, including John Zucchi (Chapter 1), Robert Bannister and Ian Dowbiggin (Chapter 6), and Robert Morrison (Introduction and Conclusion). W. Carey McWilliams and Michael Wayne also deserve my thanks for sound advice and encouragment at key points. My editor at Penn State Press, Peter J. Potter, has been consistently supportive and helpful. I am, of course, solely responsible for any errors of fact or interpretation that may mar the following pages.

I also thank the Senate of the University of Prince Edward Island for a grant that enabled me to complete my research and the Research and Graduate Studies Office at Acadia University that covered unforeseen expenses near the end of the project. The United States Embassy in Ottawa helped defray some travel expenses through their Grants in

American Studies program. The interlibrary loan departments at Alder-man Library, University of Virginia, and Erindale College, University of Toronto, saved me time and expense by locating and obtaining some very obscure nineteenth-century printed sources. Finally, Carolina Pickkers cheerfully typed most of the manuscript in short order, for which I am very grateful.

On a personal level, I owe more than I can say to my wife, Barbara Tychsen Harp, who has been a real-life model of the kind of "feminine altruism" that Comte extolled. This book is dedicated to my parents who encouraged my interest in history from an early age and inspired my faith in the power of ideas.

Portions of Chapter 2 originally appeared, in somewhat different form, in *Church History* (vol. 60, no. 4, 1991). Portions of Chapter 4 originally appeared in the *Hayes Historical Journal: A Journal of the Gilded Age* (vol. 9, no. 3, 1990), published by Rutherford B. Hayes Presidential Center, Fremont, Ohio. A much condensed version of Chapter 6 originally appeared in *Historical Reflections / Réflexions Historiques* (vol. 15, no. 3, 1988).

INTRODUCTION

This book explores a neglected chapter in American intellectual life: the shared debt of a diverse group of Americans to the thought of the French philosopher Auguste Comte (Isidore-Auguste-Marie-François-Xavier Comte) (1798–1857). While countless intellectuals in Europe and the Americas read or were otherwise influenced by Comte's work,[1] comparatively few in nineteenth-century America identified themselves explicitly as Comtean positivists.[2] Although they did not all agree about what made one a true positivist, together they represented a definable, if

1. L. L. Bernard and Jessie Bernard, *Origins of American Sociology: The Social Science Movement in the United States* (New York: Crowell, 1943); Charles D. Cashdollar, *The Transformation of Theology, 1830–1890: Positivism and Protestant Thought in Britain and America* (Princeton: Princeton University Press, 1989); D. G. Charlton, *Positivist Thought in France During the Second Empire, 1852-1870* (New York: Oxford University Press, 1959); Richmond L. Hawkins, *Auguste Comte and the United States, 1816–1853* (Cambridge: Harvard University Press, 1936); Richmond L. Hawkins, *Positivism in the United States, 1853–1861* (Cambridge: Harvard University Press, 1938); Christopher Kent, *Brains and Numbers: Elitism, Comtism and Democracy in Mid-Victorian England* (Toronto: University of Toronto Press, 1978); John Edwin McGee, *A Crusade for Humanity: The History of Organised Positivism in England* (London: Watts, 1931); Woodbridge, Riley, "La philosophie française en Amérique," *Revue philosophique de la France et de l'étranger* 87 (1919): 369–423; W. M. Simon, *European Positivism in the Nineteenth Century: An Essay in Intellectual History* (Ithaca: Cornell University Press, 1963).

2. For the purposes of this study, the term *positivism* stands for a philosophical position that embraces a wide spectrum. At one end of the spectrum are the orthodox or sectarian positivists who accepted all of Comte's scientific, social, and religious ideas. At the other end are strict empiricists such as John Stuart Mill, who, though influenced by Comte's methodology and philosophy of history, rejected his social blueprint and the Religion of Humanity. One might also identify a third group somewhere in the middle of the spectrum that was outside the official, sectarian circle, but had been profoundly affected by Comtean thought and did retain some of his political and religious ideas. I have chosen in the

changing and evolving, community of discourse. It is this Comtean community and its initial offspring that are the main subjects of this book.

The intention here, however, is not simply to demonstrate Comte's influence on a small circle of American disciples and fellow-travelers. Rather, the following analysis seeks to show how various individuals employed Comtean language to address the philosophical, social, religious, and political questions of the day. In the process, they recast Comte in a characteristically American idiom. By itself, this "translation," if you like, of Comte is an interesting story and serves to illuminate how essentially foreign intellectual systems have been integrated into native discourse. More to the point, however, the story of such a positivist "connection" reveals how different intellectuals forged, with Comtean tools, a powerful critique of Gilded Age society and politics.

While the impact of positivism upon some American intellectuals has been noted in general terms, this study seeks to demonstrate clearly a few of the concrete ways in which a distinctively Comtean influence actually functioned.[3] American Comtists were significant participants in the reconstruction of liberal ideology that occupied the last portion of the previous century and the first part of our own. To be sure, some of our subjects participated in this project more significantly than did others, but, as a collective, they provide valuable insights into how the dominant political language of nineteenth-century America was ultimately transformed.

While concentrating on this central argument, the following chapters also develop several other, related themes that cast a different light on the intellectual history of the Gilded Age and Progressive Era. For one, our Comtean "connection" affords a unique perspective on radical religion or Freethought in the United States. As philosophical radicals in nineteenth-century America, Comtists were not alone but they did speak with a distinctive voice. Certainly the ritualism and social conservatism of the orthodox element contrasted vividly with the approach of most American religious liberals.[4] So, too, this study documents how a kind

---

following pages to focus almost exclusively on American intellectuals who fall into either the first or the third category.

3. See books by Hawkins and Bernard cited above. Also, see Arthur Lipow, *Authoritarian Socialism in America: Edward Bellamy and the Nationalist Movement* (Berkeley and Los Angeles: University of California Press, 1982); R. Jeffrey Lustig, *Corporate Liberalism: The Origins of Modern American Political Theory, 1890–1920* (Berkeley and Los Angeles: University of California Press, 1982).

4. See Gillis J. Harp, " 'The Church of Humanity': New York's Worshipping Positivists," *Church History* 60 (1991): 508–23.

of fringe reform discourse moved from the cultural margins to the intellectual mainstream, as it mixed with and drew upon different American political traditions and different features of Victorian culture. This cultural and social class dimension has been pursued fruitfully in studies of Comtists outside of the United States. Christopher Kent, for instance, explains the "often misunderstood appeal of Comtism in mid-Victorian England" in these terms: "It was not the exotic aberration of a coterie of eccentrics but rather a comprehensive ideology remarkably harmonious with certain established English currents of thought and remarkably well suited to the needs of a middle-class intellectual elite. It not only legitimized their pretensions to intellectual authority but also provided a powerful ideological solvent for social irritants to those who were ready to entertain fairly radical notions of social change for essentially conservative ends—a sort of prospective conservatism rather than the more common retrospective variety."[5] The English and American experiences were, of course, profoundly different but Comtism does appear to have sometimes played a similar role in Gilded Age America, while an examination of Comte's American following can also furnish insights into this same sphere of class and culture.

Our story begins with a small cell of earnest sectarians meeting in the heavily draped parlors of several New York bourgeois. Hampered by the sectarian spirit and ritualism of Comtean orthodoxy, this initial group rarely broke out of the cultural margins. A revisionist party emerged from this metropolitan coterie, however, led by Thaddeus Wakeman and others. With the splintering of this original group, the narrative follows the activities of individual members, but eventually focuses upon a few who had only an indirect connection with the first circle of disciples. It is through the activities and writings of these latter individuals that one is afforded a new window on the internal structure of late nineteenth-century reform thought. Long before the close of the century, Comtean influences were well established in some American circles. In the writings of Lester Frank Ward and others, one recognizes Comtean categories and assumptions at work, affecting the birth and development of American sociology and, chiefly through Ward and Herbert Croly, these make a powerful contribution to Progressivism.

The following chapters seek to demonstrate how, though "Americanized" by its interaction with the political culture of American Whiggery and with the radical and reform politics of the Gilded Age, Comtean positivism helped direct the development of a new liberal discourse by the early twentieth century. In the end, it helped to reshape American

5. Kent, *Brains and Numbers*, xiii.

liberalism in some important ways. For many, it encouraged an interventionist bent, a confidence in the ability to reform; for most, it fostered a faith in technocratic elites; and, in general, it nurtured a statist or corporatist bent within American liberalism that continues to play a central role in the nation's political discourse. Therefore, by the time of the First World War, the character and shape of the new liberalism owed more to the Comtean tradition than most analysts have previously recognized.[6]

6. Lustig is the exception here; he does appear to recognize the larger significance of Comte's influence.

CHAPTER ONE

Comte and the Crisis of Gilded Age Liberalism

To sum up the matter: the theological and metaphysical philosophies are now disputing with each other the task of reorganizing society, although the task is really too hard for their united efforts; it is between these schools only that any struggle still exists in this respect. The positive philosophy has, up to the present, intervened in the contest only in order to criticize both schools; and it has accomplished this task so well as to discredit them entirely. Let us put it in a condition to play an active part, without paying any further attention to debates that have become useless. We must complete the vast intellectual operation commenced by Bacon, Descartes, and Galileo, by furnishing the positive philosophy with the system of general ideas that is destined to prevail henceforth, and for an indefinite future, among the human race. The revolutionary crisis which harasses civilized peoples will then be at an end.

—Auguste Comte, *Cours de philosophie positive*

LIBERALISM HAS DEFINED AMERICAN political culture for two centuries. From the Early National period to the present, the American ideological spectrum has been considerably narrower than that of Western Europe. Since the ratification of the Constitution, most Americans have seen the principles of individual property rights, limited government and majority rule as foundational.[1] To posit this fundamental consensus in American political life is neither to celebrate it nor deny the existence of competing discourses. The ideological consensus was never perfect, and different groups often employed shared liberal rhetoric to serve different ends. Moreover, in the past two decades, intellectual

1. These points are stressed by Thomas P. Peardon in his introduction to Locke's *Second Treatise of Government* (Indianapolis: Bobbs-Merrill, 1952), xi–ix.

historians have shown that American political thought was not so mono-
lithically Lockean as Louis Hartz believed in the 1950s.[2] The Atlantic
republican or civic humanist tradition did play a significant role in
shaping American political ideas in the eighteenth and nineteenth centuries. Nevertheless, the classical republican perspective was clearly in
gradual decline following the American Revolution. In short, as Daniel
Walker Howe has noted, "Hartz has been supplemented rather than
consigned to oblivion."[3]

In our own era, political scientists have shown that Americans continue
to enjoy greater agreement about political and economic fundamentals
than do Western Europeans.[4] Despite (apparently successful) attempts to
redefine "liberal" as a term of opprobrium during the 1988 presidential
election campaign, the partisan dialogue rarely extends beyond the
liberal mainstream. In fact, most self-styled "conservatives" in American
politics today are at most classical liberals who have had to accept the
basic outlines of the modern welfare state. Therefore, the liberal consensus that prevails today is no longer characterized by the libertarian,
laissez-faire assumptions of the nineteenth century. Sometime between
Andrew Jackson and Lyndon Johnson, American liberalism underwent a
profound change.

Most historians identify this critical transformation as having occurred
between 1880 and 1920. Although gaps remain, the story of this development has been filled out considerably by recent studies.[5] At the close of
the Civil War and with the explosive growth of American industry,
some theorists returned with a vengeance to the established verities of
classical political economy. From E. L. Godkin, to David A. Wells, to
Grover Cleveland, it is easy to find liberals of the Manchester School in
positions of cultural influence or political power during the Gilded Age.
A few went as far as to reject American exceptionalism outright and
conclude that Malthus's dire predictions now did apply to the New
World. Meanwhile, others with reform-oriented views attempted to

2. Louis Hartz, *The Liberal Tradition in America: An Interpretation of American Political Thought Since the Revolution* (New York: Harcourt, Brace and World, 1955), esp. chap. 1.

3. "European Sources of Political Ideas in Jeffersonian America," *Reviews in American History* 10 (1982): 42.

4. Hartz, *Liberal Tradition*, 10–12.

5. Dorothy Ross, "Liberalism," in *Encyclopedia of American Political History: Studies of the Principal Movements and Ideas*, ed. Jack P. Greene (New York: Scribner, 1984), 2:750–63. See also, R. Jeffery Lustig, *Corporate Liberalism: The Origins of Modern American Political Theory, 1890–1920* (Berkeley and Los Angeles: University of California Press, 1982); Martin J. Sklar, *The Corporate Reconstruction of American Capitalism, 1890–1916* (Cambridge: Cambridge University Press, 1988); Alan Trachtenberg, *The Incorporation of America: Culture and Society in the Gilded Age* (New York: Hill and Wang, 1982).

push antebellum liberalism in a more humanitarian direction. These critics were a diverse lot, composed of trade unionists, Populist farmers, Single-taxers, clerical reformers, academics, and socialists. In attempting to remain loyal to egalitarian principles, Gilded Age radicals proposed new cooperative economic structures.[6] They were especially concerned about protecting the economic independence of average Americans and they gradually grew less reluctant to use state power to secure what the free market had not produced.

By the end of World War I, a new sort of liberalism emerged, then, that had been influenced by these dissenting voices of the Gilded Age even if it was not in complete harmony with them. Like Manchester liberalism, it was more consumerist than humanistic in its social ethos and it accepted as natural a large number of dependent wage earners in the economy. Unlike classical liberalism, however, this new element believed large concentrations of corporate power were inevitable, while they affirmed the need for sustained government intervention in the private economy. From some of the elitist reformers of the late nineteenth century, the new liberals also borrowed a technocratic or managerial view of government, reflecting their increased confidence in business and scientific expertise.[7]

Such was the new liberalism that solidified in the early twentieth century; but most of the following study is concerned with the transitional era when these new ideas were first being formed and articulated. The Gilded Age was a period of flux that provides an opportunity to identify and examine the different ideological strands as they were woven together into a new liberal garment. This "reweaving" or reconstruction of liberal ideology is critical to our understanding of American culture after the Civil War. The main purpose of this work is to explore how this reconstruction occurred by highlighting one element that played a central role in the process.

Historian David A. Hollinger has suggested that one of the best ways to conceptualize the work of the intellectual historian is to understand it as the identification and examination of discreet "communities of discourse." These communities are defined, says Hollinger, by certain shared questions: "questions are the dynamisms whereby membership in a community of discourse is established, renewed, and sometimes terminated."[8] The questions selected by particular social groups, be they

6. Ross, "Liberalism," 756.
7. Ibid., 758ff.
8. "Historians and the Discourse of Intellectuals," in *New Directions in American Intellectual History*, ed. John Higham and Paul K. Conkin (Baltimore: Johns Hopkins University Press, 1979), 43.

clergymen or mechanics, and the common answers these individuals formulate, reveal much about these groups and about the larger culture in which they function. Conversely, questions not asked and answers ignored or ruled out of order can also tell one a lot about the thought of a particular aggregate.

Accordingly, this study begins with an attempt to identify the boundaries of a specific community. This community was an informal network of late nineteenth-century American intellectuals who reflected upon and wrote about social and political subjects either as professionals (i.e., academics, journalists, bureaucrats, or clerics) or as amateur commentators. At least three formative questions may be identified as having defined this large community of discourse. These three defining questions demarcate a fairly large body of Anglo-American intellectuals during the last third of the nineteenth century. This group, then, constitutes the broader milieu within which the subjects of the following chapters worked.

The first of these defining questions was a fundamental philosophical problem that had broad implications for both religion and social theory. After the Civil War, many intellectuals sought a new, rigorously naturalistic foundation for their worldview, one not tied to the pious Common Sense realism of the past. Antebellum science had been built upon a naive Baconian empiricism, Scottish Common Sense philosophy, and Anglo-American Protestantism.[9] The adherents of the Common or Moral Sense School wanted the external world to confirm their preconceived notions of divine order; practicing science and philosophical reflection were supposed to stimulate religious piety. Their empiricism made them skittish of hypothetical arguments and often restricted them to simply assembling facts and pursuing classification. The Protestantism of antebellum scientists and moral philosophers relied heavily upon natural theology. These three props that had secured American science and philosophy were kicked out by a series of important discoveries and developments between 1859 and 1880.[10]

Although Darwinian evolution was by no means the sole disruptive element, it alone undermined three long-held assumptions about the

9. Theodore D. Bozeman, *Protestants in an Age of Science: The Baconian Ideal and Antebellum American Religious Thought* (Chapel Hill: University of North Carolina Press, 1977); George H. Daniels, *American Science in the Age of Jackson* (New York: Columbia University Press, 1968); Charles D. Cashdollar, *The Transformation of Theology, 1830–1890: Positivism and Protestant Thought in Britain and America* (Princeton: Princeton University Press, 1989).

10. James Turner, *Without God, Without Creed: the Origins of Unbelief in America* (Baltimore: Johns Hopkins University Press, 1985), esp. part 2.

natural realm: a stable, created order was now viewed as changing and highly competitive; fixed species were replaced by evolving species that could as easily become extinct as flourish; and (Darwin's most important contribution) teleological assumptions were discarded for a process of "natural selection" that was random and patently amoral. Darwinism, of course, worked in tandem with other philosophical schools of European origin to break down antebellum scientific and philosophical orthodoxy. The positivism of Comte, Spencer, and Mill rejected wholesale the Christian assumptions of the Scottish School, while they dismissed as unscientific the consideration of "ultimate causes." Meanwhile, German idealism bolstered the historicism of many Darwinists. Morris Cohen aptly described the situation after 1860:

> The storm which broke the stagnant air and aroused many American minds from this [Antebellum] dogmatic torpor came with the controversy over evolution which followed the publication of Lyell's *Geology*, Darwin's *Origin of Species*, and Spencer's *First Principles*. The evolutionary philosophy was flanked on the left by the empirical or positivistic philosophy of Comte, Mill, Lewes, Buckle, and Bain, and on the right by the dialectic evolutionism of Hegel. . . . With these the history of the modern period of American philosophy begins.[11]

Although these three comparatively new schools of thought differed substantially from each other, their cumulative effect was destructive of the pious philosophies of the day. Indeed, it seemed that virtually everything was now exposed to an unrelenting historicist and scientistic analysis, and the paradigm that underlay the new skepticism was a narrowly naturalistic one.[12]

Yet in the wake of their disenchantment with older orthodoxies, most American intellectuals still conceived of truth as unitary and simply sought a more secure scientific foundation for the static, singular truth they continued to assume. Nearly all cringed at philosophical pluralism and moral relativism; they sought a way out of the debilitating doubt and far-reaching skepticism into which their loss of Christian faith could lead them. Accordingly, because of their persistent faith in absolutes, the

11. "Later Philosophy" in *Cambridge History of American Literature*, ed. William P. Trent et al. (Cambridge: Cambridge University Press, 1943), 3:229–30.

12. See Cashdollar, *Transformation*, esp. chap. 5.

discourse of many Gilded Age intellectuals remained essentially religious, though heterodox in character.[13]

Although the philosophical basis for Christianity was discredited for most members of this community, they still viewed religion as a central component of human nature. American thinkers such as Horace Bushnell, Newman Smyth, and William James all broke with traditional evangelicalism (Bushnell in a far more measured way than Smyth or James), yet all continued to affirm man's religious character.[14] Liberal theologian Borden Parker Bowne wrote in 1887 that, in dismissing religion in general, "Mankind is imposing a spiritual gag-rule on itself, denying its own nature."[15] And liberals and skeptics were not only concerned about internal or psychological questions. The external influence that traditional religious belief had exercised made many uneasy when they contemplated a society without Christian faith. Most considered religiously sanctioned mores an important societal "glue." By the turn of the century, some were reassured that popular morality had other, institutional bulwarks that would continue to promote higher values and encourage correct behavior. Still, these same individuals conceded that the larger significance or moral weight that theism had lent to personal decisions would be sadly lacking in the future.[16] In short, these intellectuals asked how one could preserve the salutary social function religion had traditionally served, without the Christian theology that had undergirded it.

Clearly, this concern for new naturalistic philosophical foundations extended into the realm of social and political thought. After the Civil War, the antebellum reform impulse needed to be translated into new scientistic terms. In particular, the meliorist or interventionist ethic of the antebellum Whigs required a different rationale in the wake of Darwin et al. American Whigs had traditionally drawn their reformism from several sources. From evangelical Protestantism they borrowed an individualistic perfectionism and their postmillennial vision. Equally, they were indebted to American revivalism for their ultraism and moralism. The Scottish School appears also to have contributed a communitar-

13. David D. Hall, "The Victorian Connection," in *Victorian America*, ed. Daniel Walker Howe (Philadelphia: University of Pennsylvania Press, 1976), 81; D. H. Meyer, "American Intellectuals and the Victorian Crisis of Faith," in *Victorian America*, ed. Howe, 61–62; Paul A. Carter, *The Spiritual Crisis of the Gilded Age* (DeKalb: Northern Illinois University Press, 1971), 18–19.

14. Sidney E. Ahlstrom, *A Religious History of the American People* (New Haven: Yale University Press, 1972), 781–83.

15. Cited by D. H. Meyer in "Victorian Crisis," 69.

16. Ibid., 71.

ian ethos and a philosophical conservatism to most Whigs. Finally, the social organicism of the Whigs is partly attributable to the Romantic idealism of the early nineteenth century.[17]

This rather eclectic edifice was toppled by the intellectual developments outlined above. In particular, the sentimental, humanitarian idealism of the pre–Civil War period was transformed, if not repudiated, during the 1860s and 1870s. George Fredrickson has shown how the war itself contributed to the demise of the separatist, moral reform movements of antebellum America. In 1878, Francis Parkman reflected that while "conviction and enthusiasm, with very little besides, served the purpose of the abolition agitators," the reformers of the Gilded Age "must be tempered with judgement and armed with knowledge."[18] Accordingly, reformist intellectuals were searching for a new theoretical foundation for their social vision after Appomattox.

A second, related question animated the intellectuals who are the subject of this study. As the corporate economy grew dramatically, many asked how economic progress could be reconciled with social order and a concern for the commonweal. American values were being undermined, some felt, while "the incorporation of America" advanced.[19] The new corporate economy did not appear to be producing social stability. Increased labor strife and violent swings in the business cycle were disquieting developments that seemed to accompany the rise of the giant corporations. First came the panic of 1873 and its subsequent recession. The nation had earlier seen its share of financial panics and depressions but the growing proportion of dependent wage earners in the economy after the Civil War made these downturns far more devastating. Then followed the Great Railroad Strike of 1877 with its alarming labor violence. As middle- and upper-class Americans blamed foreign radicals and domestic malcontents, things got worse. The labor unrest of the 1880s culminated in what some have termed the Great Upheaval of 1886.[20] Perhaps most infamous that year was Chicago's Haymarket Riot. As a result of this incident, labor leaders were often portrayed in the popular press as bomb-throwing anarchists. Nor did the conflict soon subside; the 1890s saw continued violence, especially during the Homestead and Pullman strikes of 1892 and 1894 respectively.

17. Daniel W. Howe, *The Political Culture of the American Whigs* (Chicago: University of Chicago Press, 1979), chaps. 7, 9. See also chaps. 1 and 2.

18. Cited by George Fredrickson, *The Inner Civil War: Northern Intellectuals and the Crisis of the Union* (New York: Harper and Row, 1965), 202.

19. Trachtenberg, *Incorporation*, 3ff.

20. Ibid., 70–71.

Short of overturning property relations, analysts asked how economic modernization and social peace could both be secured.

Beyond this problem of industrial strife, lay a more fundamental question about the survival of liberal democracy. A comparatively "free market" had produced huge concentrations of capital that were not responsive to the popular will. This problem underlay the monopoly issue that dominated American politics between 1880 and 1917. Some intellectuals, and not only the most radical, viewed the giant trusts as subversive of a democratic and egalitarian society. The emerging economic order looked as though it might not be compatible with American political principles and republican institutions.[21] Certainly, much of the formalism and individualism of classical liberalism looked increasingly outmoded.

While some emphasized the threat of the unregulated trusts to liberal democracy, others stressed the deleterious effect urbanization was having. In describing the role railroads played in the rise of large cities, Charles Francis Adams, Jr., commented:

> The dense aggregation of mankind may be said to necessarily result in an upper class which wants to be governed, and in a lower class which has to be governed. The extreme of luxury and the extreme of misery are equally fatal to public virtues. . . . To hope for a pure government by the people at large while ignorance and corruption are the ruling forces in these [urban] centers, is as futile as it would be to look for healthy members where the vitals are diseased. This it is which really constitutes that problem of great cities which so confounds the friends of popular government.[22]

When Adams made these remarks in 1871, the huge influx of non-British immigrants was just beginning. The unparalleled urban growth of the Gilded Age was a product of both industrialization (including the railroads Adams stressed) and the arrival of millions of European immigrants. Urban life represented an unsettling, if at times exhilarating, change for many Americans accustomed to the simpler rhythms of an agrarian lifestyle. Squalor and urban crime greeted most of the new city dwellers. An increasingly complex urban society was, in short,

21. Ross, "Liberalism," 759.
22. "The Era of Change," in *Late Nineteenth-Century American Liberalism: Representative Selections, 1880–1900*, ed. Louis Filler (New York: Bobbs-Merrill, 1962), 82.

displacing a nation of traditional "island communities."[23] The recent immigrants who filled the burgeoning cities made them seem all the more foreboding to the native-born. By 1900, immigrants represented forty percent of the total population of a dozen of the nation's biggest cities. Commented Vida Scudder: "Cleavage of classes, cleavage of race, cleavage of faiths! An inextricable confusion!"[24]

Accordingly, labor violence, corporate concentration and urbanization were all viewed as undermining republican principles and contributing to the emergence of social divisions. The advent of an industrial class society in the United States was profoundly disturbing for many because it suggested that America might not, in fact, escape Europe's social turmoil; believers in American exceptionalism were given serious pause. Walt Whitman was moved in 1879 to reflect: "If the United States, like the countries of the Old World, are also to grow vast crops of poor, desperate, dissatisfied, nomadic, miserably-waged populations, . . . then our republican experiment, notwithstanding all of its surface successes, is at heart an unhealthy failure."[25]

The third and final question that defined the community of discourse under discussion involved its social position and its members' self-understanding. The broad social and intellectual forces just outlined were also producing a "crisis of professional authority" in late Victorian America. Social workers, academics, amateur social theorists and reformers were all involved in the process of professionalization.[26] The emerging professional status of academics and civil servants, for example, was based upon their asserted technical expertise, their esoteric knowledge and skill. Thomas Haskell stresses that, as the economy underwent modernization, the interdependence of society's various component parts was increasingly recognized. This recognition of interdependence meant that older, simpler, moralistic explanations were slowly discarded in favor of a multicausal, historicist approach. Beyond boosting the assertions of expertise of some, professionalization also represented a form of membership control or even monopoly. Different groups supported different kinds of professionalization for different reasons. Members of the old gentry often supported civil service reform in order to bolster the declining political authority of their

23. Robert H. Wiebe, *The Search for Order, 1877–1920* (New York: Hill and Wang, 1967), 44ff.

24. Cited in Samuel P. Hays, *The Response to Industrialism, 1885–1914* (Chicago: University of Chicago Press, 1957), 95, 38.

25. Cited by Trachtenberg, *Incorporation*, 70.

26. Thomas L. Haskell, *The Emergence of Professional Social Science: The American Social Science Association and the Nineteenth-Century Crisis of Authority* (Urbana: University of Illinois Press, 1977), 19, 26–27.

own class. Pioneer social scientists pressed their professional claims against church-affiliated moral philosophers and amateur reformers. Regardless of their varied motives, champions of specialization were nearly all concerned about what role educated elites would play in the new sociopolitical order.[27]

What general philosophical foundation should social thought build upon? How can economic growth and social order be secured simultaneously? What role should intellectuals (social scientists in particular) play in the new industrial democracy? These questions were being asked by many within the Anglo-American intellectual community in the last third of the nineteenth century.[28] Traditionally, historians have identified Darwinism, English positivist empiricism, and German idealism as the main foreign sources Americans tapped to answer these seminal questions.[29] Given the more complete and complex view of nineteenth-century thought provided by recent studies, however, such an interpretation is now patently myopic. This conventional view has, with its narrow focus, tended to ignore other important discourses.[30] One of the most neglected currents in the American context has been the positivism of Auguste Comte. American Comtists, as the following pages will show, represented an important part of the larger community just defined. They were distinguished as a group by the Comtean answers they advanced to these same formative questions.

Comte's philosophy of science and his social theory spoke in a singular way to the questions shared by many Gilded Age intellectuals. Indeed, the three defining questions or concerns just outlined, in some respects,

27. Ibid., 87. See also chap. 5.

28. David D. Hall, "Victorian Connection," 88–94. See also Meyer, "Victorian Crisis," 68–73.

29. See, for example, Richard Hofstadter, *Social Darwinism in American Thought* (Boston: Beacon, 1955); Eric F. Goldman, *Rendezvous with Destiny: A History of Modern American Reform* (New York: Knopf, 1961), esp. 94ff; Cynthia Eagle Russett, *Darwin in America: The Intellectual Response, 1865–1912* (San Francisco: Freeman, 1976).

Ralph Gabriel is one of the few historians who did not simply dismiss Comte's American influence. Indeed, he even makes note of the New York sectarians in this regard. Nevertheless, Gabriel focuses more on O.B. Frothingham's book, *The Religion of Humanity*, and concludes "How much beyond the name the new humanism [in Gilded Age religion] owed to the French philosopher is difficult to say. . . . That his contribution to the movement was important is evident." See Gabriel, *The Course of American Democratic Thought: An Intellectual History Since 1815* (New York: Ronald Press, 1956), chap. 15, esp. 194–95.

30. Fred Matthews has made this point in *Quest for an American Sociology: Robert E. Park and the Chicago School* (Montreal: McGill-Queen's University Press, 1977), 27. See also William F. Fine, *Progressive Evolutionism and American Sociology, 1880–1920* (n.p.: UMI Research Press, 1979), 144.

constituted the very core of Comte's system. The animating force behind much of Comte's work was his determination to resolve what he viewed as the essentially philosophical crisis of his day. It is important to stress that Comte's historical milieu was early nineteenth-century France under the Bourbon Restoration. His homeland's recent past had been extraordinarily turbulent. Before Comte was eighteen, he had lived under at least four different regimes, as France attempted to reestablish political order in the wake of the Great Revolution of 1789. Nor did tranquillity return with the Bourbons. During the first half of the century, the country staggered from one political crisis to the next. This political instability was to some degree mirrored in intellectual circles. The Restoration era, for instance, was a period of intellectual ferment. Bertier de Sauvigny speaks of its "strongly marked characteristics of individualism, almost of anarchy." "In fact," he explains, "there was no one directive centre [for literature], no arbiter of taste—rather, there were so many of them that they cancelled themselves out by their very multiplicity."[31]

Viewing this political and intellectual tumult, Comte became convinced of the pressing need for a methodical plan of social reconstruction.[32] With utopian socialist Saint-Simon (for whom Comte served as secretary between 1817 and 1824), Comte concluded that social and political systems were founded upon sets of ideas. When these belief systems crumbled, as Comte believed had occurred during the French Revolution, the social and poltical order would naturally experience dislocation. As he explained in the opening pages of his monumental *Cours de philosophie positive* (1830–1842), most contemporary problems arose from the prevailing intellectual chaos:

> It can not be necessary to prove to anybody who reads this work that Ideas govern the world, or throw it into chaos; in other words, that all social mechanism rests upon Opinions. The great political and moral crisis that societies are now undergoing is shown by a rigid analysis to arise out of intellectual anarchy. While stability in fundamental maxims is the first condition of

31. Guillaume de Bertier de Sauvigny, *The Bourbon Restoration*, trans. Lynn M. Case (Philadelphia: University of Pennsylvania Press, 1966), 329.

32. Levy-Bruhl agrees that the French Revolution "dominates the period in which the positive philosophy appeared." Nearly every French intellectual "put the same question to themselves: 'What social institutions should be established after the Revolution?' . . . It is this problem in various forms which preoccupies Chateaubriand as well as Fourier and Saint-Simon, and Joseph deMaistre as well as Cousin and Comte." See *The Philosophy of Auguste Comte* (New York: Putnam, 1903), 2.

genuine social order, we are suffering under an utter disagreement which may be called universal. Till a certain number of general ideas can be acknowledged as a rallying point of social doctrine, the nations will remain in a revolutionary state, whatever palliatives may be devised; and their institutions can be only provisional. But whenever the necessary agreement on first principles can be obtained, appropriate institutions will issue from them, without shock or resistance; for the causes of disorder will have been arrested by the mere fact of the agreement. It is in this direction that those must look who desire a natural and regular, a natural state of society. [33]

Positivism represented, then, the one sure way to end this period of uncertainty and upheaval: "The Positive Philosophy offers the only solid basis for that Social Reorganization which must succeed the critical condition in which the most civilized nations are now living."[34] Herein lay the most important and practical feature of the positivist system for Comte.

Because of the importance he attached to the instrumental role of ideas, Comte began the *Cours* by addressing epistemological questions. What Ted Benton terms the seventeenth century's "systematic onslaught on traditional forms of knowledge" continued at a more advanced level in the early nineteenth century.[35] Classical empiricists such as Francis Bacon and John Locke had contended their knowledge was the product only of direct experience via the physical senses; there were no disembodied, ideal "things in themselves." In some respects, Comte stood within this empiricist tradition, and he viewed much of his work as a development of Bacon's ideas, in particular. Hence he declared in the *Cours*: "All good intellects have repeated, since Bacon's time, that there can be no real knowledge but that which is based on observed facts. This is incontestable, in our present advanced stage." Like the empiricist, the positivist restricted himself only to observable phenomenon but Comte viewed this as a liberating limitation. "The nature of beings, and the

33. Auguste Comte, *The Positive Philosophy of Auguste Comte*, trans. Harriet Martineau (New York: Blanchard, 1855), 36. Abbreviated *Positive Philosophy* below. I have chosen to quote here and elsewhere from the most popular American edition of Harriet Martineau's famous translation / abridgement of the six-volume *Cours*. Though a few of the subjects of the following chapters (such as David Croly and Lester Frank Ward) read Comte in the original French, most stayed with Martineau's condensed English version.

34. Ibid., 36.

35. *Philosophical Foundations of the Three Sociologies* (London: Routledge and Kegan Paul, 1977), 19, 29.

order and purpose of phenomenon" he dismissed as "the most inaccessible questions."[36] In this sense, then, Comtean positivism was indeed "a variant form of empiricism."[37]

But Comte's approach differed from the simple empiricism of Bacon or even the more advanced utilitarian school of Helvetius or Bentham. The latters' searching empiricism could have radical social and political implications. Classical empiricism had provided one basis for Lockean liberalism and constituted part of the foundation of the *philosophes'* theory of natural rights and individual liberty. Comte admired the rigorous empiricism of the French Enlightenment's *encyclopédistes* but he drew back from the corrosive social and moral ramifications of their thought.[38] Influenced by the rationalism of the *Encyclopédie* while a student at the Ecole Polytechnique, Comte was later drawn in a more conservative direction by Restoration critics of the Enlightenment. In order to transcend the materialism and individualism denounced by DeMaistre and others, Comte insisted on dealing with society as an organic whole; the elements that compose society were institutions for Comte, not individuals. Thus, the family was the smallest autonomous social unit and its internal relationships were reproduced at the societal level: "As every system must be composed of elements of the same nature with itself, the scientific spirit forbids us to regard society as composed of individuals. The true social unit is certainly the family . . . the family presents the true germ of the various characteristics of the social organism."[39] Society, said Comte, is characterized by relationships of subordination, arising from individuals' natural differences. Echoing the Restoration's theocratic school of DeMaistre, DeBonald and others, Comte concluded that government was a "natural" product of this tendency toward subordination within both the family and society.[40]

These two general characteristics, epistemological empiricism and social organicism, also underly the two most distinctive theoretical features of the Positive Philosophy—Comte's hierarchy of the sciences and the "Law of the Three Stages."[41] The latter, in essence, a philosophy of history, reveals simultaneously Comte's empiricist presuppositions and his willingness to break with aspects of conventional empiricism.

36. *Positive Philosophy*, 27.
37. Benton, *Foundations*, 21.
38. Ibid., 19–20, 23–24.
39. *Positive Philosophy*, 502.
40. Bertier de Sauvigny, *Bourbon Restoration*, 345–47; Levy-Bruhl, *Philosophy*, 4–10.
41. These two elements of Comte's system are isolated by Charles Cashdollar as the most familiar features of positivism for Americans at midcentury. See "European Positivism and the American Unitarians," *Church History* 45 (1976), 490–506.

Here, Comte claimed to have uncovered the law of historical development that governed the growth of human society. He announced his
"discovery" in the opening pages of the *Cours*: "From the study of the
development of human intelligence, in all directions, and through all
times, the discovery arises of a great fundamental law, to which it is
necessarily subject, and which has a solid foundation of proof, both in
the facts of our organization and in our historical experience."[42]

The three historical stages were the "theological" (men imagine divine
beings as the cause behind natural phenomena), the "metaphysical"
(anthropomorphic gods are discarded for reified ideas), and the "positive" (all phenomena are subject to rigorous scientific inquiry). Each era
is also characterized by a distinctive form of social organization: society
is ruled first by pagan priests and soldiers, then by Christian clergy and
lawyers and, finally, by industrialists and scientists. Nor did Comte
shrink from the scientific pretentions of his interpretive schema. Refer-
ring to his theory, he wrote in the *Cours*: "We can test it, as we have
tested other laws, by observation, experiment, and comparison. I have
done so through many years of meditation; and I do not hesitate to say
that all these methods of investigation will be found to concur in the
complete establishment of this historical proposition, which I maintain
to be as fully demonstrated as any other law admitted into any other
department of natural philosophy."[43]

This grand science of history underlines Comte's break with strict
empiricism. Evidently, some general theory arising from reason was
required to make sense of human history; one's method could not be
purely inductive. In a sense, Comte attempted to define a new empirical
method that expanded the meaning of simple induction. If, Comte
observed, primitive man had relied solely upon inductive reasoning, he
would have made little progress. Comte explained: "If it is true that
every theory must be based upon observed facts, it is equally true that
facts can not be observed without the guidance of some theory. Without
such guidance, our facts would be desultory and fruitless; we could not
retain them: for the most part we could not even perceive them."[44] Also,
contrary to classical empiricism, the true scientific method was discerned
by Comte through the study of its various applications in history and
not simply by the "internal observation" of an individual. Here, Comte's
position was a blending of Condorcet's Enlightenment faith in progress
and the heightened historical consciousness of Restoration conserva-

42. *Positive Philosophy*, 25.
43. Ibid., 522.
44. Ibid., 27.

tives.[45] "No conception," he wrote in the *Cours*, "can be understood otherwise than through its history."[46] In this way, Comte was both empiricist and historicist. Nevertheless, Comte's criterion for distinguishing the three stages remained the extent to which the thought of a particular period displayed a consistent empiricism. The "positive stage" was scientific because its characteristic thought met empiricist standards for scientific knowledge. First, it dealt only with phenomena subject to sensory perception. Second, invariable laws were generated to describe the relationships between these varied phenomena.[47]

Comte's hierarchical classification of the sciences was closely linked to his historicism and empiricist methodology. He held that each particular science had climbed through the three historical phases at different speeds. Thus, astronomy had attained the "positive method" before terrestrial physics, and sociology was only now aspiring to the "positive state." The Comtean hierarchy ranked mathematics first (as the most general and independent) followed by astronomy, physics, chemistry, biology, and the "Queen of the Sciences," sociology. Each of these built upon the discipline below it and thus sociology was the most complex, being the most dependent and specific. At the same time, Comte took pains to stress that he was not arguing that the various sciences were all ultimately identical:

> Because it is proposed to consolidate the whole of our acquired knowledge into one body of homogeneous doctrine, it must not be supposed that we are going to study this vast variety as proceeding from a single principle, as subjected to a single law. There is something so chimerical in attempts at universal explanation by a single law, that it may be as well to secure this Work at once from any imputation of the kind.[48]

Rather, the unity he had in view arose from an empirical method that underlay the different areas of inquiry.

45. Bertier de Sauvigny, *Bourbon Restoration*, 338–42.

46. *Positive Philosophy*, 25

47. For other important consequences of Comte's philosophy of science, see Benton, *Foundations*, 33–36. In using the term "historicism" in this study, I have in mind not Karl Popper's somewhat idiosyncratic definition but the more general understanding expressed succinctly by Maurice Mandlebaum: "historicism is the belief that an adequate understanding of the nature of anything and an adequate assessment of its value are to be gained by considering it in terms of the place it occupied and the role it played within a process of development." See "Historicism" in *The Encyclopedia of Philosophy*, ed. Paul Edwards (New York: Macmillan, 1967), 3:24.

48. *Positive Philosophy*, 37.

The only necessary unity is that of Method, which is already in great part established. As for the doctrine, it need not be *one*; it is enough that it be *homogeneous*. It is, then, under the double aspect of unity of method and homogeneousness [*sic*] of doctrine that we shall consider the different classes of positive theories in this work. While pursuing the philosophical aim of all science, the lessening of the number of general laws requisite for the explanation of natural phenomena, we shall regard as presumptuous every attempt, in all future time, to reduce them rigorously to one.[49]

Thus, although a reductionist impulse was present in his system, Comte himself rejected a simple monism.

In light of the foregoing, Comte's appeal for Victorian intellectuals should not be difficult to appreciate. As one can see, Comte attempted to be both steadfastly empirical and thoroughly naturalistic. "As we have seen," the young Comte proclaimed, "the first characteristic of the Positive Philosophy is that it regards all phenomena as subjected to invariable natural *Laws*."[50] Historian D. H. Meyer aptly describes the "fundamental and gradual *change of mind* among western thinkers" during the Victorian era as composed of two "trends," one a restrictive naturalism, and the second an emphatic scientism.[51] Comte's, certainly, was a system suited to the age of Darwin and Spencer. Another one of Comte's chief goals was to reduce the number of these particular natural laws to a small number of general laws that would cover a whole range of phenomena. Therefore, although rejecting an extreme monism that would seek to reduce everything to a single general law, Comte did appeal to the monistic aspirations of the age. Empirical certainty was afforded while a hierarchical order was imposed in Comte's classification of the sciences upon all the seemingly disparate natural phenomena. The vision of the *Cours* was encyclopaedic; it dealt with the entire sweep of natural phenomena and human history—a grand system for an era of grand systems. As disciple Lester F. Ward would later proclaim, "the work of the true philosopher is pre-eminently the synthesis of extant knowledge."[52]

Yet, Comte's system also respected and spoke to the persistent religi-

49. Ibid., 38. As I will show, Comte's disciples were not always so cautious or reserved in this respect.

50. Ibid., 28.

51. "Victorian Crisis," 62. Emphasis in the original.

52. "What Mr. Ward Was Ready to Say" in *Herbert Spencer on the Americans and the Americans on Herbert Spencer*, ed. Edward L. Youmans (New York: D. Appleton, 1883), 77.

osity of the mid-Victorian agnostic. In a sense, the Comtean approach to religion allowed intellectuals to have the best of both worlds. While he joined the skeptics in dismissing the metaphysical foundations of orthodox Christianity, Comte took care to apply his own maxim ("on ne détruit que ce qu'on remplace") by furnishing a secular surrogate for traditional faith and piety. Hence, Comtists could indulge themselves in the quasi-religious duty to doubt, while still providing for the emotional needs of individuals and preserving the moral "cement" that they believed held society together.[53] After all, Comte had placed the traditional Christian virtues of familial love and altruism at the very core of his system. Such virtues were socially necessary and could be taught, strengthened and preserved through the Religion of Humanity. The scientific understanding of society would enable one, then, to construct an ideological and even an institutional bulwark for social mores. In the wake of the dismantling of traditional belief, many intellectuals clearly shared Comte's concern for the social fallout from such a fundamental reorientation.

These cherished moral values, beyond being broadly Christian, were also characteristically Victorian. Comte was dedicated to the preservation of private property and believed in the central importance of the family unit within society.[54] Furthermore, the Victorian era was also characterized by a sentimental spirit and by what several historians have described as the "cult of domesticity."[55] Both of these themes found expression in Comte's writings. Like many Anglo-American authors, Comte held that women were morally superior to men because they were naturally altruistic. "Morally," declared Comte ". . . she [woman] merits always our loving veneration, as the purest and simplest impersonation of Humanity." Comte spoke of "the raising and purifying of the heart" as "the object of all marriage" and saw the woman's domestic role as central to the success of the family. It was axiomatic for Comte that education "must be entrusted to the spiritual power [i.e., in society, the Church], and in the family, the spiritual power is represented by Woman . . . what may be called the spontaneous training of the feelings, belongs entirely to the mother."[56] Catherine Beecher could scarcely have put it better.

53. Meyer, "Victorian Crisis," 63. See also Turner, *Without God*, chap. 7.

54. See *Positive Philosophy*, chap. 5 of book 6.

55. Daniel W. Howe, "American Victorianism as a Culture," in *Victorian America*, ed. Howe, 25–26; Katherine Kish Sklar, *Catherine Beecher: A Study in American Domesticity* (New Haven: Yale University Press, 1973).

56. Auguste Comte, *A General View of Positivism*, trans. J. H. Bridges (London: Routledge, 1910), 234, 265, 268–69.

The new empirically based moral order required a positive religion and Comte sketched out both the doctrinal basis and institutional expression of his "Religion of Humanity" in the *Système de politique positive* (1851–1854). Humanity would become the appropriate object of worship under the new faith. Referred to collectively as the "Great Being," it included all those in the past, present, and future, who had sought human betterment. To facilitate popular religion, Comte composed a new calendar that commemorated this pantheon of the past humanitarians. Love, especially altruistic motherly love, was the fundamental principal that underlay Comte's religion; he therefore stressed the emotional and nurturing characteristics of women and their proper sphere of influence in the home and family. Outside the home, a "Positivist priesthood" ran the educational system and served as both the scientific authorities and censors. Their head would be the "High Priest of Humanity" in Paris—Comte himself.[57] Though rejecting its metaphysics, Comte romanticized the Middle Ages and sought to restore the intellectual unity of medieval Europe upon a new, positive foundation, headed by a new pope.[58]

It was critical for Comte that social theory also attain the level of "positive knowledge," for only then would sociology provide the sort of scientific answers that alone could solve the contemporary crisis. Scientific sociology could deliver European civilization from this crisis by resolving the central tension of contemporary society, that is, the opposition of order and progress. His scientific sociology, Comte declared, would "bring the demands of progress into complete unison with requirements of order, representing the ultimate regeneration as consisting in the discipline of the forces evoked during the period of preparation."[59] By broadening the realm of scientific thought to include social phenomena, a science of society that could command universal acceptance would be created. The failure of various constitutional experiments in France since the Revolution was testimony to the fact that these efforts at political reform had not been based upon a positive knowledge of the social system. This new social science would circumscribe the limits of political debate by revealing what was possible to reform, as well as what was not susceptible to amelioration. Comte observed:

57. Gertrud Lenzer, ed. *Auguste Comte and Positivism: The Essential Writings* (New York: Harper and Row, 1975), xxv–xxvi. I concur with Lenzer and others regarding the essential unity of Comte's "two systems."

58. Comte was clearly influenced here by DeMaistre's *Du Pape*. See Levy-Bruhl, *Philosophy*, 5–6.

59. *System of Positive Polity*, trans. Richard Congreve (New York: Burt Franklin, 1966), 4:463.

social phenomena may, from their complexity, be more easily modified than any others. . . . This is the first scientific foundation of all rational hopes of a systematic reformation of humanity. . . . [But] still they can never be more than modifications: that is, they will always be in subjection to those fundamental laws, whether statical or dynamical, which regulate the harmony of the social elements.[60]

Comte always assumed that social progress was the inevitable result of this process:

The only ground of discussion is whether [social] development and improvement . . . are one; whether the development is necessarily accompanied by a corresponding amelioration, or progress, properly so called. To me it appears that the amelioration is as unquestionable as the development from which it proceeds, provided we regard it as subject, like the development itself, to limits general and special, which science will be found to prescribe.[61]

Scientific observation had to precede political action so that reforms would be consistent with historical trends. Then, too, a scientific sociology would give government planners the requisite tools to effect social control; technocratic manipulation could arise from a science of society. Just as nature had been tamed through science, so also social forces could be augmented or redirected to desired ends. These technocratic, interventionist themes were central to Comtean positivism.[62]

But Comte was no simple liberal reformist. Although he was concerned that social ills be eliminated through empirical study and planned intervention, real improvement for Comte could only be founded upon order, the kind of stable hierarchical order evident in nature. Comte sought to avoid the sort of unrestrained, undirected revolutionary change that France had undergone since the last part of the eighteenth century. Moreover, one can readily recognize that Comte's philosophy, although it embraced historicism, did, in fact, seek an end to history. Comte looked forward to the ultimate organization of all social life upon

60. *Positive Philosophy*, 469–70.
61. Ibid., 467.
62. Ibid., 36–37. Maurice Mandelbaum, *History, Man and Reason: A Study in Nineteenth-Century Thought* (Baltimore: Johns Hopkins University Press, 1971), 68–69.

unchanging scientific principles. Positive science alone, he believed, could bring this chaotic transitional era to a close.[63]

Comte's concern to reconcile scientifically the competing claims of order and progress dovetailed neatly with many of the questions Anglo-American intellectuals were asking. Their desire was to harness the tremendous forces of socioeconomic change for essentially conservative ends. Comte's distinctive blending of these two principles has been variously described by commentators as "prospective conservatism" or "anticipatory conservatism."[64] In addition to being apt descriptions of Comtean ideology, both are equally accurate characterizations of much of Gilded Age social thought. Though accepting prevailing property relations, the Comtist looked to a far-reaching reorganization of society along "scientific" lines. Industrial capitalism would remain but redesigned in accordance with the principles of social science and cleansed through the application of humanity's highest moral aspirations. American intellectuals alarmed by labor violence and disappointed by the greed of the "robber barons" but unwilling to consider a significant redistribution of property could find such a solution very appealing. At stake for these American intellectuals was the survival of a liberal capitalist system, placed on a more secure foundation, no longer threatened by selfish capitalists or disruptive workers.

Possibly of more significance, those social classes that aspired to positions of greater cultural influence or leadership were also predisposed to accept Comtism. During a time of professional crisis, positivism appeared to offer intellectuals a secure position of social authority. The rule of experts was central to Comte's social vision; scientists would become a "positive priesthood." And Comte could attract ambitious leaders of several types. The new positive social order would provide important places for an aspiring technocratic elite in either the spiritual / educative or administrative / economic authority. At the same time, genteel critics of the organizational politics of the Gilded Age would be attracted to a system that promised the transcendence of partisan politics by a scientifically administered state.

The transition to the Comtean system seemed to favor the amateur grand theorist. The moral and scientific revolutions that had to precede the final transition would be led, it appeared, by the erudite generalist, well-versed in all the sciences and humanities. This amateur ideal, what Kent has described as "the cult of the 'all rounder,' " was a typically

63. *Positive Philosophy*, 36–37, 399–402. See also Lenzer, *Comte*, xxxiii, xxxii.

64. Christopher Kent, *Brains and Numbers: Elitism, Comtism, and Democracy in Mid-Victorian England* (Toronto: University of Toronto Press, 1978), xiii; Lenzer, *Comte*, xxxiii.

Victorian notion and suited many Comtists.[65] Before academic specialization and professionalization gradually discredited such individuals,
the "all-rounders" were an important voice in Anglo-American social
thought. The careers of both Thaddeus Wakeman and Lester Ward are
excellent examples of this Gilded Age phenomenon.

Finally, positive-state, liberal reformists, particularly those from a
Whig background, would clearly have a powerful ally in Comte. A
central characteristic of scientific thought for Comte was, after all,
prediction (or "prevision"). "All sciences," Comte declared, "aim at
prevision. For the laws established by observation of phenomena are
generally employed to foretell their succession. . . . Such a determination
of the future should even be regarded as the direct object of political
science, as of other positive sciences." However, this would not be
simply dispassionate, scientific prediction. Rather, social science
equipped society's leaders to intervene and thereby direct social development. Observed Comte: "There is a great difference between obeying
the progress of civilization blindly and obeying it intelligently." As he
explained elsewhere, "the governing classes, clearly perceiving the end
that they are called on to realize, can [thereby] reach it directly, in place
of wasting their forces on tentative and mistaken efforts."[66] Certainly
France appeared to have only spun its wheels since 1789. Comte would
prove invaluable, then, to those interested in preserving the elite-led
reform model of the Whigs and the melioristic or perfectionist ideals of
antebellum reform upon a new, scientistic foundation.

Thus Comte addressed in a systematic way the major questions that
fueled intellectual discourse in late nineteenth-century America. Although
many in the Anglo-America community grappled with these questions,
relatively few in the United States adopted Comte's radical answers
uncritically as a comprehensive whole. The subjects of the following
chapters represent a comparatively small group of Americans who were
attracted to the Comtean system and who integrated key positivist
insights into their own viewpoint. American Comtists of the 1860s and
1870s were usually not drawn from the cultural mainstream. Perhaps the
significant proportion of foreign-born among the early sectarian group
is attributable to the exotic features of orthodox positivism. At any

65. Kent, *Brains and Numbers*, 60.

66. Comte in Lenzer, *Comte*, 56–57, xlii. Kent has summarized Comte's appeal for the
English by noting that positivism assessed "the three most central concerns of the
nineteenth-century middle-class—upholding morality, providing a means of controlling
social change, and providing a sense of identity to the individual by defining his place
within the community" (*Brains and Numbers*, 59, xiii).

rate, neither foreign- nor native-born within the early societies were characteristically American in their social outlook. The political views of some were exceedingly conservative, while the most advanced theological liberals and advocates of Freethought played a disproportionate part in the early societies. Nevertheless, others, such as Lester Frank Ward and Edward Bellamy, who usually adhered to democratic and egalitarian principals, later made important use of Comte. Historians have too often exaggerated the unattractive features of Comtean positivism while neglecting to recognize those elements that commended Comte to ninteenth-century intellectuals.[67] Drawn to Comtean thought, some grappled with those offensive aspects in an effort to recast Comte in an American mold. It was this creative encounter with Comte that forged a distinctively American Comtean language.[68]

67. See, for instance, Donald Fleming, "Social Darwinism," in *Paths of American Thought*, ed. Arthur M. Schlesinger, Jr., and Morton White (Boston: Houghton Mifflin, 1963), 127.

68. The American Comtean mind-set I have here defined could also be viewed as a "wing" of the "Reform Darwinism" Eric F. Goldman outlines in *Rendezvous with Destiny: A History of Modern American Reform* (New York: Knopf, 1963), 93–104. Goldman's choice of terms is unfortunate because the "Reform Darwinist" label encourages one to view Gilded Age intellectual discourse as simply a series of responses to Darwin and Spencer. Again, see Matthews, *Quest*, 27.

CHAPTER TWO

"The Church of Humanity"

Orthodox Positivism
in New York, 1854–1876

They seem to make of science a demi-god, and one at first feels repelled by the chilling character of their belief. Yet, on the other hand, they hold to and practically exhibit so high a faith in human nature, and such a conception of man's responsibility and duty, that their practice redeems their principles.

—*Springfield Republican*, 31 January 1872

MR. AND MRS. HENRY EDGER and their two children arrived at New York's Jersey City docks on 11 April 1851. Mrs. Edger's uncle, George Tingle, met the couple at dockside and took them both to the small community of Bloomingdale. Henry Edger, who would soon be named the only North American member of the Positive Council by Comte himself, was not a disciple when he emigrated from England. Born in Sussex of Dissenting parents in 1820, Edger had trained in London for a short time to be a lawyer before deciding that the young republic was "a promising field for social progress."[1]

New York City and its environs was a rapidly growing and energetic

1. Charles A. Codman, "History of the City of Modern Times" (Riverhead, N.Y.: Suffolk County Historical Society, n.d.), 6; Robert E. Schneider, *Positivism in the United States: The Apostleship of Henry Edger* (Argentina: Rosario, 1946), 35.

center of trade, commerce, and manufacture in the 1850s. Foreign visitors frequently commented on the bustling pace of the city and on the grasping character of New Yorkers. Thackeray wrote that New York was dominated by the "rush of life" when he visited in 1852. Certainly the city's population was growing dramatically: New York more than doubled in size between 1845 and 1860 (reaching over 800,000), while neighboring Brooklyn's growth in the same period was several times greater.[2] But, as Edward K. Spann has observed, New York was "not merely a fast growing city but a vital force in the modernization of both Europe and America." The city profited from and, to some extent, led the terrific growth that occurred in the U.S. economy after 1850. Commercial New York was also slowly becoming the Mid-Atlantic's leading manufacturing center during the 1850s.[3] Gradually, dependent wage earners became a key element within New York's working class, alongside the city's skilled artisanry. In fact, one cause of New York's labor unrest in 1850 was the concern of many artisans that they were being marginalized, reduced to a kind of "wage slavery" under the emerging economic order. Apart from frightening middle- and upper-class businessmen, however, their protests during the 1850s accomplished little.[4]

The demand of the city's manufacturers for cheap labor was, after all, answered by a steady stream of hungry and ambitious immigrants during the decade.[5] In one year (1854), for instance, well over 300,000 immigrants landed in New York. The bulk of these were, like Edger, from the British Isles, though Germany and other parts of Europe also contributed citizens. As Irish and German immigration increased, the WASP culture of the metropolis was gradually undermined. New York became one of the nation's most cosmopolitan cities. As Isabella Bird put it in 1854: "In one part [of New York] one can suppose it to be a negro town; in another, a German city; while a strange dreamy resemblance to Liverpool pervades the whole."[6] The increasing resemblance to European cities extended also to the rising incidence of crime, destitution, and vice. Some contemporary commentators argued that the freedom and individualism of the city had produced this perceived

2. Bayrd Still, *Mirror for Gotham: New York As Seen by Contemporaries From Dutch Days to the Present* (New York: University Press, 1956), 125, 129.

3. *The New Metropolis: New York City, 1840–1857* (New York: Columbia University Press, 1981), 401, 403.

4. Sean Wilentz, *Chants Democratic: New York City and the Rise of the American Working Class, 1788–1850* (New York: Oxford University Press, 1984), chap. 10.

5. Ibid., 392.

6. Quoted by Still, *Mirror*, 129, 159.

moral decline. Many agreed that such license had (in the words of Spann), "diminished civic spirit and commitment to the benefit of the me-first, ruthless, and dim-sighted individualism so evident in public places."[7]

Such was the city that greeted Henry Edger when he disembarked in 1851. Given Edger's faith in social perfection, it is perhaps not surprising that he soon sought refuge beyond the city limits. Edger found employment in Brooklyn between 1851 and 1854 and continued to read widely. After pouring over several articles by English positivist G. H. Lewes in the London *Leader* (probably in 1852), Edger became a convinced Comtist. Two years later, after corresponding with Comte himself, Edger decided not to remain a simple convert but to become an evangelist for the "positive faith." On 9 April 1854 he "consecrated" his life to "lay the foundation stone" of the Comtean "edifice" in the New World.[8]

Having determined to spread the positivist gospel, Edger and his family settled in "Modern Times," a utopian community on Long Island, near present-day Brentwood. The community had interested Edger since his arrival in America (he had visited it back in May 1851) but he had first spent a few months at the Fourierist Phalanx in Red Bank, New Jersey.[9] Not committed to Fourierism, Modern Times seemed to Edger to promise a more open atmosphere. He later wrote that the "very absence of organization," coupled with the "almost universal theological emancipation" of the inhabitants there "led me to anticipate a more favorable reception" of Comte's doctrines.[10] Although the heyday of such utopian experiments was past, Modern Times had been founded by Josiah Warren and Stephen Pearl Andrews in 1851. Warren was a disgruntled Owenite who had left New Harmony back in 1827 and, since then, had developed an anarchistic doctrine of social organization based upon the labor-cost theory of exchange. Upon moving to New York in 1850, Warren met Andrews, an antislavery radical who soon became a close disciple of Warren's individualistic philosophy. The founders of Modern Times believed that social harmony could be achieved among strong individualists if an equitable system of exchange was implemented and tolerance observed. What resulted was a less-than-successful utopian experiment of nonconformists, including advocates

7. Spann, *New Metropolis*, 423.

8. Richmond L. Hawkins, *Positivism in the United States, 1835–1861* (Cambridge: Harvard University Press, 1938), 125–27; Schneider, *Apostleship*, 47; Woodbridge Riley, "La philosophie française en Amérique," *Revue philosophique de la France et de l'étranger* 87 (1919): 407–10.

9. Schneider, *Apostleship*, 47; Hawkins, *Positivism*, 113.

10. Edger quoted by Schneider, *Apostleship*, 46. Codman, "History," 2, 4, 6–7.

of dress reform, spiritualism and free love, that lasted until the early 1860s.[11]

Edger's positivist hopes for Modern Times proved, with time, to be unrealistic. Encouraged through his intimate correspondence with Comte, Edger built an oratory and steeple onto his log cabin and there he celebrated the Comtean religious rites. He eventually organized musical activities, including a glee club and an orchestra.[12] But Edger won few converts to the new faith, save members of his own family and friends John Metcalf and Charles Codman. Indeed, the community showed itself to be decidedly unfertile ground for Edger's proselytizing. Sociologist L. L. Bernard concluded that Edger "was doubtless impeded by his lack of tact and insight . . . his literalism, ritualism and dogmatism . . . often repulsed the best minds who might have been won over."[13] The death of the Master in 1857 also appears to have devastated his recent convert.[14] Neither was Modern Times prospering as a business venture; its inhabitants were mostly urban artisans with few farming skills. This fact, combined with the area's sandy soil, meant that the initial settlers eked out a poor living.[15] All of these elements conspired to wreck Edger's dream of a Comtist colony in America.

I

Although Henry Edger's failed "apostleship" has received the attention of historians, his thought has rarely been analyzed in light of its subsequent influence.[16] Though neither an original nor an especially sophisticated thinker, Edger published several short books and articles that were

11. See William Bristol Shaw and Ernest Sutherland Bates, "Andrews, Stephen Pearl," *Dictionary of American Biography*, 1: 298–99; W. J. Ghent, "Warren, Josiah," *DAB*, 19:483–84; Codman, "History." In researching this chapter, I was unable to benefit fully from Roger Wunderlich's interesting study, *Low Living and High Thinking at Modern Times, New York* (Syracuse: Syracuse University Press, 1992).

12. Codman, "History," 2, 4, 6–7.

13. Luther Bernard made this reflection upon reading Edger's private journals. See Luther Lee Bernard, "Diary," 3:11 (1935), L. L. Bernard Papers (Box 17, File 9), Pattee Library, the Pennsylvania State University.

14. LLB, "Diary," 2:9. Bernard comments upon reading this part of Edger's journal: "It [the death of Comte] broke him up rather badly, and, as he says, filled him with despair"(9).

15. Codman, "History," 2, 4, 6–7.

16. Hawkins pays little attention to Edger's published works; Schneider briefly surveys only the *Positivist Calendar* (see *Apostleship*, 66–77).

some of the first contributions to positivist literature in the United States. As such, Edger's work exercised a formative influence over the early sectarian societies that came together in New York after the Civil War.

Edger's first book, *The Positivist Calender* (1856), began with an alarming description of the contemporary crisis. There is disorder and upheaval in the material realm, wrote Edger, because of the prevalent mental and moral anarchy. This sense of philosophical and moral collapse colors a great deal of Edger's work and that of the New York societies he helped spawn; indeed, it may well represent the central concern of the movement as a whole, at least for the period 1854–1876. Edger contended that positivism's significance lay in the fact that it alone had discovered the forces that could be employed to end this social and intellectual upheaval. Such a task would be even more difficult in America since the anarchy was "more complete" here than in the Old World. In America, Edger observed, disorder "equally affects the spiritual order and the temporal order."[17] The lack of an established national church and the proliferation of Protestant sects only exacerbated the anarchic socioeconomic conditions in the young republic. Like Comte, Edger had harsh words for the Protestant Reformation, which he held accountable for much of the spiritual disorder and confusion he perceived around him.

Edger was insistent, however, in his argument that Comte's system was not a materialistic and irreligious solution to the modern crisis. After all, Comte had repudiated much of the corrosive rationalism of the eighteenth-century *philosophes*. Religion, contended Edger, was composed of "a triple culture, at once of the heart, the mind, and the activity."[18] The first factor required worship of some kind, the second a doctrinal foundation, and the third a code of behavior. Unlike its materialistic predecessors, the glory of the Positive faith was that, in addition to providing a new empirical (and thus unassailable) dogmatic foundation for the new religion, it recognized that the key factors of heart and activity must not be discarded.[19]

Accordingly, the Comtist church would have a full sacramental system that would infuse with sanctity and meaning various stages in the growth of an individual. These were presentation (corresponding to baptism), initiation (first communion?), admission (confirmation?), destination,

17. Edger, *The Positivist Calendar: Or, Transitional System of Public Commemoration Instituted by Auguste Comte* . . . (Modern Times, N.Y.: H. Edger, 1856), 17.

18. Ibid., 6.

19. Schneider, *Apostleship*, 70.

marriage, maturity, retreat (retirement?), and transformation (death).[20] Given the nonsacramental, even antiliturgical character of much of American Protestantism at this time, it was certainly unwise for Edger to lay such emphasis upon this unabashedly Catholic feature of the church to come. Yet the first American positivist groups were evidently not repelled by such ritual; Comte's self-conscious religious rites did strike an appropriate chord for some Americans.

As for inculcating moral behavior, Edger reiterated Comte's arguments. In order to obtain upright men and women, one had to encourage an individual's "sociality" over their "personality" or self-centeredness. Outward-directed affection, Edger held with Comte, was the "true center of our existence."[21] Socialists, too, understood that atomistic, self-interested behavior had done much to promote social anarchy and they sought to redress this imbalance by teaching the fraternity or solidarity of all men. Edger sympathized with such a vision but preferred, as did Comte, to stress the historical continuity of the human race, linking the past, present and future in his definition of "Humanity."

This central principle of historical continuity was also brought home in Comte's new perpetual calendar. Like the church calendar that commemorated the lives of the saints, Comte's calendar sought to inject historical significance into each week and month of the year by naming them after great figures of religion, art, science, or government. Edger reasoned that such a device would "revive a just respect for our social antecedents" especially needed in as uprooted and disconnected a society as the United States.[22]

Nor was Edger content to remain only at the level of abstract social and philosophical criticism. "Universal [social] Reconstruction" was under way, declared Edger in The Positive Community: Glimpse of the Regenerated Future of the Human Race (1863). It was time to set forth the kind of community Comtists had in mind to build. Edger conceived of this "Reconstruction" as beginning first in thought, followed by the emotions or sentiment, and culminating finally in the fruit of new habits. Edger saw the restoration of these three elements, which together constituted all genuine religion, as his most important task. For, as he explained, "a profound social harmony necessarily implies a mental unity which it is the province of religion to institute and maintain."[23] Edger reasoned that if Humanity was recognized as the only true God

20. Edger, Calendar, 29–32.
21. Ibid., 85.
22. Ibid., 33.
23. Henry Edger, The Positive Community: Glimpse of the Regenerated Future of the Human Race (Modern Times, N.Y.: Positive Typographical Fund, 1863), 5.

then this could unify all the faithful; if individuals worshiped and served Humanity, they would be caring for each other and furthering the harmony and progress of their community.

In outlining how positive society would be ordered, Edger articulated a characteristic Comtean elitism. Since positivism could not be imposed upon society, the general public had to be educated "by the counsel and advice of trained and organized adepts." "To submit to subordination in social organization," Edger asserted, is a noble act. The community's leadership would be neatly divided into spiritual and temporal authorities, the former constituting a Positive priesthood supported by subscription. Not unlike Marx's "administration of things," Comte's civil authority would merely care for the material realm. Yet, very unlike the socialist polity, the capitalists would manage the state, having recognized their "moral trusteeship" and having become "Positive Participants." Such an arrangement was appropriate, contended Edger, because "the leadership of a society that is itself radically industrial, cannot be otherwise than also radically industrial." Edger's paternalistic model carried added responsibilities for the "captains of industry," however. They must provide for all of their workers' needs, be they housing or clothing, and not be satisfied simply to pay out subsistence wages. Edger explicitly rejected the classical economic view of labor as a commodity; job security was crucial to social stability.[24]

As for how to bring about the Positive order, Edger admitted that the utopian socialists were partly correct. "Forming a regenerated community" apart from society was a valid strategy, but it must not stand alone nor could it be purely the product of individual imaginative schemes. Under the enlightened direction of the Positive Council in Paris and with a scientific understanding of the social forces, Comtists would adopt all progressive reform measures and "carry them on, purged and purified and ennobled, to a triumphant conclusion." If Comte had understood human history correctly, then the Positive era was assured and "the final redemption of Mankind" would be realized under the Master's system.[25]

Edger's brand of positivism was clearly in the tradition of Comte's so-called second system of the *Système de politique positive*, with its concentration on the Religion of Humanity in contrast to the scientific emphasis of the *Cours*.[26] As Edger reflected revealingly in a later work

24. Ibid., 7, 33, 24, 23.
25. Ibid., 30, 35, 36.
26. Gertrud Lenzer, ed., *Auguste Comte and Positivism: The Essential Writings* (New York: Harper, 1975), xv. The Master himself wrote to Edger that his Positivist Calendar was "the most profound work on positivism that has ever been published" (Hawkins, *Positivism*, 180).

written after his return to Europe: "specialist science, whatever the intentions of the savans [sic] who cultivate it, is necessarily materialistic and atheistic in its tendencies; while synthetic science [i.e., the Comtean synthesis] is in all its bearings profoundly religious."[27]

II

Interest in Comte's ideas among the New York intelligentsia did not actually give rise to the formation of positivist societies until the late 1860s. Then, possibly as a result of an article that appeared in an issue of the *New York World*, popular interest finally bore fruit.[28] The newly appointed managing editor of the *World*, David G. Croly, invited Henry Edger to deliver a lecture on positivism during the winter of 1866–1867 and even put up the money required to procure De Garmo Hall, on the corner of 14th Street and Fifth Avenue, for the event.[29] The exact dates of this lecture and the talks that immediately followed it are uncertain, but sometime between 1867 and 1868, area Comtists formed the "First Positivist Society of New York." At the conclusion of Edger's first series of lectures, a conference was held, in the words of one of the participants, to "thank Mr. Edgar [sic] and determine what should be done." This conference was addressed by, among others, a young New York lawyer, Thaddeus Burr Wakeman, whose speech (at least according to his own accounts) galvanized the assorted "inquiring minds" into a coherent group of about a dozen. Throughout 1868, group meetings were regularly held at Croly's house on Bank Street.[30]

It would appear that a lasting formal organization was not actually created until 1869 and this seems also to have been started by a series of

27. *Auguste Comte and the Middle Ages* (Pozsony, Hungary: H. Edger, 1885), 16.
28. *New York World*, September 1867, p. 1; Riley, "Philosophie française," 410–20.
29. "In Memoriam David Goodman Croly—Estimates of the Man, His Character and His Life's Work," *Real Estate Record and Builder's Guide* 43 (18 May 1889): 3; David W. Levy, "The Life and Thought of Herbert Croly, 1869–1914" (Ph.D. dissertation, University of Wisconsin, 1967), 58–59. The hall is listed elsewhere as DeParmo.
30. Thaddeus Burr Wakeman (TBW) "The New York–Manhattan Liberal Club: The Story of Its Past and Present, and a Prophecy of Its Future," *Truth Seeker* 1 (23 January 1909): 59; *Memories of Jane Cunningham Croly—"Jenny June"* (New York: Putnam, 1904), 53; TBW, *Free Thought: Past, Present and Future* (Chicago: H. L. Green, 1899?), 26. The two accounts by Wakeman suggest that he himself was unsure about whether the conference was held in 1867 or early in 1868. See also, Edger, *Real Estate Record, and Guide*, 3. Strangely, one city directory gives Croly's address in 1870 as 37 Park Row, Vannest. See *Trow's New York City Directory*, ed. H. Wilson (New York: n.p., 1870).

David G. Croly (1829–89), early
New York positivist who edited
and published the Comtean
journal, *Modern Thinker*.

lectures by Edger.[31] Together, recent English immigrant William Owen
(as secretary) and editor H. H. Hall (as treasurer) spearheaded the
formation of the "Positive Society of North America"—later called
simply the New York Positivist Society. Though not an especially long-
lived organization itself, the society spawned a number of clubs that
enlivened the intellectual life of the metropolis, while bringing together
for the first time individuals who would play key roles in the birth and
development of a distinctively American Comtean tradition.[32]

Who composed this avant-garde community? Though incomplete,
biographical information on those most often mentioned in published
accounts of society functions suggests a relatively conventional group
(see Appendix). The club drew primarily from the comfortable upper
middle class. One of the most notable shared characteristics of these New
York Comtists was vocational: the majority were journalists, editors, or
writers of some kind. Those not involved in the print media were often

31. Schneider, *Apostleship*, 103–6. Schneider also refers to a group called "The First
Positivist Society of New York" that Edger had tried to establish in 1868. This may have
been the first informal group mentioned above. See 100–103.

32. I am inferring here that the P.S.N.A. and the N.Y.P.S. were one and the same since
Schneider appears to treat them as such. See *Apostleship*, 104, 288.

T. B. Wakeman (1834–1913) at middle age. It was as a
freethinking young lawyer that Wakeman first
encountered Comtean positivism through Henry
Edger's lectures.

professionals such as lawyers, professors, or ministers.[33] Of the fifteen
"regulars" whose birthplace could be determined nearly half were from
New England, a third were foreign-born (though most of these were
from the British Isles), and three had been born in New York State.
Interestingly, none was from New York City proper. It may have been
that the heterodoxy of some members was related to their move to
cosmopolitan New York and a rejection of rural New England or
conservative "upstate" values. In any case, except perhaps for the
number of foreign-born within the group, there is little remarkable
about its composition.

While most of the Comtists who surrounded Croly and his wife
appear to have been fairly affluent, they were clearly not of the wealthiest

33. "From New York," *Springfield Republican*, 31 January 1872, p. 5. William Leach has
an illuminating discussion of these women in *True Love and Perfect Union: The Feminist
Reform of Sex and Society* (New York: Basic Books, 1980). See especially chapter 6.

and most influential segments of New York society. David Croly's boss at the *World*, Manton Marble, represents an instructive social contrast. Marble moved in significantly more powerful and prestigious circles than did Croly. While both were active conservative Democrats, Marble helped determine national party policy. The New York State Democratic platform of 1874 and the national party platforms of 1876 and 1884 were all largely his work. In 1885, he was sent abroad as President Cleveland's special envoy.[34] Meanwhile, Croly wrote a hack election biography of Democratic presidential candidates Seymour and Blair and, earlier in 1864, co-authored a scurrilous booklet that attempted to portray the Republican party as an advocate of miscegenation.[35] Furthermore, though Marble's intellectual interests paralleled Croly's, his friends were far less marginal figures than those within Croly's immediate circle. Marble's associates included editor and publisher E. L. Youmans, Cornell president Andrew D. White, and philosopher John Fiske.[36] The young Fiske wrote to his wife Abby about visiting Marble once in New York: "Sunday I went to Marble's again, found him in bed and sat by his bedside talking for two hours. From there I went to Croly's for my aforesaid wrangle with the Comtists. Youmans was there and we had a lively time."[37] As Fiske's remarks suggest, Positivist Society meetings were not without occasional visitors of some prominence, even though most of the names of the "regulars" remain obscure today. In his autobiography, G. Stanley Hall remembered the New York group and some of its visitors:

> During this year [1867] I occasionally attended a little club of Positivists who were interested in the study of Comte. I remember particularly Stephel Pearl Andrews, a very ambitious thinker and voluminous writer whose immense book, *Universology*, I tried to understand. George Ripley occasionally came in, as did John Fiske, whose articles in the *Modern Thinker*, a progressive journal printed in many hues of paper and ink, undertook to spread this cult.

34. "Manton Marble," *Dictionary of American Biography* (New York: Scribner, 1933), 6:267.

35. Sidney Kaplan, "The Miscegenation Issue in the Election of 1874," *Journal of Negro History* 34 (July 1949): 274–343. Croly, himself, coined the word "miscegenation."

36. George T. McJimsey, *Genteel Partisan: Manton Marble, 1834–1917* (Ames: Iowa State University Press, 1971), 76.

37. Ethel F. Fisk, ed., *The Letters of John Fiske* (New York: MacMillan, 1940), 192–93.

Other notable visitors included author James Parton and scientist John William Draper.[38]

On the whole, this portrait of the New York Comtists suggests a group marginal enough to entertain heterodox ideas but respectable enough to want to attract the intellectual establishment. The few extant accounts of their meetings tend to corroborate this portrait of the society as a collection of earnest upper-middle-class philosophical radicals in search of a surrogate faith. In addition to fortnightly public meetings at Plimpton Hall, services were held every Sunday for a time in addition to special observances on particular days in the Comtist calendar. The latter festivals took on a primarily social air, with dinner parties at members' homes (usually in Brooklyn or Harlem).[39] Dinner was followed by a series of toasts and / or short addresses and, if Fiske's experience was at all typical, by animated discussion.

At one vernal celebration in the spring of 1872, more than forty guests were present at the home of a "Mr. Wreaks" in Brooklyn. The centerpiece of the evening's events was an address by T. B. Wakeman concerning the astronomical significance of the religious festivals of the major world faiths. "The speaker concluded," wrote a reporter in attendance, "by claiming for Positivism the highest philosophical completeness among all existing religions as well as the greatest adaptability to the practical needs of mankind." Concluding this "striking and scholarly address," Wakeman presented Mrs. Wreaks with a giant bouquet that "represented by its varied hues the historic evolution of the religious sentiment of the race." Wakeman's talk was followed by music, dramatic readings, and prayer (or what Comtists called "aspiration" or "invocation"). Such an evening moved a *Springfield Republican* reporter to conclude:

> I find them [the New York Comtists] to be practically [a] very good sort of people, and far more genial and warm-hearted than many of their less heretical neighbors. . . . They seem to make of science a demi-god, and one at first feels repelled by the chilling character of their belief. Yet, on the other hand, they hold to and practically exhibit so high a faith in human nature, and such a

38. G. Stanley Hall, *Life and Confessions of a Psychologist* (New York: D. Appleton, 1924), 179; R. Jackson Wilson, *In Quest of Community: Social Philosophy in the United States, 1860–1920* (New York: Wiley, 1968), 123; TBW, "The New York–Manhattan Liberal Club," 50; William Leach, *True Love and Perfect Union* (New York: Basic Books, 1980), 139.

39. "From New York," *Springfield Republican*, 8 April 1872.

conception of man's responsibility and duty, that their practice redeems their principles.[40]

Evidently, the devotees of Science could be as fervent and idealistic as their evangelical opponents.

Accounts of two other festival gatherings suggest a slightly different pattern of activities but a similar atmosphere. Here, an evening meeting at a member's home began with an observance of a particular Comtean rite or sacrament followed by a lengthy series of toasts each with a commentary or response by individual members. Comte's birthday, for instance, was celebrated by the New York society on 27 January 1872 by a meeting of some thirty-five people at a member's home in Harlem. The guests gathered at 8:00 P.M. for an elegant dinner that included a ritual meal of bread and water (a rite practiced by Comte to remind him of the needy).

The topics of the toasts made after dinner further illustrate the religiosity of the New York society, as well as revealing their distinctly Comtean perspective on social issues. David Croly offered one of the first toasts to

the day we celebrate, the birthday of Auguste Comte—the incomparable man, for it was he who founded for us: A Faith resting upon the philosophy of positive science, A Hope resting on the proved Laws of human progress, and, greater than all, a Love ever fed by human needs, and ever flowing to supply them (based on 1 Corinthians: 13).

Other toasts were offered involving "the new golden rule—'Live for Others,'" "the new moral safeguard—'Live in the open day,'" and "Woman—the Queen and Priestess of the home—the spiritual and creative Providence of mankind." These religious themes were summed up in a call for leadership in this important sphere: "The early advent of a true Spiritual Power—the normal organ of public opinion—which can inform our understandings by science, and guide and inform our lives by the religion of humanity, love and duty."

Toasts emphasizing social themes commended both the "Working Bees of the Social Hive—the Proletariat—hereafter to include the mass of mankind—the source of wealth and the objects to whose welfare it should be chiefly devoted" and "Reformers" for championing progressive change. The latter group must realize, the toastmaster cautioned,

40. "Comte's Birthday," *New York World*, 23 January 1872; "From New York," *Springfield Republican*, 31 January 1872.

that humanity could be elevated only "by the Religion of Humanity, which can insure the cooperation of all hearts, heads and hands." A conciliatory, if patronizing, statement asking patience and charity from "Theologians, Christians, Materialists, Spirituralists, Atheists, Rationalists, etc." ended the long series of toasts. "Only a faith according knowledge can," the toast read, "further sustain human progress and hope."[41]

Once again, the reporter in attendance was moved to remark on the intense yet respectable, even conservative mood of the gathering:

> The evident earnestness of the speakers impressed me much, however I might differ from some of their expressed views. . . . A decidedly conservative spirit was manifested, particularly in the references to the family, marriage, and the safeguards of society. Upon philosophical themes radical views were advanced . . . but there was no rampant iconoclasm, or fierce fanaticism, such as is common in the leaders of most founders of new faiths.[42]

Observers were often struck by how a godless scientism could be such a passionate faith. One commentator later wrote of society member Courtlandt Palmer: "I recollect the eager pleasure with which he was wont to discuss the Comtian doctrines, and with how great an intensity of devotion he sought to understand and accept them in their true spirit and their highest significance."[43] How, observers asked, could philosophical radicalism be advanced while profoundly conservative social views were still espoused? Moreover, the socioeconomic conservatism of the Comtists did not displace a seemingly genuine concern for the welfare of the laboring classes. This unusual mixture of piety and science, atheism and morality, and conservatism and social reform must have confused the uninitiated, yet it was probably these very themes that made Comtism attractive to the Victorian middle classes in both Britain and America. After all, positivism legitimized science without destroying religious fervor or traditional morality. In addition, it provided a scientific answer to the labor question that sounded both orderly and humane.

A similar pattern, the observance of a Comtean sacrament followed

41. "From New York," *Springfield Republican*, 31 January 1872.
42. *Courtlandt Palmer: Tributes Offered by Members of the Nineteenth Century Club to its Founder and First President* (New York: F. W. Christern, 1889), 155.
43. Charles Hirschfeld, "The Memoirs of Herbert Croly: An Unpublished Document," *New York History* 58 (July 1977): 320.

by a lengthy series of toasts, obtained the following year at a celebration of the Festival of Humanity by New York Comtists. At this particular gathering, the rite of presentation was administered. The candidate may in fact have been the infant son of David and Jane Croly. Herbert Croly, who remembered little about this "tiny but pretentious religious sect" to which his parents belonged, was apparently not the only child of the New York group to undergo this rite.[44] President Henry Evans conducted the service as "priest."

The liturgy used was probably that employed by religious positivists in England under Dr. Richard Congreve who read a form adapted from the Anglican service. With the parents, there were to be two other couples, one called protectors, the other called patrons. The latter couple was to be drawn one from "the father's family and representing the practical servants of Humanity, the other from the mother's family and from the theoretical servants of humanity."[45] Throughout the service, Christian references to God were replaced by invocations of "divine Humanity." "By this first sacrament," the priest was to explain, "religion gives a systematic consecration to every birth, and binds anew the fundamental ties that bind us one to another, and all to Humanity." A reading followed from Comte's *Positivist Catechism*; then, instead of renouncing the devil, the parents were asked to reject "all the sins of inordinate selfishness." The "presentation" concluded with "the sign of Love, Order and Progress" being made upon the child's forehead and a recitation of a positivist version of the Lord's Prayer.[46]

The high humanism of the baptismal rite was underlined by Evans's lengthy prayer addressed to "divine Humanity" following the ceremony. Evans's rhetoric, like the above liturgy, sounded almost as metaphysical as a traditional Christian sermon. "We come to ask entrance into the arcana of thy mysteries," Evans began, "accept us, we pray thee . . . assist us to understand the blessedness of the future." But, though the religious rhetoric was quite elaborate, the Comtean humanist element remained central. "We gladly find our friend," declared Evans, our brother, our savior, our Christ, our helper, everywhere . . . wherever

44. Joseph Lonchampt, *Positivist Prayer*, trans. John G. Mills (Goshen, N.Y.: Independent Republican Job Office, 1877), 29.

45. Ibid., 29–31. The prayer read: "Holy Humanity, who art in all human time and space, Hallowed be thy Name, may thy recognition come to all men, and thy labors glorify the heavens and the earth. Grant us power to earn our daily bread, and deter us from erring as we strive to serve others aright, and teach us how to deliver each other from every evil. Amen" (31).

46. *The Modern Thinker: An Organ for the Most Advanced Speculations in Philosophy, Science, Sociology and Religion* 2 (1873), endleaf.

men have given utterance to true thought, and lived noble, selfsacrific-
ing lives."[47]

After the sacrament was administered, several toasts or "sentiments"
were read and commented upon at some length by appointed members
of the society. The subjects of these toasts included Humanity ("the
Great Being"), Auguste Comte ("founder of the human faith"), positivism ("the great religious synthesis of the present"), Woman ("the moral
providence of the race"), "The New Priests" ("the philosophers, men of
science and artists"), and "The Patriciate" ("our rich men"). Having
discussed the last toast, the members dispersed, David Croly later calling
the gathering "a very pleasant occasion."[48]

Despite members' involvement in the city's journalistic life, New
York's Comtists had little distinctively Comtean impact on the mainstream media. Croly was perhaps best positioned to influence what
appeared in print with his prominent position at the *World*. But due to
Marble's tight reins on his city editor and perhaps Croly's own sense of
propriety, the *World* never became anything like a mouthpiece for the
positivists. Nevertheless, Croly's beliefs obviously did affect his work.
J. M. Bloch notes that Comtism "strongly colored Croly's choice and
treatment of news, and undoubtedly provided the fundamental impulse
of his humanitarian crusades." In fact, Croly hoped that the *World* might
one day displace Greeley's *Tribune* as the "*Reform* paper of the country."[49]

Thus, although Croly's boss, Manton Marble, was not usually supportive of organized labor, Croly showed considerable sympathy toward
workers involved in industrial disputes. Even when Marble's editorials
sounded censorious, Croly often quoted the statements of union leaders
at considerable length, which certainly made the *World's* treatment more
balanced than most of the other city dailies.[50]

III

The positivism taught by the New York society was the reflection of an
intellectual fellowship that was part religious cult and part adult discus-

---

47. Ibid.

48. J. M. Bloch, "The Rise of the New York World" (Ph.D. dissertation, Harvard
University, 1941), 489, 511.

49. Ibid., 511–17. Note that Croly commended English positivist E. S. Beesly's work
on unions to his readers. Croly also showed a more open attitude to feminist reformers
(see Bloch, "Rise," 524, 506–10).

50. Schneider, *Apostleship*, 101–2.

sion group. Though the subjects discussed at meetings were eclectic, the published writings of society members reveal a singular interest in philosophical and religious questions. New York's Comtists sought first to discover the true "Nature and Limits of human knowledge and its Divisions." Their interest here centered on, in Edger's words, "the Nature and Scope of Religion and Science as such."[51] Comtists were concerned with redrawing the dividing line between science and religion in order to rehabilitate the latter in a form consistent with a new positivistic understanding of empirical truth.

As representatives of, in David Croly's words, "the religious element of the Positive school in this country," the society held out the orthodox Comtean solution to this modern dilemma.[52] Rationalists and skeptics had been right in dismissing theology and metaphysics but they had failed to appreciate the legitimate place of religion in the life of the individual and of society. Heretofore, science had been destructive of traditional religion but positivism was not the enemy of that which was true and authentic in the religious systems of the past. While they rejected a personal deity or "First Cause" as not subject to empirical investigation, Comtists equally dismissed the agnosticism of Huxley or Spencer. After all, how could one worship an "Unknowable," a mere possibility? Croly held to the central Comtean assumptions regarding the religious nature of man and the centrality of worship to religion. Nor were idealist, liberal religionists excused. Subsequent American positivists would view the likes of Channing, Emerson, Parker, Beecher, and Frothingham as allies in the broadest sense; but, consistent with Comte's perspective, Croly held these religious leaders accountable for the religious "disintegration" and intellectual "anarchy" that, in his words, "reign[ed] supreme in Church, State and Social Life." Though their approaches differ, wrote Croly, they all agree in discrediting the past—in denying that "any objective basis of belief is possible or desirable as a bond of union—in exalting the individual at the expense of society—in appealing to the inner light rather than the outer form. And see what has resulted!"[53]

Croly lamented the amount of intellectual energy spent considering such questions as "Creation, God, Soul [and] Hereafter" not subject to empirical verification.[54] The absence of an afterlife need not lead one to despondence or to an iconoclastic rationalism. If human feelings were

51. C. G. David [David G. Croly], *A Positivist Primer: Being a Series of Familiar Conversations on the Religion of Humanity* (New York: David Wesley, 1872), 5.

52. DGC, "Religion Reconstructed," *Modern Thinker* 1 (1870): 7; *Positivist Primer*, 12.

53. DGC, "Creation, God, Soul, Hereafter: The Four Fruitless Problems," *Modern Thinker* 2 (1873), 91.

54. DGC, *Positivist Primer*, 15.

not discarded and a new tangible god was substituted for the old metaphysical one, religion could again be meaningful. Accordingly, the worship of a Supreme Being of some kind was highly beneficial to human society; what was wrong was basing that faith upon outmoded theological or metaphysical systems. If, as Croly contended, there was only "one real religion of man," then it would be one founded upon Positive science and have humanity as its god.[55]

Yet, while the Religion of Humanity was founded upon empirical fact, it provided an important place for art and emotion within its system. Positivism was truly then a "religion of the heart"; indeed, Croly termed it "the most emotional . . . of all religions" in its hagiolatry and elaborate ritual. Croly was actually most critical of Unitarians for their tepid eighteenth-century rationalism and rejection of human emotion as a legitimate part of worship. In fact, Croly preferred the "orthodox Christian creed to the rationalism, skepticism, and atheism of the modern mind. Man is made to believe."[56] Similarly, Croly disagreed with J. S. Mill's critique of Comte's religious system as a ridiculous attempt to stimulate and control emotions artificially. It is possible, Croly countered, to exercise one's feelings of sympathy or gratitude and thereby cultivate the moralistic altruism that is the product of all authentic faith. Throughout his exposition of the Comtean system, Croly appeared to be most concerned with dispelling the popular misconception of religious positivism as simply a base, iconoclastic materialism.

The New York Comtists were therefore involved in an effort to construct a surrogate religion for late Victorian skeptics. Consistent with Comte's vision, the faith they put forward was a truly comprehensive replacement. As one New York disciple put it, "the Religion of Humanity is at once the result and essence of all preceding faiths . . . so far as they are either good, true or imperishable."[57] Most important, the surrogate had to meet both the intellectual and emotional needs of individuals. Like Comte, however, they faced the challenge of making atheistic humanism a vital, passionate religion. To do so, they followed Comte's model of a "positivized" Catholicism complete with liturgical worship and a sacramental system. But how could traditional forms of prayer and worship be adapted to serve the needs of the positivist faithful?

One answer to this important question was furnished by society member John G. Mills who in 1877 translated and published *Positivist*

55. Ibid., 46.
56. Lonchampt, *Positivist Prayer*, 4.
57. Ibid., 3, 6, 7.

Prayer, composed earlier by French Comtist Joseph Lonchampt. Petitionary prayer to a personal God may have been rejected by Comte as fanciful but Lonchampt stressed that the "nobler functions of Aspiration and of Commemoration" were legitimate parts of prayer for Comtists and these functions "make it essential to religious life." Lonchampt concurred with Comte that worship was the proper response to the Humanity to whom "we are indebted for all that sweetens, exalts, ennobles and charms our life." Daily private prayer was advocated by Lonchampt as the best way "of consecrating all our efforts to the service of the New Great Being [i.e., Humanity]." "Pouring out our gratitude and our love," Lonchampt explained, would promote "a noble development of our soul." Sounding more than a little like a forerunner of Norman Vincent Peale, Lonchampt wrote that this sort of positive mental exercise was always the "guarantee of an infallible success" in any endeavor.[58] Hence such "prayer" or meditation would be an instrument to ensure individual and social improvement.

As one can readily recognize in the above reference to the "soul," some Comtists were not averse to employ explicitly metaphysical language when expounding the Religion of Humanity. The Comtist penchant for borrowing extensively from Roman Catholic liturgical forms was similarly evident in the prayers Lonchampt composed for each day of the week. Based upon the Hail Mary, each prayer began: "Holy Humanity, our mother and our benefactress, blessed be thou in this _____ day of the week, for . . ." The daily prayers, though beginning with this formula, had a particular theme depending on the day of the week. Marriage, for example, was the focus of adoration and invocation for Monday, paternity for Tuesday, filial love for Wednesday, fraternal love for Thursday, the Supreme Being (Humanity) for Friday, woman for Saturday, and Holy Humanity (or "the religious bond") for Sunday, designated sabbath.[59]

The prayer book closed with a "Positivist Decalogue" composed by an American disciple, J. D. Bell. The American's composition is notable for its emphasis upon individual piety and self-improvement. For instance, one was enjoined to contemplate "the masterpieces of painting and sculpture," read "the great poems in prose and verse," in addition to studying "the laws of the world," learning "the laws of biology, sociology, and morality," and acquainting oneself with "the laws of human development, mental, political and moral." Other typically Comtean commands included "Worship thy mother" and live "without

58. Ibid., 9.
59. Ibid., 32.

concealment." The ninth commandment stipulated that "the active classes must provide for the affective and speculative [i.e., women and priests, respectively]" lest "the important social functions discharged by them . . . be neglected." Most of the traditional biblical injunctions against lying, stealing and murder were collected together under the eighth commandment.

Perhaps nothing better illustrates the thoroughly Victorian spirit of the early Comtists than Lonchampt's prayers. Besides the florid, sentimental style, the prayers also typify their era in other interesting ways. Their picture of woman's nature and social role was, in line with Comte's vision, almost a caricature of the Victorian image. Weaker physically and intellectually, women were more emotional and sensitive; they had a more highly developed religious sensibility. Their sympathetic, nurturing character accordingly made women more altruistic than men—a character trait Positivists held to be crucial. All of these alleged features of the feminine personality suited women for the "domestic sanctuary," which Comtists, with their paeans to the familial bonds, viewed as a lofty calling indeed.[60] Note, for example, these lines from the prayers for Monday and Saturday:

> Woman gives to man the cares and pleasures of the domestic fireside, and receives from him, in exchange, all the means of existence which labor procures; woman inspires man with the amenities and tenderness of her heart, and receives from him in exchange, energy of character and the light of intelligence . . . it is under her sympathetic features that she appears at the sick-bed to comfort the sufferer; it is by her sweet tears that she consoles the afflicted in sharing his sorrows . . . into this haven [i.e., woman's heart] we are gathered after the tempest, and here we draw new strength to enable us to confront renewedly the dangers of the perilous passage of this life towards immortality.[61]

In some sense, then, the Comtist worship of the idealized Woman was but a logical development of the Victorian cult of domesticity and glorification of feminine sentiment.[62]

60. Ibid., 16.

61. Ibid., 9–10, 20.

62. T. J. Jackson Lears interprets G. Stanley Hall's "admiration of 'feminine' values" as part of his "revolt against positivism" (see *No Place of Grace: Antimodernism and the Transformation of American Culture, 1880–1920* [New York: Parthenon, 1981], 247–51.) This element of Hall's thought could, however, be viewed instead as a product of his youthful exposure to orthodox Comtean positivism. Comte's system was a complex blend of

Other characteristically Victorian concerns of the Comtists that surfaced in these prayers are a profound belief in progress and an obsession with personal duty and self-improvement. "We have no doubts of success," Lonchampt asserted, "since we second the Great Being in its irresistible progress. To work, then, and behold already our obscure names shining in letters of gold on the pedestal of the future."[63] Apparently, a good part of the uplift sought from positivist prayers was to come from "casting our looks into the splendors of thy [i.e., Humanity's] future." Such a future would be the product of the orchestrated efforts of many individuals. The duties of prayer and study had to be inculcated, for they were the means of attaining individual and social perfection. Hence, Bell's tenth positivist commandment read in part: "Thou art not only a member or officer of a community but posterity's trustee. Work because it is thy duty to work, and let no solid hope of reward or fear of punishment here or hereafter, tempt thee to do thy duty, much less to leave it undone."[64]

The set prayers and quasi-Roman ritual lent a cultic air to the early New York group, an air reinforced by the dogmatic and exclusivist claims made by its leaders. Croly contended that Comte's Religion of Humanity afforded "the only solution—of nearly all the problems now puzzling and distracting the race."[65] "Ours is the only true church," wrote Croly elsewhere, "the church infallible—universal. We tolerate no dissent and insist upon subordination, but our weapons are moral— spiritual."[66] The final qualifying phrase about "moral weapons" fails to offset the triumphalism and illiberal thrust of Croly's words. Formed in the image of their founder, Henry Edger, the early New York groups adhered loyally to Comte's religious views as set out in the *Système*.

Equally, in the realm of social and political thought, the early American Comtists deviated little from the Master's position. Of course for the Comtist, the religious and philosophical crisis was inextricably linked to the age's socioeconomic crisis; Comte's solution was designed to meet both challenges. The religious system was crucial, explained Croly, because "the only hope is in the growth of a religion and a philosophy more in accord with the higher instincts of humanity. These in time will

---

Romantic and Enlightenment elements; it valued "feminine" sentiment and would, in that respect, appeal to the antimodernist.

63. Ibid., 13, 23.
64. Ibid., 32.
65. DGC, *Positivist Primer*, 4.
66. DGC, "Religion Reconstructed," 7.

indicate a policy which will restore health and soundness to the state."[67]
As with Comte, then, social instability was held to be the direct product
of intellectual and moral anarchy or dislocation. Consequently, the
Religion of Humanity was not merely a new sect but rather a radical and
scientific way to bring about social reform. Or as Croly put it in *The
Modern Thinker* (a short-lived Comtist journal he edited): "We are now
living in anarchy, brought about by our Liberals and Skeptics of all
schools—philosophical, scientific and religious . . . while the disintegrating process continues in theology, public corruption increases with it."
Croly concluded, "The time demands such a cure for that immorality as
is based on the conception of human duty . . . that conception Positivism
only supplies."[68] Here, the first American positivists' loyalty to Comte
created tactical problems for them. After all, this moralism and social
organicism would be much more likely to attract religious conservatives
who were hostile to the new positivist science. Later positivists would
escape this dilemma by aligning with radical reform politics but, for the
orthodox Comtist, it remained a persistent problem.

David Croly was again the most articulate and prolific spokesman of
the orthodox group on social and political topics. Comte clearly struck
responsive chords in the heart of this conservative, pro-Southern Democrat. Croly's critique of the American political system drew out the anti-
majoritarian thrust of Comte's thought. He listed, for example, the
deficiencies of the American electoral process as its tendency to "inten-
sify partisan conflicts" and award "mediocrities," and its encouragement
of both "demagogism" and tyranny of the majority.[69] A proportional
system, similar to that proposed by Mill for Britain, was preferable
because it would produce a more moral and meritocratic system. It
would, Croly believed, "dethrone King Caucus" in state and national
legislatures, "rob minority votes, such as the 'Irish vote,' 'soldiers' vote,'
'workingmen's vote,' and the like, of the undue influence they now
exert; . . . increase the intellectual and moral power of Congress . . .
[and] would ensure us the first minds in the country as executive
officers." Finally, the "demoralizing political contests" of the present
would give way to "efforts of honorable emulation between candidates."[70] Croly's assessment of Gilded Age politics, its elitist, antiparty
spirit and its criticism of ethnic bloc voting anticipated the position of
many Mugwump reformers of the 1880s.

67. [David G. Croly], "Remarks by Editor," *Modern Thinker* 1 (1870): 184.
68. [David G. Croly], "What the Matter Is," *Modern Thinker* 2 (1873): 1020. Emphasis
mine.
69. DGC, "Personal Representation," *Galaxy* 4 (July 1867): 307.
70. Ibid., 312–13.

The solution to America's political and economic predicament constructed by Croly represented a faithful application of Comtean principles. Croly called upon his countrymen to reconcile themselves to the future political rule of the "captains of industry." Now, the industrial entrepreneurs rule by corrupting state and national legislators; why not remove the "middle-men" and formalize the political power of capital, Croly asked.[71] Similarly, Croly composed an open letter to three multimillionaires which appeared in the *Modern Thinker* and argued that political power was rightfully theirs. But Croly took care to lecture each on the social responsibilities of wealth. If wealth is social and not individual in nature, then the capitalist has a weighty responsibility to use his wealth for the benefit of his employees and society at large. As important trustees of social wealth, the awakening of businessmen to their wider duties was critical, explained Croly, because the choice looming before them was either positivism or communism. Public opinion and exposure to the high-minded altruism of positivism could make statesmen out of robber barons.[72] Nor was Croly afraid (at least when writing under a pseudonym) to confront the implications his positivist critique held for American liberal democratic values. "Let it be distinctly understood, then," Croly observed,

> that there is a class of thinkers in this country who are profound dis-believers in the whole republican or democratic theory of government. But we are not, therefore, either Imperialists or Monarchists. We do not advocate going back to any obsolete political institutions. Progress is our motto. There is something in the future as much better than republicanism as republicanism is better than monarchy, and that is the rule of wealth controlled by moral considerations.[73]

Why was "the ideal of a self-respecting, well-intentioned, frugal, Republican Government" now obsolete? Croly answered that "the conditions have widely changed" since the foundation of the republic; there were huge cities now, thousands of recent immigrants, persons without property or local ties. Positivism, Croly felt, furnished a scientific response to modernity that an ideology founded upon a metaphysical

71. D. Goodman [David G. Croly], "King Wealth Coming," *Modern Thinker* 1 (1870): 45–47.

72. [David G. Croly], "Stewart–Astor–Vanderbilt: Letters Addressed to Three Millionaires on the Social Function of Wealth," *Modern Thinker* 2 (1873): 24.

73. DGC, "King Wealth," 47.

notion of natural rights simply could not provide.[74] "We believe,"
declared Croly on behalf of his fellow Comtists, "in a government of
the people, and for the people, but not by the people . . . ; government
by counting noses is to us a preposterous government."[75]

The elitist thrust of Croly's positivism was especially evident in this
emphasis upon the division of labor. Croly rejected the collectivism of
the Paris Commune and the utopianism of other socialist schemes
because they allegedly failed to understand how essential was a hierarchical division of labor to ensuring social order and progress. Employing a
favorite metaphor, Croly observed that "it is impossible for an army to
direct its own movements—it must have a general." Or, to put it
another way, "the bees in the hive represent the Positivist conception of
government"[76] Schemes involving radical land or monetary reform
were dismissed in the *Primer* as wrongheaded and dangerous. Croly's
arguments sounded more European than American. For Croly, members of the working class had no inherent right to rise above their current
social station and "get out of their class"; to teach them that they
should seek upward mobility was "immoral."[77] Positivist society would
probably retain a stratified class structure but all of its classes would
together serve the commonwealth.

With the trusts wielding formal political power, Croly's theory of the
state was active and interventionist. He was an outspoken critic of both
classical and Spencerian laissez-faire. Calls for freedom from governmental restriction were "ridiculous," said Croly, "when the very supposition
of a highly organized, differentiated [economic] structure also included
the idea of one highly integrated, and, as such, necessarily subject to a
new set of limitations."[78] New realities demanded that the state not just
intervene occasionally but become an integral part of the economic
system. "Our government," Croly wrote in 1869,

> from natural and inevitable causes, has got to be one of excessive
> powers. The maladministration of the federal power under Adams
> or Jackson was not of much account, so little were the people at
> large affected by its action; but now it is very different. The
> authority of the central government has grown so enormously
> large, that its action upon the business of the country has become

74. Ibid.
75. DGC, *Positivist Primer*, 103.
76. Ibid., 63, 85.
77. Ibid., 46.
78. Ibid., 68–69, 85.

vital. Hence the necessity of a more scientific government than that we had before the rebellion.[79]

But, unlike Spencer's critics on the Left, Croly sought this "scientific" integration of state authority with corporate capital through elitist and even antidemocratic means.

In its initial step from utopian community to middle-class parlor, American Comtism remained faithful to the sectarian vision of the Master's "second system." The New York disciples were, moreover, able to draw upon key elements of Victorian culture as they constructed a scientistic religiosity to replace America's dominant evangelical Protestant piety. As Jane Cunningham Croly summarized the attraction of the early group for one of its members: "He was particularly attracted to it from three points of view: first, the recognition of the value of all existing and preceding religions; second, its cultivation of duty and the spirit of humanity among men; third, the absence of personal motive, except that of growth in character, as aids to goodness."[80] The historicism and moralism of such a surrogate faith spoke to the Victorian mind and heart. A religion that addressed the Anglo-American middle classes in these terms—a faith both profoundly conservative and yet committed to social progress—was bound to attract some New York intellectuals.

And yet, though one may see how well suited to Victorian culture Comtism was in some respects, it is not difficult to appreciate the failure of sectarian positivism in America. Its ill-concealed atheism and Roman ritual seemed designed to alienate both the traditionalist and the iconoclast.[81] As Joseph H. Allen commented concerning Comtist worship: "These performances, as reported, seem a poor and cold imitation of the least attractive portions of sacerdotal Christianity."[82] Surely for those disenchanted with traditional theism, there were many less alarming alternatives. Henry Edger even appeared to understand that the Protestant piety and anti-authoritarian, individualistic habits of most Americans would make them unlikely converts to orthodox Comtism. In an 1872 letter written to his brother Ebenezer, Edger conceded: "I myself recognize readily enough that the style of the *Positive Catechism*, or rather perhaps its form, is but ill adapted to win the immediate sympathies of

79. DGC , "King Wealth," 47.
80. *Courtland Palmer: Tributes Offered*, 114–15.
81. L. L. Bernard and Jessie Bernard, *Origins of American Sociology: The Social Science Movement in the United States* (New York: Crowell, 1943), 175.
82. Joseph Henry Allen, *Positive Religion: Essays, Fragments and Hints* (Boston: Robert Bros., 1891), 206.

our special social surroundings. I mean especially our ultra protestant and free thinking contemporaries with whom the very idea of theoretical authority is such an immense bugbear!"[83] These very features of Comtean orthodoxy—its bizarre ritual, papal pretensions, and ultraconservative politics—would be purged by the next set of New York positivists.

83. H. Edger, quoted by Schneider, *Apostleship*, 156. For other explanations of the failure of orthodox positivism in the United States, see Frederic Harrison, "Auguste Comte in America," *Positivist Review* 102 (1 June 1901): 121–25; Hawkins, *Positivism*, 215–25.

CHAPTER THREE

"The Mother and Nurse of All Reforms"

Comtean Revisionism, 1876–1883

> . . . so we are compelled to remove the obstructions which we find in the path of religious and political progress. But nothing should be destroyed for the mere sake of destruction. Destruction is only a preparation for construction. The problem of the nineteenth century is just as distinctly reconstruction as that of the eighteenth century was destruction.
> —Lead editorial, *The Evolution* 1 (6 January 1877): 1

DURING THE 1870s, the sectarian spirit of the early New York societies dissipated. Some members of the original body channeled their energies into different causes, which ensured that Comtean thought would eventually influence different parts of the nation's intellectual life. In New York City alone, Comtists helped spawn organizations such as the New York Liberal Club, the Society of Humanity, the Nineteenth Century Club, the Commonwealth Club, and publications such as the *Positive Thinker* and the *Evolution*. These societies served different constituencies but were nurseries of a sort for many influential reformers and social scientists of the Gilded Age and later.[1] The writings and

---

1. Thaddeus Burr Wakeman, *Free Thought: Past, Present and Future* (Chicago: H.L. Green, 1899?), 26–27; *Memories of Jane Cunningham Croly—"Jenny June"* (New York: Putnam, 1904), 53–54.

activities of the revisionists brought Comtean perspectives into the ideological mix of their era. Those groups that sought to retain some of the style of the original society had far less success; while breaking with official Comtism, they could not shake their cultic image. Religious positivism, therefore, even in revised form, attracted little popular interest. But, as the final section of this chapter demonstrates, projects directed by positivists of various stripes that addressed the larger political and cultural concerns of the city's elites had a far broader impact. Comte gave the reform-minded a unique perspective on the country's freewheeling capitalist economy and its deleterious social consequences. He furnished the tools with which to attack the prophets of laissez-faire and allowed the socially and culturally conservative to consider the need for fundamental change.

I

After encouraging the formation of the New York Positivist Society, Henry Edger remained rather distant from its activities. Edger's lack of direct participation seems to have stemmed from three causes. For one, the English immigrant viewed himself as an itinerant evangelist, not the shepherd of established groups. Nor did Edger think highly of the New York society's leadership. To someone like Croly, Edger wrote to English Comtist leader Richard Congreve, "the idea of devotedness is utterly incomprehensible." In this same letter, Edger described the "personal hostility" between himself and society secretary Henry Evans as "based upon personal ambition" and "rivalry" for leadership.[2]

Finally, Edger's illicit affair with Clara Oborne, the wife of his follower John Metcalf, discredited him among some of the New York Comtists and encouraged Edger to seek a "low profile" for several years. As Edger explained in a letter to Metcalf: "They [the Comtists] are just beginning to have a chance; especially the English Branch. I don't want anything Oborne or anybody else can do to mar prospects or give them any more worry than can possibly be helped." To ensure, in Edger's words, "that the general work here in America also may go on independently of my own special action," he took pains to establish "some correspondence between the New York Positivists and Dr. Congreve."[3]

2. Robert E. Schneider, *Positivism in the United States: The Apostleship of Henry Edger* (Argentina: Rosario, 1946), 161–62, 167–68.
3. Ibid., 128–29.

Some formal ties appear to have been established at least by 1871 when David Croly wrote in his *Positivist Primer*: "The head of our church is M. Pierre Lafitte in Paris . . . , our head in England is Dr. Richard Congreve."[4] Perhaps his own personal turmoil, what with Comte's death, the Oborne scandal, and his wife Millicent's mental problems, meant that Edger could no longer manage the New York group nor command respect among its members.[5]

It is difficult to determine how long after its formation the New York Positivist Society survived. There appears to have been some internal dissension (in addition to that involving Edger) almost from the very beginning. Even before there may have been a formal organization, factions emerged among these New York students of Comte. Wrote T. B. Wakeman years later:

> Differences soon arose which made the meetings [at Croly's home in 1867 or 1868] very earnest and interesting. The Crolys and Henry Evans tended towards Comtean Catholicism, others inclined, with Mr. [Courtlandt] Palmer, John Elderkin, and myself towards a republican Positivism; others, with Mr. Ingalls, looked towards some phase of Socialism for the lead of the race in the future.[6]

As a result of these differences, when the orthodox element coalesced to form the Positive Society of North America in 1869, Wakeman secretly backed the creation of the New York Liberal Club. This latter group was designed to provide a less dogmatic and more open forum to

4. C. G. David [David G. Croly], *A Positivist Primer: Being a Series of Familiar Conversations on the Religion of Humanity* (New York: David Wesley, 1871), 111.

5. Millicent Edger died in an insane asylum in Connecticut in 1870 during one of Edger's trips to England (see LLB, *Diary*, 5:7). L. L. Bernard observed after reading Edger's private journals for these years: ". . . but after his [Comte's] death and the ascendancy of Lafitte and Richard Congreve he [Edger] seemed to have a good deal of inner conflict and gradually to lose interest. He would never admit this to himself even[?]; so he worked spasmodically and cooked up more or less grandiose schemes and wrote propaganda letters to ease his conscience and give a good impression to the European contingent. But it is interesting to note that his entries in his journals are less complete and tangible and objective after Comte has been dead a year or two and some ten years afterwards they cease altogether without any explanation in the Journals themselves. . . . It is possible that the movement, which he tried so hard to dominate ruthlessly while it was growing, finally grew out of his hands" (LLB, *Diary*, 3:11–12). Given the publication of strongly Comtean articles by Edger during the seventies, it seems unlikely that he simply lost interest in the 'Cause.'

6. TBW, "The New York–Manhattan Liberal Club: The Story of Its Past and Present, and a Prophecy of its Future," *Truth Seeker* 1 (23 January 1909): 50.

discuss the whole spectrum of radical philosophical thought. For the time being, however, Wakeman continued his affiliation with his orthodox Comtean brethren.[7] Alluding to the persistent factionalism within the society, Elizabeth Dudley wrote that the New York Positivists were finding it "so difficult to create true social feeling among themselves."[8] Then, in July 1873, the society was reorganized. Lelia, Edger's daughter then in London, described the situation this way in a letter to her father:

> [T]he Positivist Society in New York has quite changed its position. Mr. [Thaddeus B.] Wakeman, the great disturbing element, has been expelled (if I understand Dr. C. [Congreve] rightly) and Mr. [Henry] Evans has been chosen leader and the whole Society seems quite ready to place itself in subordination to Mr. Lafitte [Comte's successor in Paris]; thro' him, in fact they have done so already, and have sent subscriptions to a considerable amount and profess to hold themselves in readiness to do anything Dr. Congreve may suggest.[9]

Reasons for the Wakeman schism were probably twofold. To begin with, it appears from Lelia's letter that some in the society (led by Wakeman) opposed any affiliation with Edger in the wake of the Clara Oborne scandal. In fact, to prevent the New York Society from severing its ties altogether with orthodox positivism as represented by Laffitte and Congreve, Edger had earlier resigned his position on the Positive Committee.[10] The exclusion of Wakeman also doubtless arose from his critical attitude toward his co-religionists' aping Roman Catholic ritual, their idealization of the medieval church, and their conception of the role of the positivist priesthood in the future polity. Wakeman's other political views also appear to have been more liberal than those of the society's leadership. Nonetheless, while officially excluded from the New York society, Wakeman would not remain inactive.

In May 1876, a new group was formed which took as its name The First Congregation of the Religion of Humanity (or simply, the Society of Humanity). It is unclear as to whether the first society founded by Edger was still in existence at this time (Edger left New York permanently for Europe in 1879) and whether this new group was formed primarily by dissidents from the original body. At any rate, Wakeman

7. Ibid.
8. "The New York Positivists," *Old and New*, 3 (1873): 304.
9. Schneider, *Positivism*, 161.
10. Ibid., 191.

was instrumental in establishing the new society and he clearly saw it as a successor to the initial group. The intention originally, Wakeman later reflected, had been "to establish a nucleus of positive philosophy and human religion in the City of New York" and the mission of the new body was essentially the same.[11] Wakeman and his associates now maintained a more independent relationship vis-à-vis Comtean orthodoxy centered in Paris and London. Writing from Europe, Edger referred to Wakeman et al. as one of "the scattered forces . . . who without directly co-operating in the essential task, the organization of the new Priesthood, are still working, whether consciously or not, in the same direction."[12]

Besides Wakeman, the two prime movers of the society were G. L. Henderson and H. B. Brown. Henderson, "a Scotch Freethinker and Positivist," rented in 1876 an edifice on Eighth Street in Manhattan that contained a large meeting room. The building was promptly renamed Science Hall and became the office for a Freethought paper, the *Truth Seeker*, as well as the main meeting place for the Society of Humanity, the Manhattan Liberal Club, and (the latter's press) the New York Liberal Publishing Company. Brown was a New York journalist who shared Wakeman's Comtean revisionism.[13] Together, Henderson and Brown put out a short-lived Comtist periodical called the *Positive Thinker*, described in advertisements as a "semi-monthly, radical, constructive journal." The Liberal Publishing Company also released a short book by Henderson called the *Positive Catechism* and a number of Wakeman's monographs. On top of this ambitious publishing activity, the Society continued the original group's habit of holding Sunday worship services (now in Science Hall) led by Wakeman and T. C. Edwards, a stalwart of the earlier society.[14]

The constitution of the Society of Humanity suggests some ways in which the new body differed from its predecessors. For instance, the objects of the society were defined quite broadly in Article II of the document:

1. To develop and extend a knowledge of the synthetic or religious value of SCIENCE and HUMANITY.

11. TBW, *Epitome of the Positive Philosophy and Religion* (New York: Society of Humanity, 1877), i; TBW, *Free Thought*, 26.

12. Schneider, *Positivism*, 200.

13. George E. MacDonald, *Fifty Years of Freethought: Being the Story of the Truth Seeker, with the Natural History of its Third Editor* (New York: Truth Seeker, 1929), 1:179; "The Death and Funeral of Hugh Byron Brown," *Truth Seeker* 25 (6 August 1898): 504.

14. G. L. Henderson, *The Positive Catechism: A Text Book on Religion, Philosophy and*

2. To present them, instead of Theology, as the basis and substance of Religion.
3. To practice and promote such Religion, as the foundation of individual and social duty, and of human welfare and progress.[15]

A number of committees were established by the constitution, including one for "Exercises and Religious Affairs," one on "Womanhood," and one on "Humanity." The concerns of this last committee suggest that the sectarian ethos of the group was being displaced by a broad social reform impulse. Members of the committee were to be both lobbyists and muckrakers. They were to endeavor, by "legal or legislative means, to aid in having the evils by which Humanity is afflicted or debased mitigated or removed . . . [and] investigate and bring to justice or public obloquy special instances of cruelty, wrong, baseness, or inhumanity in any form." There was, moreover, no mention of Comte in the articles, though positivism was referred to in Article VI as the penultimate stage "of the religious and social development of Humanity."[16] The society grew even less sectarian as the years passed. In 1887, having received a gift of $10,000 from a wealthy supporter, the society moved into new premises on 28 Lafayette Street. George MacDonald described the meetings there that he covered for the *Truth Seeker*: "on the parlor floor meetings and sociables that might almost be called receptions were held. Birthdays of Paine and Jefferson were celebrated, their services and principles expounded, and then there were musical and literary offerings, followed by dancing. They were quite brilliant functions."[17] Evidently, American skeptics and deists were replacing the saints of the Comtean calendar as the focus of society functions.

In attempting to become less sectarian, the society gradually attached itself to a broad spectrum of Gilded Age Freethought and reform groups. Henry George was, for example, reported to have attended one of their soirées. A reform journal, *Commonwealth*, established its office in the society's Lafayette Street address in the 1890s. Subtitled first "a monthly magazine and library of sociology," for slightly over a year, its masthead proclaimed it to be the "Official Organ of the Society of Humanity." A year or so earlier, a journal advertisement for the society had noted:

Morals (New York: New York Liberal Publishing, 1878), 2:38; James D. Bell, ed., *The Evolution: A Weekly Review of Politics Religion, Science, Literature and Art* 1 (1877): 2.

15. TBW, *Epitome*, 51.
16. Ibid., 54.
17. MacDonald, *Fifty Years*, 2:416–17.

The work of the Society and of the Commonwealth being along similar lines, they have co-operated in many ways with good results, and hope, by continued co-operation, to accomplish much more, and to soon realize that future which cheered the last days of Harriet Martineau when she said: "The world as it is grows somewhat dim before my eyes, but the world that is to be looks brighter every day."[18]

These growing links between New York Comtists and Gilded Age Freethought and reform closely paralleled Wakeman's evolving concerns between the Civil War and the turn of the century. As for the Society of Humanity, though the Commonwealth continued to be published for several years, there is no record of such an organization after May 1896.

II

Consonant with these organizational changes, the positivism of the Society of Humanity represented a significant departure from the Comtean orthodoxy of its predecessors. Wakeman and others associated with the society wanted to Americanize positivism, to remove its dogmatism, its cultic or sectarian features, and its exclusivist claims. A more open, pluralistic, and democratic spirit is evident among these "Americanists," though the illiberal, authoritarian spirit of an Edger or Croly was never entirely absent.

Most striking, to begin with, was the new attitude to Comte himself and the Master's relationship to the positivist system. In An Epitome of the Positive Philosophy and Religion, Wakeman gave notice that his new society would not represent the cult of the now-deceased French philosopher. Careful to proclaim Comte's Cours "still the most useful initiative and outline," Wakeman nevertheless asserted "that the true philosophy and religion of our race is not, and cannot be, the pendant of any personality, however great."[19] Since Comte's system was "in no sense to be regarded as a finality," it had to be supplemented with the insights garnered by subsequent thinkers. Such an open perspective was not

18. "The Society of Humanity," Commonwealth: A Monthly Magazine and Library of Sociology 1 (1893): 3.

19. TBW, Epitome, ii–iii; TBW, The Religion of Humanity (New York: New York Liberal Publishing, 1878), 29.

disloyal to positivism, Wakeman contended, but was, in fact, "a religious duty."[20]

Having cut himself free from official Comtism, Wakeman was able to develop his critique of the Comtean system; this is how he later described his revisionist efforts at the funeral of his associate, H. B. Brown: "The Positivism of Auguste Comte, as therefore introduced into this country by his disciple, Mr. Henry Edgar [*sic*], was made to change its base from the attempt to revive Catholicism, plus science but minus theology, to a new and broader position in harmony with republican evolution."[21] How could such a brilliant thinker, the "father of sociology," have been so misled? Wakeman's answer seemed to suggest Gallic inferiority. Such a misbegotten authoritarian scheme was probably the product "of his Catholic ancestry and of his personal environment."[22] This "personal limitation" of Comte's need not distract American students, however. After all, if Comte "had been 'caught when young,' his disciples would never had had occasion to call upon us 'to accept' such absurdities."[23]

The more critical stance of later American positivists did leave them open to a host of new philosophical currents that were not strictly Comtean. For T. B. Wakeman, these non-Comtean currents included the writings of Johann Wolfgang von Goethe (1749–1832). Being fond of the German master's poetry, Wakeman translated much of his work and quoted it frequently. From the quotations that he placed along excerpts from Comte's *Catechism* in one of his works, it appears that Goethe's enthusiastic humanism and epigrammatic style most attracted Wakeman. His interest in Goethe may help account for Wakeman's Germanophilia and monism, but how he reconciled Goethe's pantheism and Kantianism with Comtean positivism remains unclear in his early work.[24] Wakeman simply pictured Comte and Goethe "as prominent founders of the new faith." While "contrasts of each other," Wakeman believed that, understood properly, Goethe and Comte were "the supplements of each other. He who can best combine the free growth of the one with the method and social purposes of the other will be our completest man. Their works are an inexhaustible storehouse of suggestions in and toward the new culture."[25]

The eclecticism of the new positivists is also evident in their increased concern for scientific classification, empirical method, and positivist

20. TBW, *Epitome*, iii.
21. "Death and Funeral," 504.
22. TBW, *Epitome*, viii.
23. TBW, *Religion of Humanity*, 29.
24. TBW, *Epitome*, 3–6.
25. Ibid., 34–35.

epistemology. Much of Wakeman's early work was, for example, largely concerned with the question of classification. Accordingly, Wakeman found the "synthetic outlines" of Spencer and Fiske especially attractive; in fact, his monistic vocabularly often sounds more Spencerian than Comtean. Where possible, though, Wakeman still wanted to reconcile these contemporary grand theories with the Comtean system. For example, Wakeman was particularly concerned that the seemingly contradictory Spencerian and Comtean classifications of the sciences be somehow fitted together. Wakeman did criticize Spencer's hierarchy but, if viewed as merely a subjective or logical classification, he believed it could be reconciled to Comte's objective or empirical model. In Wakeman's words, "the Logical principle of Spencer's classification, may be retained and substantially harmonized with the Objective and cumulative orders of the Positive Classification, by recognizing as he [Spencer] does not, the plain distinction between the abstract and the concrete in each Science."[26] Similarly, society cofounder G. L. Henderson's *Positive Catechism* spent much of its sixty pages classifying different aspects of man and nature, or categorizing scientific theories that attempted to explain these two.[27]

For Wakeman and Henderson, such classification represented the very essence of Positive science and was closely linked to the inductive method. When induction discovers something, Henderson explained, it classifies it and this is called Science; such knowledge of verified and classified facts is called "Positive Knowledge"; those who attain such knowledge are called "Positive Thinkers."[28] Therefore, part of the concern for classification was an attempt to remain loyal to an inductive method, which for these positivists defined true science. Another part of their concern seems to have arisen out of the characteristic philosophical monism of the period. By the 1880s, positivists were increasingly fascinated with integrating into some sort of monolithic structure the varied forms of scientific knowledge. Such monism had, after all, profound religious implications. "The more this scale [the classification of the sciences] is used," declared Wakeman, "the more will it crystalize the mind and bring order out of chaos. It is the backbone of the new faith."[29] The work of Wakeman and others reflect this gradual transition of Comtism into a kind of cosmic monism.[30]

26. TBW, *An Extension and Enlargement of the Positive Classification of the Sciences* (New York: New York Liberal Publishing, 1881), 8.

27. Henderson, *Positive Catechism*; see esp. 10–11.

28. Ibid., 6.

29. TBW, *Epitome*, 14.

30. See Leszek Kolakowski, *The Alienation of Reason: A History of Positivist Thought*, trans. Norman Guterman (New York: Doubleday, 1968), 101, for an analysis of this trend.

The religious thought of Wakeman's circle again demonstrates how Comte was Americanized and how the new groups were less narrow or sectarian in character. Wakeman's positivists were still profoundly interested in Comtism as surrogate religion. They, too, viewed their era as one of religious and intellectual upheavel. Henderson saw "individuals losing their peace of mind" and interpreted this as "the evidence of the decay and death of a system of religion."[31] When he asked how intellectual unity could be reestablished, the following exchange appeared in the *Positive Catechism*:

A. Through the intellect and the affections.

Q. Where must the intellect look for a sure foundation?
A. To science.

Q. Where will the affections find full satisfaction?
A. In the love and service of Humanity.

Q. What name would you give to a religion which relied on these?
A. The Religion of Humanity.[32]

Even those positivists who openly dissociated their religious ideas from Comte's vision, continued to seek a scientific surrogate for Christianity. Most explicit in this regard was Wakeman's friend Courtlandt Palmer who credited his fellow lawyer with delivering him "from the superstitions of the old theology" and giving him an "abiding sense of salvation in the new faith of science." In *The Cause of Humanity, Or, The Waning and Rising Faith* (1879), Palmer wrote that his Religion of Humanity was not exactly that of Comte, though he accorded "that most noble and most able man the first place in this connection."[33] Palmer also acknowledged Spencer and Francis E. Abbot as "powerful auxillaries" to his main argument. If the present is indeed a period of philosophical upheaval and religious decline, then, Palmer contended, skeptics must be careful. For the character of the coming era depends, Palmer observed, on what one constructs now. Quoting Comte's dictum "To destroy, you must replace," Palmer stressed that an iconoclastic rationalism was no longer enough. Nor could the new religious synthesis be based upon "natural theology." "Let me conjure both Christian and Liberal thinkers that they deceive not themselves," Palmer cautioned. "Between science

31. Henderson, *Positive Catechism*, 18.
32. Ibid., 3.
33. *The Cause of Humanity, Or, the Waning and Rising Faith: An Essay From the Standpoint of the Positive Philosophy* (New York: New York Liberal Publishing, 1879), 8.

and doctrinal theology there can be no truce."[34] For Palmer, the only sure foundation for the new faith was positivist science.

Besides its exclusively empirical foundation, Palmer believed that his Religion of Humanity was superior to Christianity in two other respects. For one, it was progressive and hopeful. It accepted the evolution both of man and of his moral and religious systems. "The ape progressive opens boundless vistas for the Future of the Race," Palmer reflected, "the angel fallen tolls the knell of human hope."[35] But, though there is no fall from grace, the "Great Being," Humanity, does fulfill Christ's role in some respects. Following Comte, Palmer understood Humanity as a kind of symbolic mediator between the objective, external world and the subjective individual.[36] As Comte had done, Palmer's religion retained and recast some traditional images humans had long found meaningful, while it discarded those doctrines that were deemed backward.

Though agreeing that Comte's attempt to make the new positivist religion a sort of "Catholicism minus theology" was misguided, Wakeman's cohort was divided about the Master's assessment of Protestantism. Henderson's view was largely negative (as Comte's had been) but the conflict between the church and science was now given considerably more emphasis. The *Positive Catechism* examined the cases of Copernicus, Bruno, and Galileo at some length and the author took pains to show that the Catholic church had not been any more cruel or repressive than had Protestants and that the Reformers should in no way be viewed as progressive. For instance, Henderson concluded that the result of Luther's teaching regarding the Bible and the "priesthood of all believers" was that

> Popes were multiplied, their doctrine maintained by force, because the Bible contained them, and not because they were right or reasonable . . . [the Reformers] carried them [i.e., Protestants] back to the cradle of the church and compelled them to read the "Primer," containing the myths of the orient, as a literal statement of facts, which was like compelling a man of fifty to receive instruction from a babe.[37]

Evidently, Henderson felt the need to disabuse his American readers of the idea that the Protestant reformers were champions of freedom of

34. Ibid., 8, 17.
35. Ibid., 27.
36. Ibid., 32–33, 38.
37. Henderson, *Positive Catechism*, 13.

thought. Though more critical of the medieval church than Comte had been, Henderson still saw the Reformation as the triumph of destructive and chaotic forces, including a primitive bibliolatry and anarchic individualism.

Palmer, on the other hand, broke with Comte, Edger, Croly, and Henderson and identified the "twin Saviors" of humanity from the tyranny of dogmatic Christianity as "Protestantism and Science." It was Protestantism, Palmer contended, that "with its dogma of the right of private judgement, shouted revolt against authority, the destruction of idol worship, [and] the overthrow of all false Gods." Similarly, Palmer saw Unitarianism as a progressive development from Protestantism, just as the latter had been "an advance upon Romanism."[38] But Palmer was careful to reiterate that the simple nay-saying of liberal Christianity was inadequate; only science could provide alternative principles upon which to construct the new ethical / religious synthesis. Nevertheless, Protestantism and Unitarianism for Palmer were, contrary to Comte, genuinely progressive developments and not destructive missteps.

Nor was Henderson reluctant to criticize Comte's idealization of medieval Roman Catholicism. Though he agreed with Comte's interpretation of the Reformation, Henderson did not admire the monolithic ideological consensus of the Middle Ages. Sounding more like Mill than Comte, Henderson argued that citizens be left free to pick and choose their own preferences in the "market place of ideas":

A. It is much more safe to permit truth and error to contend freely together than to establish an authority to decide what is true and persecute all who oppose it.

Q. How can you make this apparent?

A. By an appeal to history which shows that established authority condemned as false what later generations accepted as true.[39]

Of course, part of Comte's admiration for the Catholic church was in fact based upon its far-reaching control of cultural and intellectual life in medieval Europe. Indeed, Henderson's formulation of the right of rebellion seems to have owed more to Locke than to Comte. When asked whether it was wise to rebel against the state, Henderson declared: "It is wise to resist any power which suppresses the brain, the hand, or the

38. Palmer, *Cause*, 43, 48.
39. Henderson, *Positive Catechism*, 28.

heart. One who lives and is not free to exercise these is a slave."[40] Certainly one of the persistent tensions in the political discourse of American positivism was this interaction between a Romantic or scientistic authoritarianism and the libertarian impulse of classical liberalism.

Americanization also meant that Comte's social and political thought would have to be purified of much of its conservative, European character. Again, while the individual routes taken by society members varied in this regard, they shared an essentially Comtean understanding of the fundamental questions.

Here, Wakeman's critique of Comte was again the most developed. His main criticisms were directed at Comte's inordinate admiration for the Roman Catholic church and his advocacy of a hierarchical papal model for the future Positive polity. Other members of the New York societies had earlier expressed misgivings about these features of the Master's work, but none had really articulated their views in a coherent way. For Wakeman, such a structure "as set forth in his [Comte's] Catechism and the fourth volume of his Positive Polity [was] . . . clearly a mistaken deduction in Sociology." History demonstrates, Wakeman believed, that an autocratic structure such as the papacy could only exist under the theological dispensation; today, secular governments must exercise all temporal authority. In a backward thrust at Henry Edger, Wakeman described the attempt to realize such a papal system in America as "retrograde and worse than useless." As for what the future polity would look like, Wakeman had few doubts. "It is useless to deny," he declared, "that the Republic is the great modern fact in Sociology, and the great hope and ideal of the world." In light of these facts, Wakeman concluded, "it may be proper to distinguish Positivism, with its progressive Republic, from Comtism with its retrograde Papacy."[41]

Sociology and history suggest rather that the "true [political] order" will most likely arise "from the Germanic Anglo-Saxon American town, nation and republic, with its appeal to the people, a jury and a parliament. . . . Those who would organize the future of Humanity cannot be reminded too often that the Germans did defeat the legions of Varus, and that no people who escaped the Roman Empire have ever been governed by its methods, spiritual or temporal."[42] On top of this Teutonic chauvinism, Wakeman added a touch of American patriotism. "Our own federal union is the type," Wakeman thought, of what he

40. Ibid., 31.
41. TBW, *Epitome*, vii–viii.
42. Ibid., 36–37.

elsewhere called "the Grand Federal Republic of Mankind."[43] As a model
for the future world order, the United States rightfully has a "leading
place" among nations. This emphasis upon republicanism and national
pride represents one of Wakeman's most important contributions to the
American Comtean tradition. "Patriotism," he wrote in the *Religion of
Humanity*, "is part of the Religion of Earth and it rests upon some
knowledge of the benefits of republican government; and that, and the
consequent duties, must rest upon some theory of human progress and
of history." The schools must therefore teach Positive Science if patriotism is to be fostered and "the future of the great republic is to be
worthily upheld."[44]

Aside from differing with Comte as to the precise character and shape
of the Positive polity, Wakeman also rejected the Master's tactics for
establishing the new world order. Comte's attempt to secure conservative support for his cause had been "fruitless" and was based upon false
assumptions. Men of means remain selfish, Wakeman observed. "The
Conservatives have shown, again and again, that they will force a
revolution," he wrote, "if they can, rather than relinquish a profitable
injustice. Upon them the Religion of Humanity has been chiefly
wasted."[45] So much for Comte's suggestion to Edger that he seek out
Jesuits in New York as potential converts, or Croly's open letters to
leading industrial entrepreneurs. Wakeman did not abandon his elitist
social ties, but as the years passed he increasingly looked elsewhere
for leadership.[46]

The natural allies of positivism were, Wakeman believed, the very
groups Comte had dismissed as "Revolutionists"—the "Evolutionists,
Scientists, Liberals, democrats and Socialists." Comtists must not alienate such individuals, for they are "the only people who have either the
power or the will to secure progress and thereby develop order."[47] Only
the progressive, freethinking element in politics or religion would be
likely to entertain the positivist perspective. Cooperating with these
groups, positivism could become a kind of liberal umbrella, or in
Wakeman's own words, "the mother and nurse of all reforms, and of all
beneficent, political and social changes." As part of a larger reform
movement, positivists need not be tied to a specific utopian blueprint;

---

43. TBW, *Religion*, 30; TBW, *Epitome*, v.
44. TBW, *Religion*, 25.
45. TBW, *Epitome*, ix.
46. Wakeman was, after all, a member of Courtlandt Palmer's socially exclusive Nineteenth Century Club for several years.
47. TBW, *Epitome*, ix.

such "details of organization" would doubtless appear as society progressed. Such an approach was not a repudiation of Comte, Wakeman argued, but was, rather, consistent with his own "law of adaptation and adjustment."[48]

Wakeman's critical stance obviously implied severing relations with official Comtism and its leaders in Paris and London. Wakeman accordingly repudiated any official connections between the Society of Humanity and Laffitte or Congreve (though there may still have been some communication between these groups). Wakeman insisted that, unlike its predecessor, his society was not a foreign satellite, "but an independent growth from the seed—and on American Soil." "The new wine," he wrote, "has been largely wasted by attempts to force it into old bottles."[49]

Yet Wakeman did not throw out Comte's idea of a "spiritual power" or priesthood completely. This "new wine" of Comte's needed simply to be placed in a new bottle, one consistent with "a republican point of view." Wakeman believed that America's universities were the probable "centers of the new theoretical power." All that was required was for these institutions to be secularized and run by men dedicated to science. Under such a system of higher education, the nation would attain a social and intellectual cohesion as an outgrowth "of the positive method itself."[50] The faculty of such universities could properly be called priests, being all exponents of the true faith of humanity. Although Wakeman neglected to develop such a plan in his early writings, this would prove to be a not uncommon way to interpolate Comte in the American milieu.[51]

Meanwhile, Courtlandt Palmer's attempts to refurbish Comte's social and political ideas showed an even more eclectic spirit. Although he employed many of the same corporatist and organic analogies as had Comte, Palmer was not reluctant to adopt new terminology. Industry, he wrote, "must be changed from competition to some form of cooperation. Individualism must give way to socialism." Positivism, Palmer concluded, "sets the seal of its approval on the vast trend of republicanism now so triumphant through the world."[52] It is difficult to imagine David Croly drawing a similar lesson from recent history. Indeed, Palmer defended in most un-Comtean terms the people's "natu-

48. Ibid., xii, ix.
49. Ibid., x, viii.
50. Ibid, x–xi.
51. The following chapter recounts Wakeman's efforts to help establish the Freethought "Liberal University" in Oregon.
52. Courtlandt Palmer (CP), *The Spiritual Life* (New York: n.p., 1883?), 30–31.

ral right of self-rule" and portrayed the general public as "the court of last resort" within the polity.[53]

So, as some positivists ran to embrace the reform politics of the 1870s and 1880s, their social theory became a sometimes contradictory amalgam of discourses.

III

By the 1870s, there was much about life in New York that disturbed the city's middle and upper classes. There was glaring social inequality, a rising crime rate and alarming growth among the so-called dangerous classes. Even members of the city's patrician class found it difficult to insulate themselves entirely from this disquieting scene. Mindful of their position, some intellectual elites sought to address this perceived social crisis. As Thomas Bender has shown, the social responsibility and cultural leadership of the urban gentry were two issues that defined the intellectual discourse of New York in the 1870s and 1880s. How should the community's "natural leaders" channel or control worsening class conflict? How could intellectuals "establish themselves as authoritative" in the mass politics and culture of a rapidly changing city? Moreover, because New York was the journalistic capital of the country, these questions inevitably became topics of national concern.[54]

One publication that became a vehicle for these concerns was E. L. Godkin's *Nation*. Consistently in the pages of the *Nation*, Godkin extolled the virtues of limited government, while he attacked the class politics of the disinherited. Godkin's regular targets included organized labor, ethnic voters, currency reformers, and feminists. Against these "particular interests," Godkin asserted the "common good," as defined by the educated and propertied classes. And the *Nation* proved to be enormously influential.[55] Bender aptly characterizes its achievement this way: "In New York during the 1860s and 1870s, the metropolitan gentry, responding to their local circumstances, redefined the domain of political discourse, greatly reducing its territory. Writing for the nation's middle classes as well as for those of their own city, New York's political

53. CP, "European Aristocracy: Its Responsibilities and Opportunities," *Westminster Review* 128 (August 1887): 622.

54. Thomas Bender, *New York Intellect: A History of Intellectual Life in New York City from 1750 to the Beginnings of Our Own Time* (New York: Knopf, 1987), 3, 171.

55. Ibid., 187, 183.

journalists were able to propagate a liberal opinion that advanced their own interest, as a class and as intellectuals, while denying the legitimacy of any other interests." Godkin eventually used the word "Liberalism" (a comparatively new term in this context, at least before the 1870s) to describe his laissez-faire politics.[56]

There were, however, dissenting voices within New York's intellectual community, and positivists were prominent among them.[57] In fact, positivists James D. Bell and Henry Evans founded and ran (albeit briefly) a reform-oriented alternative to the *Nation*. The *Evolution*, which described itself as a "Weekly Review of Politics, Religion, Science, Literature and Art," was begun in early 1877 under the editorship of Bell and represented one of the most ambitious efforts on the part of New York's positivists to enter the mainstream of the country's political and cultural discourse. Apparently modeled after the English *Fortnightly*, the *Evolution's* regular contributors included (besides Bell and Evans) several who had earlier attended Comtist meetings, such as Augusta Cooper Bristol and John G. Mills. Lester Ward was also a contributor, although only his initials appeared on his contributions and on the review's masthead. Even new articles penned by Edger himself appeared regularly.[58]

In fact, it seems that the number of positivists on the publication's editorial board caused some controversy at first. When Asa K. Butts, a liberal-minded New York publisher, took over the editorial reins from Bell, the new editor found it necessary to deny that the *Evolution* was a party mouthpiece of the Comtists. "In answer to many inquiries," Butts wrote, "we say: First, that the EVOLUTION is not an organ of the Positivists, any more than it is of the Free Religionists, the Materialists, or even the Christians. . . . The leading Positivists in this country as in Europe stand in the front ranks of Science and Literature. No first-class literary enterprise is started without the co-operation of several. As we could not conduct this journal without them it does become their *medium* while it is the *organ* of no none." Butts closed his open letter to the readership with a defense of regular contributor, Henry Edger. Although he admitted that Edger was a positivist "in a sectarian sense," Butts

56. Ibid., 189. Regarding the use of the term 'liberal' in a political context, see Dorothy Ross, "Liberalism," in *Encyclopedia of American Political History*, ed. Jack P. Greene (New York: Scribner, 1984), 2:750.

57. Bender does mention William Dean Howells as one of the few dissenters from this gentry consensus. See *New York Intellect*, 191–94.

58. Conspicuously absent from the masthead were David Croly and T. B. Wakeman, although the latter did receive a favorable reference in the journal's first number. See *Evolution* 1:2.

characterized Edger's articles as "masterly" and concluded: "If mankind must have a religion they can find none better than the one he elucidates."[59]

The pages of the *Evolution* provide a unique insight into how the revisionists sought to apply Comtean social theory to the political and cultural questions of their day.[60] Clearly, they shared much of Godkin's concern that educated elites provide national leadership and, like the *Nation*, they sought to speak primarily to that class. "That wing of the instructed classes," declared Bell in his opening editorial, "which is thoroughly emancipated in religion and politics is the only really earnest, faithful, constructive, hopeful, thankful portion of modern society. It is for its members that we propose to publish THE EVOLUTION." According to Bell, the "speculative and religious organs" of these freethinking Mugwumps "are unworthy of them" because they continued to mouth the "exploded" natural rights philosophy of the eighteenth century. As for their "more purely political organs," these have failed to be truly independent, notwithstanding their claims of nonpartisanship. To drive his point home, Bell attacked the partisan spirit of the *Nation* (without mentioning it by name), denouncing its editorial stance during the Tilden–Hayes presidential contest of 1876 as "bitter and unscrupulous."[61]

Like the *Nation*, the *Evolution* believed that "the wider the basis of suffrage the more necessary are proper safeguards about its exercise." But Bell's positivists regularly assaulted the selfish, negative liberalism of Godkin and company. Regarding Spencer, Bell wrote, "while showing himself keenly alive to the despotic tendencies of the general and national executives, he entirely overlooks the germs of those tendencies in individuals and corporations pursuing certain lines of industry. For me despotism is despotism, whatever be its source or origin, and I can not imagine why the tyranny of a railroad president should be sacred and beyond discussion."[62] Also like the *Nation*, the *Evolution* praised the

59. *Evolution*, 1:260.

60. Bell and his positivist colleagues also used the pages of the *Evolution* to defend Comte's religious and philosophical teaching against the critical or unappreciative. For example, Bell excoriated Francis Bowen for criticizing Comte in his *Modern Philosophy* and rejected Spencer's "Unknowable" as nonsense while defending "the legitimacy of a religion of humanity." Also, he attacked English positivist George Henry Lewes for borrowing key concepts from Comte without acknowledging his debt to the Frenchman. As Bell said in closing: "it is very distasteful to me to appear as an advocate in such a matter, but so long as a thinker is unduly depreciated and neglected so long is it needful to reassert his claims and defend his originality" (*Evolution*, 1:235; for above material, see *Evolution*, 1:295–96, 214).

61. *Evolution*, 1:1, 2.

62. Ibid., 1:1, 214. The social position of the *Evolution's* contributors was, on the whole,

initiative and ability of entrepreneurs like Cornelius Vanderbilt but balanced its eulogy (in the case of Vanderbilt) with sharp criticism of a lack of "public spirit" and a predilection for corporate secrecy. In light of the power of private interests, these positivists argued that the state had to wield substantial authority. Government, Bell contended, had always been a natural part of human society and, therefore, asked only to be used intelligently and creatively. Declared Bell, "There is no escape from the conclusion that governments, in origin, at least, are products of man's social needs . . . but if we treat all government as evil, and fondly dream that we ought to be able to get along without it, government will not die, but it will go from bad to worse."[63]

Similarly, although the *Evolution* decried, along with the *Nation*, the violent tactics of some labor unions, its treatment of organized labor was far more sympathetic than the *Nation* and its allies. In its premiere issue, Bell declared his intention "to treat the labor question, in all its aspects, and with perfect freedom from bias towards either party to the controversy."[64] Certainly in his handling of the Great Railroad Strike of 1877, Bell (by then, no longer editor) appears to have kept his promise. At the height of the strike, Bell observed: "The railroad corporations have all the talking elements on their side." The newspapers and the lawyers shamefully denounced the strikers as "fiends who should be shot down in their tracks." Bell showed no reluctance in assailing "the greedy and grinding self-seeking of railroad officials," whose methods appeared to him "far from an improvement on the slave system." If the railroad bosses could not keep their employees happy, "the obvious inference is not that their power is now too small . . . but that it is much larger than they have abilities to execute, and should be curtailed." Unlike most mainstream commentators at the time, Bell also recognized that larger issues were at stake: "Is all our boasted civilization and liberty to end in piling up colossal fortunes, and making a permanent pauper class? This is the real question." For Bell, the state was the logical agency to put the railroads in their place but he observed sadly that "the government truckles altogether too much to the railroads." Bell's conclusion was a typical Comtean balancing act: though he sympathized with the aspirations of labor, "anarchy should not be tolerated for a moment."[65] Social progress demanded state action but order was the prerequisite of all genuine progress.

---

more modest than those at the *Nation* and this class dimension may help account for some of the outspokenness of the former on socioeconomic issues.

63. Ibid., 1:20, 34.
64. Ibid., 1:15.
65. Ibid., 1:221–22.

Throughout the short life of the *Evolution*, Bell and his associates argued that their radicalism in politics (and in religion, for that matter) was a conservative, constructive radicalism. Echoing Comte, they were highly critical of the continuation by some Gilded Age reformers of the largely negative, destructive approach of eighteenth-century radicals. "Nothing should be destroyed," Bell proclaimed in the premier issue, "for the mere sake of destruction. Destruction is only a preparation for construction. The problem of the nineteenth century is just as distinctly reconstruction as that of the eighteenth century was destruction."[66] Rather than return with Godkin et al. to the negative liberalism of the previous century, the staff of the *Evolution* sought a reconstruction of liberalism in America along essentially Comtean lines.

The other major venture spearheaded by Wakeman's circle of Comtean revisionists addressed, even more directly and successfully, the cultural and intellectual concerns of the New York gentry during the last two decades of the century. With the encouragement of Wakeman, Court-landt Palmer founded the Nineteenth Century Club in 1882. Under the patronage of the well-heeled Palmer, the society thrived for many years. Profoundly influenced by Wakeman's religious and political views, Palmer's own philosophy was a typically Comtean mixture of reformist rhetoric and elitist principles. "The body political," he once wrote, "must have its organs—that is, its directors—as well as the body human . . . ; most of the individuals born into this world are born, not to lead, but to follow."[67] Like his more conservative predecessors, Palmer valued elite leadership and a hierarchical division of labor. In fact, Palmer attempted to resurrect Comte's notion of a ruling "spiritual power" in his creation of the Nineteenth Century Club in 1882. As Palmer envisaged it, "Such clubs . . . seem to me to indicate the possible inauguration of what might be called a supplementary spiritual power on the earth based on the average conscience, common sense, aestheticism of the advanced souls of all faiths, philosophies and politics; . . . a power which, while responsive to, would yet mold and lead public opinion towards all that is excellent."[68]

On one level, the club was supposed to be an open evening discussion group to foster greater tolerance for radical philosophical viewpoints. Under Palmer's roof, New Yorkers of varied opinion could hear and discuss the central philosophical, political, and artistic questions of the day. For its motto, the club chose the Pauline injunction favored of

66. Ibid., 1:1.
67. CP, "European Aristocracy," 622.
68. Ibid, 625.

positivists: "Prove all things; hold fast that which is good." Although
the club was to "promulgate no 'ism' as its own" and entertain addresses
from any person "whether he be orthodox or heterodox," the Comtist
in Palmer could not help add "that ultimately out of the chaos of
conflicting schools of thought, some final basis of agreement on important questions may be evolved."[69]

Palmer described the club as "a coalition of all classes on the basis of
liberty and good manners," but, actually, it had few members who were
not part of the urban gentry. Nevertheless, though never really a forum
for class interaction, the club did serve Palmer's Comtean aims by
introducing business and intellectual elites to avant-garde religious and
political ideas, while it encouraged a strong sense of leadership and social
responsibility among these groups.[70] "The basic idea of the New York
Club," conceded one member, "is to surround intellectual freedom with
the refined atmosphere of the drawing room. . . . Ladies of distinguished
social and literary position in our metropolis are [therefore]
members. . . . It became fashionable from the start." Indeed, Julia Ward
Howe, after her lecture at the club's first meeting, remarked: "You are
too fashionable, and I have never found that a good element in the
beginnings of a literary enterprise." In the drawing room of Palmer's
stately Gramercy Park home, gathered "the young lawyers, doctors,
merchants, artists and architects, professors, teachers and men of the
future."[71]

On one level, Palmer succeeded where his sectarian predecessors had
failed. The most elite circles of metropolitan society that had eluded the
sectarian Comtists were attracted to Palmer's gatherings. And, although
Julia Ward Howe failed to understand the rationale behind the club,
Palmer's vision seems to have been calculated along Comtean lines. What
better way to educate the "patriciate" of the future Positive order in
their social responsibilities than to present liberal speakers as part of a
fashionable evening's entertainment? This way, elites who exercised
political and economic power could be exposed as a group in a friendly
environment to new ways of looking at nature and human society.
Accordingly, some members believed that, in their words, "we were not
fashionable enough, and that we should be glad for a few more of the
leaders of society."[72] Reflected one member, "it was by no means an
easy or congenial task to induce Conservatism to come out of its shell

69. CP, *Aims, Objects and Methods of the Nineteenth Century Club of New York* (New York:
n.p., 1886), i.
70. CP, "European Aristocracy," 625.
71. CP, *Aims*, i–ii; *Courtlandt Palmer Tributes*, 56.
72. *Courtlandt Palmer Tributes*, 56.

and consider the untrammeled attitudes and undraped fancies of free thought." But Palmer appears to have been deeply committed to such a course. As Jane Croly put it perceptively, the club "was an effort at intellectual redemption."[73]

A perusal of the list of speakers and their topics for the club's first few seasons lends credence to this understanding of Palmer's larger purpose. Speakers and discussants included Palmer, Henry George, Felix Adler, William G. Sumner, Wakeman, James Parton, Oliver Wendell Holmes, Jr., Parke Godwin, Andrew Carnegie, John Swinton, Theodore Roosevelt, Thomas W. Higginson, Charles W. Eliot, James McCosh, John Fiske, Andrew D. White, Woodrow Wilson, Lawrence Gronlund, and Jane Addams, to name only a few.[74] Discussion topics reflected a typically positivist mixture, from philosophical and religious subjects to sociology and politics or literature and the arts. The balance of the talks in the first several seasons, however, was probably from the first two categories and the featured speakers, while not uniformly positivists, were rarely from the traditional Christian camp. "Courtlandt Palmer," wrote one of his admirers, "caught this [positivist] spirit of our age and wrought it into a new and powerful educational institution."[75] Therefore, though avoiding sectarianism, the club's "beneficient and important mission" was firmly founded upon Comtist ideals.

American Comtists nearly all discarded a narrow Comtean orthodoxy by 1880. The "Americanist" impulse of the New York community found expression in both the formation of new societies independent of official positivism and in the production of a varied revisionist literature. The parallel movement toward reform politics also gathered strength during the 1880s, as Chapter 4 confirms. Yet, despite the radicalism some entertained, Comte had left a deep-enough imprint that the new liberalism they fashioned never quite escaped its elitist and paternalistic foundation. This fundamental tension characterized liberal political discourse at the turn of the century and permeated the thought of the individuals who are the subjects of the remaining chapters.

73. Ibid., 155, 144.
74. *Officers, Members and Constitutiton of the Nineteenth Century Club . . . 1899–1900* (New York: n.p., n.d.), 32–49.
75. *Courtlandt Palmer Tributes*, 4.

CHAPTER FOUR

T. B. Wakeman

Comtist as Radical

The astonishing thing about Goethe, Comte, and Haeckel is that they in religion so thoroughly emancipated themselves from theology and metaphysics; and two of them were Germans! The result is that they and their school of *general* scientists and reformers are, as we enter the new era, the chief sources of any true enlightenment or guidance, especially in religious, social, or political affairs.

—TBW, 1891

THE SUBSEQUENT LIFE AND WORK of New York positivist T. B. Wakeman brings into sharper focus the contribution to the reconstruction of liberal thought in America made by the Comtean "connection" described in the preceding chapters. During the ideological ferment of the Gilded Age, Wakeman and others fashioned a reform ideology that, though it departed from Comte in important respects, owed much to Comte's original vision. While not so significant a figure as fellow critics of late nineteenth-century American capitalism Edward Bellamy, Henry George, or Lester Frank Ward, Wakeman was part of their informal circle. He contributed to many of the same publications they did, shared political platforms and corresponded with them over many years. Wakeman did not achieve their prominence but an analysis of his career and writings sheds new light on the reform thought of the Gilded Age, its complex, sometimes contradictory character, and the role of Comtean ideas in this hybrid discourse. Wakeman clearly pushed Comtean social thought to the left, while strengthening the statism that had characterized some within the original New York circle. Moreover, Wakeman's keen interest in religious and philosophical questions provides the historian with a unique opportunity to examine the theoretical foundation of reform politics. Here again, Comte had a lasting effect, despite Wakeman's obvious openness to other influences.

I

Wakeman's published writings on religious and philosophical subjects during the 1880s and 1890s do reflect important changes in his perspec-

T. B. Wakeman in his later years. He pushed Comtean social thought to the left, while strengthening the statism that had characterized some within the original New York circle.

tive. In some ways, these changes demonstrate a further drift away from Comtean orthodoxy. The following analysis highlights two key developments in Wakeman's thought during this period. For one, he became a more conventional freethinker, indulging in anticlerical rhetoric and expressing uncompromising opposition to institutional Christianity. And, two, Wakeman's general philosophical position approached, under the influence of Ernst Haeckel, German scientist and materialist philosopher, an almost pantheistic monism. Indeed, Wakeman's increasing intolerance of philosophical systems that were pluralistic or open to the nonmaterial in any form appears to have had an indirect effect on his political theory, strengthening his unitary, almost monolithic conception of the state.

With the decline in the activity of the sectarian Comtean societies in New York, Wakeman appears to have been drawn to more broadly based or inclusive Freethought groups. In addition to his long-standing affiliation with the Manhattan Liberal Club and more recent involvement with Palmer's Nineteenth Century Club, Wakeman gradually grew more active in the National Liberal League after its founding in 1876. Indeed, the Manhattan Liberal Club may have been instrumental in arranging (along with Francis E. Abbot) the first organizational meeting of the league in Philadelphia during the centennial year.[1]

1. TBW, *Free Thought: Past, Present and Future* (Chicago: H. L. Green, 1899), 26–27. Formed as a society to promote secularism, the league was at first dominated by more conservative freethinkers such as Abbot, O. B. Frothingham, and Minot Savage. Serious differences soon surfaced, however, over the Comstock Postal Laws. The Comstock Laws had been enacted to facilitate the exclusion from the mails of obscene materials, but broadly construed, they posed a threat against Freethought literature (in fact *Truth Seeker* editor D. M. Bennett had been arrested in November 1877 under this legislation). The majority of more radical league members who favored repeal of such laws repudiated the leadership of Abbot and his sympathizers during a tumultuous convention in Syracuse in 1878. Wakeman was an outspoken critic of Comstock and it was probably at this time that he rose to a position of some influence within the league (see Sidney Warren, *American Freethought, 1860–1914* [New York: Columbia University Press, 1943], 162–65).

Besides the Comstock controversy, the league was also divided over its political role and sponsorship of social reforms. At its 1879 convention, the league decided to support the formation of a liberal political party, but enthusiasm for the venture seemed to evaporate almost as soon as the measure was passed. A similar proposal came up again in 1883, but Wakeman (then president of the league) spoke against the plan, explaining that the society could not support such a venture financially. The question of political activity and social reform was finally resolved in 1884 when it was agreed that the society should concentrate exclusively on promoting Abbot's "Nine Demands of Liberalism." The demands addressed none of the socioeconomic issues of the Gilded Age, but rather concentrated on advocating a thoroughgoing secularism on the part of federal and state governments. Consistent with the sharpened focus of the league, a new name was adopted: the American Secular Union. With its less ambiguous title, the organization survived until the turn of the century (Warren, *American Freethought*, 161). Wakeman was named treasurer

Wakeman's affiliation with the National Liberal League underlines his increasingly uncompromising secularism. Indeed, although he had never followed Comte in fawning over medieval Roman Catholicism, Wakeman seems to have become more polemically anti-Christian in the 1880s and 1890s. Casting aside the more subtle, sympathetic, and conservative attitudes of an Edger or a Croly toward traditional religion, Wakeman appears often to have opted for a dogmatic scientism. As a result, he sometimes sounded more like Robert Ingersoll than Auguste Comte. "Theology is the past tense," he proclaimed in 1883, "Science is king." Wakeman championed the omnicompetence of science in the most sweeping terms. "The custom of prayer," he wrote in the same article, "is simply evidence of man's weakness and needs, and of the childish views he once entertained of the world and of God. As far as the needs remain, science will supply them under intelligent human effort." Illusions such as prayer, observed Wakeman, are "common enough now in uncivilized countries and among the more ignorant Roman Catholic people."[2]

Wakeman often appeared to lose patience with anyone (or, at least those of Northern European ancestry) who still insisted on clinging to a traditional faith. "How," Wakeman asked with evident impatience, "after all that evolution has done for us in science, history, and religion, anyone who supposes himself to be a gentleman, and therefore a fair and honest man, could continue to shut down this old theologic environment of falsehood, and horror upon the human soul of the Nineteenth century . . . ?"[3]

Contrary to Comte, Wakeman seemed sometimes to imply that Christian monotheism was little better than the simple superstitions of primitive man. Not until "the telescopes of Galileo" was the "ancient cave environment" transcended, he wrote. The history of man under all previous faiths was characterized by "terror, darkness, and selfishness, [during which] human brothers trampled, persecuted, and wronged each other into misery and suicide."[4]

In fact, Wakeman appeared to grow quite impatient with the persistence of traditional Christianity in republican America. In *Science is Religion*, Wakeman fulminated that if indeed the "welfare of the people is the supreme law" in a republic, then the state must outlaw or at least

---

of the league in 1880 and served as president from 1881 to 1883. In these capacities and as editor, Wakeman made numerous contributions to the league's newspaper, *Man*.

2. "Science and Prayer," *North American Review* 137 (July 1883): 193, 201, 200.

3. "The Universal Faith: A Memorial Address . . . ," *Open Court* 2 (3 January 1889): 1392.

4. Ibid., 1393.

regulate, any sect that "educates adherents into social enemies, law violators, drones, and the useless creatures of 'spiritual' and 'other-world' despotisms."[5] If Americans could not abide Mormon polygamy, then what of "celibacy," "confession," "indulgences," and frauds by "miracles" and "relics" of the Christian church? To objections that such a policy would violate the principle of religious liberty, Wakeman countered that such religious practices "are of themselves, at the very start, deprivations of the liberty that every citizen must enjoy as a condition of safety for all." Wakeman went on to conclude that "the robbing of the young, the innocent and the ignorant, by the various phases of duress and fraud referred to calls for the protection of the victims by common law, in their interest as well as that of the community."[6]

Rather than viewing the Judeo-Christian faith with Comte as a beneficent (albeit now outdated) product of the pre-scientific mind, Wakeman's perspective was overwhelmingly negative. "The most terrible blunder," wrote Wakeman only months before his death, "made by mankind (and in his childhood) was that man was created in the image of God." Such a notion, Wakeman believed, served not to heighten man's sense of self-worth; rather, it rendered his God "a distorted shadow of himself, filled up with all the darkness he could image."[7]

Wakeman's strident anticlericalism and his increasing concern about the influence of Christianity in American society are also underlined by his involvement in efforts to found a Freethought college during the late 1890s. Liberal University was begun in 1896 by J. E. Hosmer, a secularist reformer from the Midwest and by others affiliated with the *Torch of Reason*, a leading Freethought newspaper. The college was located in Silverton, Oregon, and by 1900 it had its own classroom building and student dormitory. College secretary P. W. Geer persuaded Wakeman and his family to come west and join the faculty in 1899. President Hosmer evidently had qualms about Wakeman's philosophical radicalism from the start and soon after the Wakemans' arrival, controversy erupted. During a tumultuous meeting of the board of directors, Hosmer resigned and Wakeman assumed the presidency. Then, in late February 1903, the school removed to Kansas City, Missouri, where it had purchased a large downtown building. The struggling college did not last long in its new location, however. Shortly after its move, Liberal University folded,

5. *Science Is Religion* (Los Angeles: Singleton W. Davis, 1905), 14–15.
6. Ibid., 15.
7. *Addresses of Thaddeus Burr Wakeman At and In Reference to The First Monist Congress.* (Cos Cob. Conn.: by the author, 1913), 55.

a victim of internal squabbling, declining enrollments, the Wakemans' poor health, and a fire that destroyed much of its library.[8]

A militant secularism was the driving force behind the college. "There is not today," declared the Liberal University catalogue for 1900–1901, "outside of the little city of Silverton, a college or university that is not bound and gagged, or rendered impotent of the highest good, by some form of dogmatism." The new institution represented a unique experiment because it was, in the words of the catalogue, "founded on a Scientific basis, that is on the TRUE SOLUTION AND EXPLANATION OF THE UNIVERSE. All other schools are silent, try to harmonize so-called revelation and science, or are directly opposed to evolution and are building on the quicksands of the old and thoroughly exploded orthodox dogmas." Wakeman was a natural supporter of such a venture, for the denominational ties of most major American universities had long concerned him. As he had argued: "All of the education which leaves it to theology to say what it shall do . . . can only end by increasing our difficulties. . . . The education that leaves these errors undisturbed is simply surface work and illusory."[9]

Thus, Wakeman entered into his work at L.U. with a deep sense of commitment and mission. As superintendent of the Department of Sociology and Law, Wakeman taught a variety of courses and lectured on the "Religion of Science and Humanity." After he was forced to close down L.U., Wakeman continued to hold informal classes in his home in Connecticut. There, he continued his efforts to draw students away from the theological and metaphysical systems of the past by introducing them to the works of Comte, Spencer, Ward, and Haeckel.[10]

Perhaps Wakeman's growing intolerance of orthodoxy was the product of decades of opposition and indifference to his message. The complete victory of science and secularism had not come with the dawn of the twentieth century and Wakeman sometimes sounded bitter about it all. Though he often appeared to prize his role as lonely prophet, the

8. Down, *A History of the Silverton Country* (Portland, Oreg.: Berniff, 1926), 218, 221; Letter, TBW to Lester F. Ward, 9 January 1908, Brown University, Ward Papers, Appendix B; Letter, TBW to Lester F. Ward, 26 November 1907, Brown University, Ward Papers, Appendix B. See also Letter, Pearl W. Geer to Lester F. Ward, 6 July 1899, Brown University, Ward Papers, Appendix B. This letter documents secretary Geer's attempts to elicit the support of both Ward and Wakeman for L.U.

9. *Annual Catalogue of the Liberal University*, (n.p., Torch of Reason Printing Office, 1900), 10, 22, 20.

10. Letter, TBW to Lester F. Ward, 20 August 1908, Brown University, Ward Papers, Appendix B. Wakeman praised Ward in this letter as "the successor and *Corrector* of Comte, Spencer[,] Fiske and of the *past* Sociologists generally, and the Chief Instructor of the *present*."

concomitant social and intellectual isolation probably took its toll. He once admitted that "sometimes it seems that we must retire and leave the result to the inhuman and unaided chances of nature." In concluding an address to the Manhattan Liberal Club on his seventieth birthday, Wakeman reflected:

> Some people say that I have failed—that I "came to my own and they received me not." . . . I have been said to be fifty years before my time, but yet I hope against hope and am not discouraged. . . . Time will remove the evil, this inattention and unbelief, which rests chiefly upon ignorance, tradition, habit and selfish social conventionalism.[11]

And yet, although he increasingly indulged in the kind of anti-Christian polemics that Comte and Edger had found distasteful and impolitic, Wakeman's later writings continued to reflect many of the religious themes peculiar to the Comtean perspective. Regarding the social necessity of religion and the basic configuration of the new positive faith, Wakeman remained a Comtist. Even when writing for the National Liberal League's organ, *Man*, Wakeman seems to have followed the Comtean maxim "On ne détruit que ce qu'on remplace." In other words, Wakeman continued to view the simple nay-saying of the free-thinkers and secularists as inadequate. As noted in the previous chapter, his goal was to articulate a "constructive liberalism" that transcended simple Enlightenment skepticism. Clearly, a neutral empiricism was insufficient to provide the creed of the modern era; Wakeman was confident as to what would constitute the new surrogate religion: "let none fear that modern civilization will die for want of the old faith. The Gospel or Religion of Humanity, a pure human secular religion—with its pure, human, natural, healthy, just morality and life—will gradually displace the old superstition."[12]

Wakeman thoroughly revised the papal outlines of Comte's scheme, but he always spoke of the Religion of Humanity as the true Positive faith. Indeed, Wakeman was not reluctant to defend Comte when the doctrine of the *Système* was assailed. It is unfair and improper, contended Wakeman, for critics to "ridicule some extravagance, error or idiosyncrasy of some individual scientist or reformer; for example, the papal scheme of Auguste Comte; as tho [*sic*] such deficits availed ought against

11. *Science Is Religion*, 70.
12. *Man: A Weekly Journal of Progress and Reform* (January 1882): 8.

the TRUE or the GOOD."[13] "Is it not time," asked Wakeman in an article for the *Open Court*, "for the second thought of this generation to end all envious or idle criticisms, and to begin the practical work of constructing, teaching, and living the new religion?"[14]

Moreover, Wakeman appears to have never doubted that both individuals and society needed religion. Man's religious questioning constituted for Wakeman "the highest of issues" and its constructive solution was crucial to continued human progress.[15] "The three H's and the three P's still confront us," Wakeman reflected in 1889.

> The Head must have a true Philosophy.
> The Heart must have a satisfying Poesy.
> The Hand must have a beneficent Polity.[16]

In fact, it seemed to remain important to Wakeman, as it had been for Edger and Croly, to furnish a positivist substitute for each of the essential component parts of Christianity. Thus, Wakeman explained,

> In a particular way we saw the Personal Historical Christ enlarged [under positivism] to the Ideal Christ or Humanity, the Synthesis of the Human Race, the epitome of all human History.
>
> The Holy Spirit became the Altruism, Love Sympathy, Charity, which makes that human Synthesis possible.
>
> The Holy Mother re-appears as Womanhood. The Hebrew-Greek Bible extended to include the good and useful of the books of the race.
>
> The Heaven imagined above became the Ideal Heaven germinating in the heart. . . . The Hells were seen as the shadows of the evils which obstruct the incoming of this Heaven.
>
> The Creeds became the Laws and Truths of science, classified into a Positive Philosophy. . . .

Here, concluded Wakeman, was "a solid religion," a scientific surrogate for Christianity that would satisfy the intellect and the emotions.[17] Hence, while it rejected Croly's "Catholicism minus theology," the thrust of Wakeman's Religion of Humanity differed little from the

13. *Evolution or Creation?* (New York: National Liberal League, 1883), 95.
14. "The Universal Faith: A Monistic, Positive, Human, Constructive Religion," *Open Court* 3 (April 1889): 1585.
15. "The Universal Faith: A Memorial Address . . . ," 1391–92.
16. "The Universal Faith: A Monistic . . . ," 1584.
17. "The Universal Faith: A Memorial Address . . . ," 1393.

essentials of Comte's model. Despite the tensions inherent in such a hybrid system, Wakeman's religious thought appeared both American and, in its key assumptions, fundamentally Comtean.

With respect to Wakeman's broader philosophical position, a similar picture becomes clear. After the 1880s, Wakeman dropped much of his distinctively Comtean language and borrowed more freely from Spencer and Haeckel. In an 1883 contribution to the *North American Review*, for instance, Wakeman sounded more Spencerian than strictly Comtean. It is "the law of evolution," Wakeman declared, that "is now recognized as the backbone of the organic, the social, the mental, the moral, and the religious sciences." Wakeman cited Spencer and not Comte as the thinker who best understood this truth and how it related to the other "fundamental laws of modern science."[18]

Similarly, a speech delivered in the same year by Wakeman focused almost exclusively upon evolution as the summation of all scientific truth. Asked Wakeman: "Is evolution the solution of the world, or is creation the solution?" Empirical method and positivist epistemology were, for Wakeman, both completely encompassed by evolution.

> The word "Science" has come now to mean substantially Evolution. It means that the known world about us has come to be as it is, without creation or miracle, but always in consequences of previous facts, states and conditions, which we are able to follow and to trace by knowable laws.[19]

Furthermore, for a definition of this central scientific principle, Wakeman opted for Spencer's words from *First Principles*: "a change from an indefinite and incoherent homogeneity to a definite coherent heterogeneity." The remainder of the speech was simply an attempt to test the explanatory powers of evolutionary theory. In turn, Wakeman examined astronomy, geology, biology, and sociology and found each best understood under this great principle. Surprisingly, Wakeman failed to cite Comte at all when discussing human society, but chose instead to quote Henry Carey's conclusion that evolution "is as true of societies as it is of plants and animals in reference to which it was written." Wakeman consequently surmised that evolution gave "the true solution to all the known phenomena of the world" and that, as such, "Science is the true creed and the Bible of the world."[20]

18. "Science and Prayer," 194.
19. *Evolution*, 5.
20. Ibid., 9, 10, 6–7. Both Spencer and Haeckel subscribed to what Maurice Mandelbaum calls a "total evolution" doctrine. See Mandelbaum, *History, Man and Reason: A*

Yet, Wakeman's sometimes Spencerian vocabulary appears to have been laid over essentially Comtean foundations. Echoing Comte's maxim *savoir pour prevoir*, Wakeman conceived science—and, specifically, evolutionary theory—as "the true solution of all the known phenomena of the world about us." Accordingly, "by virtue of it [i.e., science], we can predict the general future of the human race and determine what even its true heaven itself shall be." Again, the significance for Wakeman of the all-encompassing explanatory and predictive powers of science was that these legitimized science's claims as a surrogate faith. If, Wakeman reasoned, science could in fact foresee and secure the new "heaven on earth,"

> why then Science is the true creed and the Bible of the world, and it must at once take the place of the old creeds and Bibles with every intelligent man. Evolution now not only undertakes to do everythinq that theology has done in the past, but it has substantially done it.[21]

Despite his Spencerian rhetoric, Wakeman clearly continued to envisage his philosophical position as basically Comtean. Comte, not Spencer was chosen by Wakeman (along with Goethe and Washington) as one of "the three fundamental, fruitful representative men of that [i.e., the modern] era."[22] For Wakeman, writing in 1889, "the four fundamental corner stones" of modern philosophy had all been laid by Comte:

(a) The relativity of human knowledge, and its consequent limitation to the correlative and phenomenal as the knowable.
(b) The classification of the sciences, . . .
(c) The evolution of human history and civilization, . . .
(d) The conception of humanity as a great social organic being, . . .
(e) The superstructure upon these corner stones can be none other than the new religion, the Monistic Universal Faith; the Religion of Science, and Humanity.[23]

As for "the attacks of 'Spencer and Co.' upon these corner stones," Wakeman held they had never made a convincing case. The criticisms or

---

Study in Nineteenth Century Thought (Baltimore: Johns Hopkins University Press, 1971), 401 n. 33.

21. *Evolution*, 7.

22. "Auguste Comte and Philosophy in America," *Open Court* 3 (24 October 1889): 1903.

23. "The Universal Faith: A Monistic . . . ," 1585.

additions only demonstrated that Fiske and Spencer had succumbed to dualism and metaphysics. "Comte," Wakeman observed, "insufficient, verbose, and crude as he may be, avoided their capital error: he nowhere breaks the back of the world." That is, Comte did not, like Spencer, make provision for a separate Unknowable reality. In fact, Wakeman went as far as to say that Spencer and Fiske were primarily valuable as "useful commentators upon, and amenders of the unitary positive philosophy which Comte founded, and which still stands as the base of the scientific philosophy."[24]

Wakeman also remained determined, as Comte had been, to exclude from scientific inquiry the search for a first or ultimate cause. When challenged whether scientists must explain the origins of protoplasm, Wakeman replied: "Not at all! It is enough that we find it as a natural product endowed with this property of continuous reaction." Explained Wakeman: "Science is based on the continuance of the processes of the world, not on their origins. If it had any supposition to make about them it would be that they are limitless and beyond the capacity of man to fathom." An ultimate cause or Creator thus struck Wakeman as inconceivable. "Who," he asked, "can break this mighty Law of correlation, who can create or uncreate a particle of matter or a correlation of force?"[25]

In addition to his seemingly rigid positivist empiricism, Wakeman remained a steadfast Comtist in other key respects. Perhaps he was most identifiably Comtean in his consistent historicism. All intellectuals, he declared, echoing Comte's own phrasing, "are now as thoroughly convinced that there is a law of historic progress and evolution as they

24. Ibid., 1585, 1584, 1585. Nor did Wakeman only assail Spencer in the course of defending Comte. By the turn of the century, Wakeman had developed a thorough critique of "Spencerism." Here, Wakeman's main target was Spencer's notion of the Unknowable and the broader epistemological and religious implications this concept presented. Spencer had, Wakeman contended, moved in his later writings from a materialistic or correlative theory of knowledge to a position inconsistent with positivist empiricism. Spencer's (and especially Fiske's) recourse to the Unknowable—particularly when seeking to account for human consciousness—deeply alarmed Wakeman. Wakeman viewed Fiske's references to unknown "psychic" phenomena as tantamount to "a public confession of philosophical bankruptcy." (See TBW, "The Latest Phase of Herbert Spencer's Philosophy," Open Court 5 [13 August 1891]: 2909.) Wakeman was not interested in entertaining for a moment that there might be some phenomena not susceptible to scientific explanation: "There is no room for an unknowable, or a spook of any kind, and that [sic] this ghost-world simply does not exist, except in the imagination of agnostic philosophers." For Wakeman, a scientist could not, in this sense, be an agnostic. If science could not ultimately explain everything, then the door to spiritualism of one form or another was left open (see TBW, "The Nature of the Soul," Open Court 5 [17 December 1891], 3058).

25. Evolution, 43, 44.

are that there is a law of gravity."[26] Consistent with Comte, Wakeman viewed sociology as "the realization of the evolution of human history."[27] Although Wakeman often did employ distinctly Darwinian language, his understanding of human history was built primarily upon Comtean foundations. Wakeman's "five great stages or religions" of history ("Fetishism, Astrolatry, Polytheism, Monotheism, and Humanity") were clearly derived from Comte's categories. To gain insights into the first of these eras, Wakeman recommended reading Comte along with others, such as Spencer, Tylor, Muller, and Lubbock. Astrolatry Wakeman conceived of as simply a "higher Fetishism" that grew naturally out of more primitive forms. Similarly, polytheism constituted a progressive historical development and, so too, monotheism. Here, however, Wakeman usually took care to elaborate what a mixed blessing the advent of Christianity had been. Though it was presumably the product of progressive evolution, Wakeman often spent more time documenting how Christianity was "the religion of blood."[28] Hence, while his historical understanding was colored by Comte, Wakeman's religious polemics seldom seemed to owe much to his mentor.

Wakeman's understanding of the development of Freethought itself was founded upon Comte's Law of the Three Stages. In an address given in 1899 to the Manhattan Liberal Club, Wakeman laid out an essentially Comtean history of Freethought. Liberal religious thought, Wakeman contended, had begun in the theological or deistic phase, moved to the metaphysical or spiritualistic and was now "verging toward the Scientific or Positive state." Like Comte, Wakeman conceded that these stages were not neatly coterminous. "They largely began together," he wrote, ". . . and have continued to evolute [sic] together." Wakeman added, nevertheless, that "each of them has had the lead and emphasis in Free Thought in the order given above." "We must never forget," Wakeman noted, "that our first modern Freethinkers were chiefly bona fide Deists." Contemporary Freethought owes much to the likes of Paine and Jefferson, but it must remember that their philosophy was built upon theistic assumptions. So too, metaphysics underlay the beautiful Romantic poetry of Wordsworth, Coleridge, Shelley, and Keats, yet it must be discarded when attempting to explain any natural phenomenon. Distinct from its precursors, contemporary Freethought furnishes "a new Philosophy, built out of the special sciences, which is our creed—ever grow-

26. Ibid., 53.
27. *Free Thought,* 17.
28. *Evolution,* 53, 56, 71.

ing—yet verifiable, true and trustworthy. This world Bacon and Comte forfelt."[29]

Yet, undoubtedly the most important single trend in the later philosophical writings of T. B. Wakeman was an increasingly monistic perspective. Leszek Kolakowski has noted this strong monistic element in late nineteenth-century positivism, suggesting the German evolutionary philosopher Ernst Haeckel as a representative exponent of this school. German zoologist and evolutionist, Ernst Haeckel (1834–1919), had been one of the first German biologists to accept and propagate Darwin's theory of evolution. Haeckel taught zoology at the university at Jena for most of his life but was perhaps better known in Anglo-American circles for his materialist philosophy and strident attacks on religious belief. Perhaps his best-known work was an ambitious philosophical tome, *The Riddle of the Universe*, published in English translation in 1899. Here, Haeckel developed a rigid philosophical monism that sought a singular explanation for all phenomena.[30]

Comte had, of course, in the *Cours* articulated a philosophy of science that stressed the unity of all knowledge. But, as Kolakowski observes: "unity in the sources of cognition as a premise and unity in the results of cognition as a postulate" were two very different philosophical "aspirations."[31] The former aspiration Comte shared, the latter he could not, especially if it sought to distill natural laws into a single, ultimate causal law.[32] Spencer, however, did espouse such reductionism and it was probably his reading of Spencer, Fiske, and, certainly, his study of Haeckel that drew Wakeman's thought in a monistic direction. Yet, for many other positivists, Haeckel's monism, in Kolakowski's words, "savoured of metaphysics" in its "totalitarian . . . aspirations to a universal accounting of phenomena."[33] Accordingly, Wakeman's identi-

29. *Free Thought*, 2, 5, 17.

30. See Leszek Kolakowski, *The Alienation of Reason: A History of Positivist Thought*, trans. Norman Guterman (Garden City, N.Y.: Doubleday, 1968), 101; Wilhelm Boelsche, *Haeckel: His Life and Work*, trans. Joseph McCabe (Philadelphia: G. W. Jacobs, 1906); Daniel Gasman's *The Scientific Origins of National Socialism: Social Darwinism in Ernst Haeckel and the German Monist League* (New York: American Elsevier, 1971) examines the political implications of Haeckel's thought. Wakeman definitely encountered Haeckel before 1899 and probably, therefore, read him initially in German.

31. Kolakowski, *Alienation*, 101.

32. See Mandelbaum, *History, Man and Reason*, 401, for an explanation of this question.

33. Kolakowski, *Alienation*, 101. Though appropriately grouped by Mandelbaum with Spencer under the "systematic" label, orthodox Comtean positivism would be inclined to reject the causal monism and mystical pantheism of Haeckel (see Mandelbaum, *History, Man and Reason*, 401). Also, Mandelbaum places the "systematic" school in the early nineteenth century and the "critical" school later, near the turn of the century. Mandelbaum's categories of "systematic" and "critical" positivism should *not*, therefore, be

fication with this particular strand of positivism may have served to ensure his isolation from the intellectual mainstream. The dogmatism and almost mystical character of Wakeman's later philosophy would hold little appeal to those who followed positivism in a critical or radical empiricist direction.

Wakeman was actually quite open about choosing monism as the new name of his philosophical/religious system. Monism, he wrote in the *Open Court*, "is a new and beneficent revelation and power in our land, with which it becomes every person of free thought and a good heart to become personally acquainted as soon as possible. It is an improvement upon the forms of Positivism heretofore presented in America, for it is real instead of phenomenal, infinite instead of dual and finite."[34]

At the same time, though, Wakeman seems often to have intentionally minimized the changes implied by the title "monism." Haeckel, Wakeman pointed out, first adopted the term simply because it avoided "the limitations that seem to inhere in the words Materialism, Positivism, Secularism, Cosmism, etc."[35] It seems that Wakeman held all of these terms, properly understood, as roughly synonymous. "Because," explained Wakeman, "it [the new philosophy] is based upon verified science, it is *positive* monism; because it depends upon the objective unity of the world, it is *monistic* positivism."[36] Wakeman once described the personal faith of his friend Courtlandt Palmer as "the Positive and Monistic Religion of Science." Frequently, he would leave out the positivist adjective entirely and what Wakeman once referred to as Comte's Religion of Humanity, he later termed "the Universal, Monistic, Republican Religion."[37]

---

confused with those used by Kolakowski (i.e., "monistic" and "empirical") in chap. 4 of his *Alienation of Reason*.

34. "Only One World After All!—But That Infinite," *Open Court* 3 (7 November 1889): 1926. Note here how Wakeman wrote "forms of Positivism," perhaps meaning to include his own earlier revisionism as well as the orthodoxy of Edger or Croly. In the brief article "Our Unchurched Millions" for the October 1890 issue of the *Arena*, Wakeman made some disingenuous remarks about the "new light" *Open Court* was shedding upon the philosophical questions of the day by employing the new term. It was, in fact, Wakeman himself who authored most of these pieces for *Open Court*.

35. "Our Unchurched Millions," 609.

36. *Ernst Haeckel*, 41. As Wakeman revealingly concluded: "We find the religious history of our race to consist, therefore, of a gradual evolution of its leading peoples from a broad base of general animism and fetishism, thence to astrology, thence to polytheism, thence to monotheism, and thence to *scientism*, expressed chiefly to us in the pantheism of Goethe, the positivism of Comte, the synthetism of Spencer, the cosmism of Fiske, and finally by the *monism* of Haeckel" (41).

37. "The Universal Faith: A Monistic . . . ," 1583. In fact, Wakeman wrote elsewhere that Thomas Paine had actually anticipated Comte in using the term "Religion of Humanity." Explained Wakeman: "The First Part of the 'Age of Reason' is the first and in some

Whether Wakeman really believed that the monistic direction in which he was drawing his positivism was consistent with Comte's own approach, or whether he ever grasped the subtle philosophical issues involved, is not clear. At any rate, Wakeman did begin in the late 1880s to articulate a philosophy of science much more akin to that of Haeckel (and, in some respects, to that of Spencer) than to anything Comte had constructed.[38] Explained Wakeman in an article entitled "The Universal Faith: A Monistic, Positive, Human, Constructive Religion":

> the "phenomenal" changes which we sense and call "matter": these changes are found to be correlates of each other, and the law of "the equivalence of forces" results. Each change is the centre of changes correlative in its environment and which extend by similar correlations in ever widening circles as we trace them, until they are lost in the infinite. Thus, science leaves us only a *Monistic* world.
>
> These things being so, every other philosophy, except the correlative or scientific is ousted.[39]

Moreover, the character of Wakeman's religious thought was also transformed by Haeckelian monism. The fervid humanism of Comte often appeared overshadowed in Wakeman's later writings by an almost mystical pantheism: "God and the World [note: *not* Humanity] are one Infinite Being or Existence." The same individual who had once considered Comtean humanism as the definitive scientific modification of traditional theism, wrote in 1889: "There can be no Theism but Pantheism. So Spinoza taught and Goethe sung, and all the great men in thought of the world are following their lead; as Haeckel implies, Monism is the word of Science which separates the new true world from the old and false idea about it."[40]

Wakeman may have come to prefer Haeckel for, ironically, the same reasons he had originally been attracted to Comte. Like Comte's positivism, Haeckel's monism purported to be, in Wakeman's words, "the final

respects the broadest, shortest, and clearest statement of the 'Positive Philosophy' ever made for religious purposes." Wakeman valued Paine, in part, because he had not sought to express his radical religious views through institutions derived from Roman Catholicism, as Comte had mistakenly done. See TBW, *Thomas Paine: The Father of Republics* (New York: Truth Seeker, 1899), 26.

38. Similar at least to Spencer's earlier thought. See Kolakowski, *Alienation*, 91; and Mandelbaum, *History, Man and Reason*, 400–401 n. 32.

39. "The Universal Faith: A Monistic . . . ," 1584.

40. "Only One World," 1925.

philosophy and religion of evolution and science." As a thorough historicist, Wakeman could no longer look upon Comte's work of some forty years ago as definitive. "Monism," wrote Wakeman, "claims to be the last and most consistent word of science in philosophy"; as such, every true positivist had also to be a monist. Unlike all of his valuable but limited predecessors, Haeckel struck Wakeman as "the only complete evolutionist."[41] The comprehensiveness and closed character of Haeckel's philosophic vision seemed to validate its own lofty claims.

By the first decade of the twentieth century, Wakeman was articulating a philosophical position that was virtually an echo of Haeckel's and with barely even a backward glance at Comte. In *Science Is Religion: The Monistic Religion* (1905), numerous references to Haeckel supplanted the usual citations of Comte. Indeed, the few times Comte was quoted it was now without ascription. The whole tone of the book (which was actually the text of an address to the Manhattan Liberal Club) was extremely adulatory of Haeckel, and the philosophical position therein developed was blatantly derivative. Wakeman's address was a systematic elaboration of a series of philosophical theses recently published in a liberal review. Describing the German professor of biology as "among the great men of our day and generation," Wakeman sought to explain and apply Haeckel's system to an American audience less familiar with this brand of European monism.[42]

Wakeman now characterized science as simply correlation. "The universality, certainty, continuity and equivalence" of all changes of matter was, claimed Wakeman, "the bottom law of all science." Unlike his radical empiricist brethren, Wakeman came also to affirm philosophical determinism. As "a correlating organism" there was no "room for a chance or chaos in the universe." If "everything and motion is related organically to every other, and has its place," then surely there was little room for contingency or human free will. The closed, unqualified character of this philosophy is striking, but Wakeman believed that these were the only possible conclusions to be drawn from modern scientific enquiry. Only Haeckel, Wakeman believed, had in "the fullness of time" successfully constructed a philosophical system that "avoided the pitfalls and stumbling-blocks upon which Liberals have usually been led, to fall into or over."[43]

41. *Haeckel*, 21, 33, 31.
42. *Science Is Religion*, 5.
43. Ibid., 9, 42. Even in his later writing, however, Wakeman did occasionally pause to give Comte his due credit. In his monograph, *Ernst Haeckel*, Wakeman took pains to acknowledge monism's debt to Comte. "We have from him," Wakeman admitted, "some indispensible things lying at the base of monism, . . . without which monism can not be

As a result of his interest in and promotion of Haeckel's writings, Wakeman was invited to attend the first Monist Congress at Hamburg, Germany in the fall of 1911. Wakeman's addresses at the congress further illustrate the depth of his intellectual commitment to Haeckelian monism and particularly underline his concern with the religious implications of that philosophy. Visiting Haeckel's home in Jena, Wakeman addressed the German monist in revealing terms:

> Our Great Emancipator!
> Rightly Honoured and Worshipful Sir:
> Right before our eyes and others you have done it! Quietly, patiently, modestly you have worked out our emancipation—our salvation—in time to become that of the Human Race. [44]

For Wakeman, the larger significance of any philosophical system still lay in its ability to provide a scientific surrogate for traditional religious faith. The individual who constructed such a system would truly be mankind's emancipator. This characteristically Comtean idea regarding the religious import of science led Wakeman to embrace enthusiastically the monism of Haeckel. Furthermore, the integrating, systematizing impulse that had long characterized Wakeman's thought (and which may account for his initial attraction to the *Cours*) seems to have found its logical culmination in Haeckel's unitary philosophical vision. Finally, as a champion of Haeckel, perhaps Wakeman was relieved not to have to apologize for or explain away Comte's papalism or his pre-Darwinian biology.

II

Wakeman's significance for historians of the Gilded Age is not based exclusively upon his largely amateur philosophical musings. His political

---

understood or appreciated." These key insights of Comte, Wakeman listed as: the relativity of knowledge, the classification of the sciences, the "law of the three stages," the "supremacy of humanity," the "general law of interdependence," and the complementary character of individual rights and social duties. Wakeman continued to believe that Comte had been insufficiently appreciated. While arguing in his later work for Haeckel's preeminence, Wakeman still believed that, together, "Goethe, Comte and Haeckel . . . [were] the chief sources of any true enlightenment or guidance, especially in religious, social or political affairs."(See TBW, *Haeckel*, 43, 43–44, 45.)

44. *Addresses*, 44. These sentiments would appear to contradict Wakeman's remarks quoted on page 55.

theory and reform activities during the 1880s and 1890s are particularly valuable for the new light they shed upon late nineteenth-century American liberal thought. Several commentators have described the appearance of a native democratic-collectivist ideal during the last quarter of the century.[45] This emergent ideology was an evocative blend of themes new and old but was also fraught with internal tensions. In it, egalitarian rhetoric was often joined to an elitist or paternalist model to produce a peculiar hybrid. This mixture was characteristic of Wakeman's political theory, as it was that of Bellamy and Ward. In varying degrees, this undemocratic or paternalistic strand in the work of all three can be attributed to the influence of Comtean social thought. Wakeman's political thought, in particular, shows clearly how Comte contributed to the revised liberalism. Comtism bolstered its organicist and interventionist impulse; at the same time, however, Comte added an elitist, hierarchical and bureaucratic twist that is usually understood as unique to the later reformism of the Progressives. The wedding of "conservative doctrine" and "collective perspective" that Arthur Lipow sees in the social vision of Bellamy and his followers represents, in fact, a vivid illustration of positivism's interaction with the varied strands of Gilded Age thought.[46] Recognition of this key Comtean thread should, therefore, render a more subtle and complex picture of late nineteenth-century liberalism and clarify how it both anticipated and contributed to Progressivism.

For the purpose of analysis, Wakeman's social and political thought can readily be divided into three periods: c. 1854–1866 (before reading Comte); c. 1867–1888 (after Comte); and c. 1888–1913 (after reading Edward Bellamy's *Looking Backward*). Very little is known about Wakeman's politics during the first period other than his antislavery sentiments and his involvement with his older brother, Abram, in the early organization of the Republican Party in New York. In 1872, Wakeman joined Horace Greeley in supporting the Liberal Republicans. From then until his nomination for New York attorney general by the Progressive Labor party in 1887 (roughly the second period noted above), there is no record

45. See, among others Chester M. Destler, *American Radicalism, 1865–1901* (Chicago: Quadrangle Books, 1966 [1946]); Lawrence Goodwyn, *The Populist Moment: A Short History of the Agrarian Revolt in America* (New York: Oxford University Press, 1978); Arthur Lipow, *Authoritarian Socialism in America: Edward Bellamy and the Nationalist Movement* (Berkeley and Los Angeles: University of California Press, 1982); Bruce Palmer, *"Man Over Money": The Southern Populist Critique of American Capitalism* (Chapel Hill: University of North Carolina Press, 1980); and John L. Thomas, *Alternative America* (Cambridge: Harvard University Press, 1983).

46. Lipow, *Authoritarian Socialism,* 245 n. 73.

of his political activities.[47] But a number of articles and addresses published between these years can furnish some insights on Wakeman's evolving social and political vision. Chapter 3 has already suggested some of the chief characteristics of Wakeman's Comtean revisionism. Ideologically, Wakeman was a fierce champion of republican institutions; he was nationalistic and sympathetic with labor and other radical or reform causes. These themes, together with newer concerns, defined Wakeman's social philosophy during the 1880s.

Wakeman's arguments in favor of a high protective tariff, for instance, show him employing a kind of republican rhetoric more suited to Jefferson or Jackson; his conclusions were decidedly un-Jacksonian, however. The chief end of government, Wakeman argued in 1888, "is the welfare of the people, which depends upon their independence." Such independence can only be secured through a diversified economy since a "one-product producing people" is dependent upon others and thus "cannot be one of any great culture, wealth or happiness." Perhaps more important, however, Wakeman believed that agriculture and manufacturing were "the chief *productive* employments of mankind." Most commerce, he argued, was but "a *waste* of human life, energy and capital" because merely transporting "really produces nothing." A system of free trade would force the United States to accept the wage levels and living standards of less civilized nations in order to compete properly with them. Such a competition would force American workers to become a

> dependent class, become serfs or slaves, like the cooley Chinese or imported Italians, under masters or importers. When the labor of a country is chiefly performed by such a class, a republican democracy cannot exist. The names may be changed, but the master and slave will reappear, and the Republic must end under the poverty of its producers and their consequent degradation.[48]

It was no coincidence, observed Wakeman, that the slave economy of the Southern Confederacy had been built upon the principle of free trade. Nor had the threat to the republic disappeared with the end of the

47. Down, *Silverthorn Country*, 221–22 n. 12; TBW, *Free Thought*, 24–27. Brother Abram's connections with the Republican Party were well known; an angry crowd set fire to his house during the antidraft riots of 1863 (W. Hartley, Interview).

48. "The Sociology of Free Trade and Protection," *Social Science Review* 2 (28 April 1888): 3, 4. On this subject, Wakeman sounded much like political economist Henry C. Carey. Wakeman appears to have been familiar with Carey but was not a disciple.

war and defeat of secession. "The trouble is," noted Wakeman with alarm, "that the Free Trade party and influence now seeking control of our country, is the direct political, social and economic successor of the slaveocracy, and is working in the same spirit and for the same ends."[49]

Nor was Wakeman's republican sympathy for the small, independent producer simply a rhetorical ruse to hide the vested interests of industrialists. Wakeman continued to champion the rights of labor and propose radical measures to improve the lot of workers. If protection benefited only the wealthy few, "then the remedy is by a proper limitation of wealth by taxation or to inaugurate cooperation to take the place of the captain of industry. Free Trade is no remedy for this trouble, it gives us a new set of capitalists—the merchant, importer and banker, against whom no remedy is possible under Free Trade."[50] Again, his primary concern appears to have been for the wage laborer; Wakeman noted several times that protection tended to raise and sustain higher wages.

Wakeman's arguments here about a protective tariff are intriguing because they are a blend of traditional democratic and republican principles with Gilded Age social science. Not only was free trade unrepublican and un-American, it was unscientific, Wakeman contended. "Political Economy," he wrote, "has become a branch of Social Science or Sociology" where scientific and historical laws determine one's conclusions. Consequently, the negative individualism and deductive character of the Manchester School had been transcended by a "larger social view of human relations and progress." The question then became whether protection was or was not "the true economy of Social Science." Wakeman had no doubt that the "higher standpoint" of the new political economy pronounced protection scientific.[51]

For Wakeman, the appeal of the economics of Carey, Ely, and Walker was essentially Comtean. Such systems were scientific, empirical, historical, organic, and altruistic. These last three features of the new social science could, however, create tensions within Wakeman's political thought if he sought to remain loyal to the liberal, egalitarian, and individualistic principles that defined American political culture. Not unlike his more orthodox Comtean predecessors, Wakeman grew fond of using the beehive analogy to argue for cooperation in human society. In the same lecture on the tariff, Wakeman declared that one must not

49. Ibid., 4.

50. Ibid., 5. For a discussion of how Republicans viewed protectionism as a prolabor policy, see James L. Huston, "A Political Response to Industrialism: The Republican Embrace of Protectionist Labor Doctrine," *Journal of American History* 70 (June 1983): 35–57.

51. Ibid., 3.

adopt "the point of view of individual selfishness, instead of the point of view of social welfare and the advantage to the commonwealth in the long run." After all, he reasoned, was not "the lot, fate, and welfare of every individual bee . . . indissolubly connected with that of the hive?"[52] Sociology, it seemed, always taught that the good of the social "hive" was the primary consideration. Both Comte's teaching about altruism and Nature itself appeared to confirm this truth for Wakeman. The potentially illiberal and elitist character of such a model was only brought out in bold relief in Wakeman's later work.

Another, not unrelated ideological tension evident in Wakeman's political writings of the 1880s arose from his Comtean conception of social reform as scientifically conceived, directed, and, in some larger historical sense, inevitable. Wakeman reckoned that the "discovery" of a "Logic of History" had made sociology possible.[53] This "Logic of History" was a fusion of Comte's Law of the Three Stages with Spencer's evolutionary sociology. Social scientists were now generally agreed, explained Wakeman, "that there is a law of historic progress and evolution, . . . [just as] there is a law of gravity." Moreover, like Comte, Wakeman's logic of history was explicitly teleological. "The voice of science," he concluded, "is that this humanistic kingdom, or better, this Republic of Man, is the outcome of the logic of history."

Yet, though inevitable, the progress of society toward a truly Positive polity could be smooth and logical, or it could be socially disruptive and haphazard. Like Comte, Wakeman believed that one of the greatest blessings of sociology was that it allowed one to anticipate and even stimulate social development. "The revolution," reflected Wakeman, "if it is understood, organized and manned, is gradual and safe; it is but another name for the growth and progress of man." Without scientific leadership and direction, progress would "be the result of blind facts, forcing events and revolutions like the broken and dammed up ice in the mountain gorge." The body, for instance, cannot advance, cannot even function properly "without limbs or organs."[54] As for who would provide this leadership for social reform, Wakeman's answer, while not explicitly antidemocratic, was often elitist. Clearly for Wakeman, it was the freethinkers, scientists, and other cognoscenti who would constitute the revolutionary vanguard and lead human society toward the Positive state.

So, then, Wakeman's Comtism already had within it significant deter-

52. Ibid.
53. *Evolution*, 53, 54.
54. *Man: A Weekly Journal of Progress and Reform* (September–October 1881): 10.

ministic and elitist elements before it encountered Bellamy's Nationalism. Wakeman's notion of scientific prevision and his image of social
reform as elite-led were both primarily derived from Comte; they would
make him very receptive to the social vision of Bellamy's *Looking
Backward*.

When Edward Bellamy, novelist and reform journalist, published his
utopian novel, *Looking Backward, 2000–1887*, in 1888, it proved to be an
enormous hit. The book soon sold a million copies and almost five
hundred local societies, or Nationalist clubs, were formed across the
country. Many Americans, Wakeman among them, were attracted to
Bellamy's humane resolution of the "labor question" and his idyllic
picture of a rationally organized, harmonious society.[55]

The characteristic tension within the American Comtean tradition
between democratic and elitist or bureaucratic themes emerges most
clearly in Wakeman's Nationalist writings. Bellamy appears to have had
an ambiguous effect upon Wakeman; he seemed to reinforce some of the
social conservatism and organicism originally drawn from Comte, while
he eventually pulled Wakeman in a more egalitarian or socialistic direction. These sometimes conflicting tendencies are especially interesting in
the politics of a positivist concerned with "republicanizing" Comtean
ideology.

Among the newer themes that emerged in Wakeman's work during
this period was a pointed critique of contemporary partisan politics. The
American political process, Wakeman believed, had been thoroughly
corrupted—from within by the bosses and from without by the trusts.
"Ours is no longer a government of the people," Wakeman lamented.
Political power had passed out of the hands of the people and into those
of the political and economic elites. Under such a system, the future
looked bleak. "Parties must more and more," Wakeman posited, "become subjected to the control of Trusts and Monopolies and popular
elections can be little more than the record of their wishes and interests."
Such was not the intent of the republic's founders. Wakeman held that
"the original plan of our government" was to have it "rest upon practical
democracy." What had undermined this arrangement was the advent of
national political party organizations in the 1830s. Such mass organizational structures were "more irresponsible and independent of the people
than any King." As trusts and monopolies arose, the parties became
their agents and legislatures were corrupted just as the Roman senate and
British parliament had been before them. Since government by such

55. John L. Thomas, introduction to *Looking Backward, 2000–1887*, by Edward Bellamy
(Cambridge: Belknap Press, Harvard University Press, 1967).

parties was certainly not government by the people, the initiative of governing had to be somehow returned to the people.[56]

One may be struck by the antidemocratic thrust of Wakeman's proposed solution to this problem, but what is perhaps even more interesting is the republican rhetoric employed in the argument.[57] The way Wakeman articulates the problem, his democratic sympathies seem clear. Nationalists must resolve this question using practical means, declared Wakeman; to do so, they would benefit from reading Patrick Henry. While most of the Founding Fathers failed to foresee the form of corruption the republic would take, Henry had anticipated some of these developments in his criticisms of the Constitution. The sheer size of the electoral districts and complexity of the country would ensure "a government of parties and partisans" undercutting "democratic principles." Republican government must rest, Wakeman agreed with Henry, "upon small districts of the people able to meet and vote in primary assemblages."[58]

Yet the socioeconomic ends Wakeman sought were vastly different from those of an eighteenth-century republican such as Henry. The sort of system Wakeman envisaged would have spelled tyranny to Henry or most any of his contemporaries. Wakeman did propose that town assemblies gather to elect state legislators and name delegates who would in turn assemble in convention to elect Congress. The president would be elected by Congress itself and all political activity outside the local assemblies would be carefully proscribed. Such an arrangement might warm the heart of a traditional antiparty republican; however, Wakeman did not seek to curtail governmental power. Rather, the state would administer all those things "necessary to secure the general welfare of the people, such as transportation, and the production and distribution of the common means of living."[59] Thus, not unlike Bellamy, Wakeman adopted traditional republican and antimonopoly means to serve statist ends.

How Wakeman responded to criticisms of Nationalism also underlines the tension within his political theory, between egalitarian and hierarchical impulses. To those who doubted whether some form of socialism would be the product of social evolution, Wakeman answered that such a system was the inevitable outcome of "the fundamental law of history and Sociology." Nor did it represent the negation of the individual;

56. TBW, "Politics and the People," *Nationalist* 2 (December 1889): 11, 12–13.

57. Lipow stresses only the former antidemocratic element. See *Authoritarian Socialism*, 241–45.

58. TBW, "Politics," 14–15.

59. Ibid., 16.

social "integration," said Wakeman, "is the inevitable counterpart of individuation." Not publicly managed integration, but privately controlled monopoly most threatened individual liberty. "The lesson of history," Wakeman wrote, "is that Republics and Liberty always go down when the necessary integrations of civilization and progress, military or other, pass from the control of the people." If huge concentrations of capital were the inescapable products of modernization, then the question was, Shall the people become the slaves of this capital, or its masters? The issue of personal liberty was as central to this conflict as to those of 1775 and 1861, and to do nothing would threaten liberty far more than the proposed measures. Neither was Bellamy's military model something to be feared. An industrial 'army' was not identical with a military army—Nationalists simply used these terms as metaphors. Explained Wakeman: "The word 'army' is short poetry for the order, economy, punctuality and reliable co-operation and *co*, not *sub*-ordination of the public administration of industries." Nationalist government, Wakeman contended, would most definitely not be one "of force or of authoritarianism."[60]

But, although Wakeman assured the skeptical that "every priest, sect, fanatic and phase of thought and opinion" would be tolerated under Nationalism, this did not include partisan political activity outside government or electoral assemblies. Like Comte, Wakeman did not value political pluralism. Wakeman's reason for his proscription of partisan politics usually centered upon "bossism" and related corruptions of the American system. Wakeman's chief concerns, though, often appear to have been civil service reform and a more efficient electoral system (two goals both secured by eliminating national political parties). When listing the benefits of his proposals, for example, Wakeman stressed that they would "save the people an immense amount of money, time, worry, disappointment, corruption, and deviltry of nearly every description."[61] Wakeman noticeably did not say that the mass of citizens would have a greater voice in the decision-making process or that social inequality would be lessened. Furthermore, Wakeman's ascending scale of indirect elections could easily be turned to elitist ends. Such "forced atomization of the electorate" and the "substitution [of] bureaucratic administration for politics" would probably purge the nation of party "bossism" but it could also destroy genuine political freedom.[62] Having eliminated parties, Wakeman's utopia takes on a unitary, authoritarian character. Under

60. "Emancipation by Nationalism," *Arena* 4 (October 1891): 592, 594, 595, 596.
61. "Politics," 16; Lipow, *Authoritarian Socialism*, 244.
62. Lipow, *Authoritarian Socialism*, 242–43.

such a system, Wakeman observed chillingly, "the state becomes the true Church."[63]

One should avoid, however, overdrawing the antidemocratic features of Wakeman's reformism. Wakeman and his fellow Bellamyites did seek to organize as "a party above parties" but their attitudes here were strongly colored by the political corruption of the Gilded Age. While certainly favored by some genteel reformers to serve their own narrow class interests, the plebiscitary system suggested by Wakeman could also conceivably benefit the working classes. It is therefore misleading to conclude that Wakeman disdained "the urban working class, particularly the swelling number of non-English speaking immigrant workers."[64] Although Wakeman was not without ethnic prejudice, such an attitude cannot be deduced from his political writings. Moreover, Wakeman's political association with the Progressive Labor and Populist parties in New York City (including running as a candidate under both banners at different times) does not suggest a hatred of the urban proletariat.[65] Later, Wakeman was active in the People's Party at the state level in New York. Notably, New York Populists were among the most advanced and socialistic of the various state parties.[66]

63. "Our Unchurched Millions," 612. Wakeman was fond of quoting James Parton's dictum: "The proper and practical religion of a citizen of the United States is, in the first instance, The United States of America." See TBW, "Auguste Comte and Philosophy," 1586.

64. Lipow, *Authoritarian Socialism*, 243.

65. TBW, *Free Thought*, 25; Down, *Silverton Country*, 222; Howard H. Quint, *The Forging of American Socialism: Origins of the Modern Movement* (Columbia: University of South Carolina Press, 1953), 50–53. The former party was a non-Marxian socialist splinter group which had broken away from the United Labor Party in 1887. The exodus came as a result of the takeover of the ULP by Henry George's Single-taxers at their Syracuse convention. Progressive Labor Party (PLP) leaders included labor journalist John Swinton (who had visited Comtist meetings in New York during the late 1860s) and Wakeman, who was named to run for state attorney general. Anti-George labor unions represented the party's main constituency and Wakeman's association with the PLP underlines his sympathy for urban workers.

66. Quint, *Forging*, 225, 243. Lipow neglects, as he does with Bellamy, to identify or explain the foreign and domestic sources of Wakeman's alleged authoritarianism. This omission is curious since he refers to "the American Comtean tradition" in his introduction and Wakeman's Comtean writings are more numerous than his explicitly Nationalist work. Wakeman did not, as Lipow claims, merely "borrow his ideas" from the Mugwumps. Rather, Comte's influence best explains the elitism and organizational emphasis Lipow identifies. The wedding of "conservative doctrine" and "a collectivist perspective" that Lipow discovers here represents an excellent illustration of American Comtism's encounter with the varied strands of Gilded Age reform thought (*Authoritarian Socialism*, 245 n. 73). Nor, as the preceding chapters demonstrate, should one simply lump together all American Comtists into a single undifferentiated mass. The "reactionary political and social views"

The best portrait of Wakeman's political orientation during the early 1890s is provided by a short piece contributed to the *Open Court* in April 1891. Entitled "Our Future Polity," the article is partly Wakeman's reflections upon his earlier critique of Comte's political theory. "Many of the open minds and hearts of the more aspiring students of sociology in America, and especially in New York, gave this new [Comtean] Gospel a thoughtful consideration," Wakeman remembered. But Comte's polity, he lamented, "was the stumbling-block over which there was no passing for many of us." The critique, declared Wakeman, that he had articulated some ten or more years ago remained relevant. Wakeman still contended that "the Utopia of the future will be finally a re-integration of Plutocracy and Catholicism into some form of 'Socialism'—a Republic of social industrialism." Comte's "American students have never been able to agree with their French Master in this realm and thus," Wakeman lamented, "Positivism, or Constructive Liberalism received a check in its hopeful progress from which it has never recovered." Spencer's "Monopolistic Feudality [*sic*] or Anarchy" were certainly not the answer. The future lay instead (just as it had ten years ago) in the direction of Comtean revisionism. Wakeman had then argued for and still proposed "the continuance of our Republic, saved by gradually passing to the people the monopolistic powers" that had once gone to the "nobility of blood or of wealth."[67]

Wakeman, then, did not repudiate his earlier attempts to apply Comte to American society but, in fact, saw his involvement in the reform causes of the 1880s and 1890s as a practical application of his revisionist principles. By extension, Wakeman also conceived of his Populist activities as a practical way to realize the goals he had found so attractively outlined in *Looking Backward*. Nationalism and Populism, declared Wakeman, were "two distinct though not divergent lines," both directed toward "economic freedom in America." For him, the People's Party was the only political vehicle that could be employed to realize a few of the "ultimate ideals of *Looking Backward*."[68] Under Populism, Nationalism would be extended only to limited sectors of the economy. Many would agree that natural monopolies such as transportation and communication must be nationalized and for this the Populists labored.

All the same, Wakeman was still willing to argue under the Populist flag for Nationalism on what he termed "advanced ground." Wakeman

---

Lipow ascribes to David Croly were not bequeathed *unchanged* to Wakeman, Lester Ward, or to David's son, Herbert Croly (*Authoritarian Socialism*, 13).

67. "Our Future Polity," *Open Court* 5 (30 April 1891): 2791.

68. "A New Nation," *Commonwealth* 1 (4 February 1893): 3.

here supported a publicly owned and managed economy akin to Bellamy's utopia. All of the basic requirements for free and civilized existence should be provided, Wakeman believed, by the government. Wakeman's rationale for this wholesale nationalization was less Comtean (at least when addressing political audiences) than it was couched in the rhetoric of equal rights and antimonopoly. "Monopolies," explained Wakeman, "are built by giving franchises to a few, and these few turn around and dictate the cost of living to the many. It is an unjust and unfair arrangement."[69] Although the organizational and systematizing ends of Wakeman's proposals clearly owed much to Comte and Bellamy, his rhetoric frequently sounded more Jacksonian than Comtean. Wakeman seems, then, to have had an authentic democratic impulse that moved in a collectivist direction during the 1880s along with much Gilded Age reform thought. Yet, there remained in his system a hierarchical, bureaucratic principle, a deep commitment to rational order, derived largely from Comte and bolstered by parts of Bellamy's work.

These same tensions, so evident in Wakeman's political writings, also appear in Edward Bellamy's work, though for Bellamy, the case is much more inferential. Again, Comte seems to have played a significant role, both in Bellamy's religious ideas and in his social thought. One is struck by the similarities between Edward Bellamy's personal background and that of Wakeman. Though Bellamy was sixteen years Wakeman's junior, both were the products of fairly strict Calvinist upbringings. Both attended colleges with Protestant denominational ties (though Bellamy only for one year); both rejected the faith of their parents as young adults; and both became lawyers and journalists (though Bellamy practiced law for less than a year). More important, both men seemed concerned for much of their adult lives with recapturing the fervor and security that orthodox belief had once provided them. Like Wakeman, Bellamy often appeared (in the words of John L. Thomas) on a "search for a substitute for inherited Christian doctrine."[70] In their quest for a meaningful modern substitute, both men found Comte's theories very attractive.

Comtean positivism clearly did not have the kind of profound impact upon Bellamy as it had upon Wakeman. Nevertheless, the imprint Comtism left upon Bellamy's thought is unmistakable.[71] In a slight,

69. Ibid., 4. See also *Commonwealth* 1 (18 February 1893): 7, for an account of a party rally for General Weaver at which Wakeman spoke.

70. John L. Thomas, Introduction to *Looking Backward 2000–1887* by Edward Bellamy, 12. All following references to *Looking Backward* are to this edition.

71. Curiously, Bellamy's major biographers merely note that he read Comte and may have been influenced by some of the French philosopher's religious ideas; see, for example, Sylvia E. Bowman, *The Year 2000: A Critical Biography of Edward Bellamy* (New York:

though strangely engaging short story published a year and a half after *Looking Backward*, Bellamy dealt with Comtean religious thought. In addition to testifying to his continued interest in positivism, the story also suggests those elements of Comte's system Bellamy found most valuable. The story is essentially a conversation between two characters, one of whom relates a lengthy anecdote about his college days and his encounter with Comte's Religion of Humanity. Like Bellamy, the college youth attends a small, orthodox institution and is the son of a minister; these autobiographical details encourage one to accept the student's remarks regarding positivism as reflecting the author's own views. What, said Bellamy's character, he found most attractive was "the ethical side of Positivism—the idea of the essential unity of the individual with the immortal race of man and his obvious duty to forget self in its service."[72]

Bellamy, or at least this character, seemed to understand Comte's veneration of women; he agreed that they were in some important sense, worthy of worship. Or, as the student concludes, he was overwhelmed by woman's "perpetual consecration and everlasting martyrdom to my race."[73] For Bellamy, as for Comte, women deserved adulation because they were the very embodiment of the values of altruism and self-sacrifice that gave meaning to life.

Such a worshipful attitude toward women, and thus toward compassionate humanity in general, was important for what it did to develop the impersonal or universal spirit within an individual. By cultivating "the instinct of solidarity," one participated more and more deeply in "infinite being." This mystical notion of Bellamy's, a sort of "Oversoul," certainly owed much more to Emerson than to Comte. "Personalities cannot," Bellamy admitted sadly, "absorb each other; their essence is diversity." But this separateness could be transcended during "occasional realizations of an ecstasy of ineffable tenderness, transitory glimpses of that oneness of our universal parts which overarches and includes all individual diversities."[74]

Although the transcendentalist way in which Bellamy articulated this

Bookman, 1958), 36. Joseph Schiffman has gone beyond most commentators by noting that Bellamy followed Comte in his emphasis of "the solidaristic concept of living for others as well as living in the past and in the future." He notes that both "came to the conclusion that humanity fulfilled the place of God"; see Schiffman, ed., *Edward Bellamy: Selected Writings on Religion and Society* (New York: Liberal Arts, 1955), xx. Yet, important as such a conclusion was for Bellamy, humanism was not all that he drew from Comte.

72. Edward Bellamy, "A Positive Romance," *Century* (August 1889): 626.

73. Ibid., 629. Bellamy's character even reflected glowingly upon the role of Mariolatry in medieval culture.

74. Schiffman, *Bellamy*, 22, 25, 15.

idea was quite un-Comtean, the notion of finding one's personal meaning only in relation to the collective is compatible with Comte's perspective. Furthermore, Bellamy's understanding of death dovetailed with the Comtean notion of the timelessness of Humanity. For in dying, Bellamy believed, one simply put aside individual personality and joined the larger existence. "By this higher life," Bellamy wrote, ". . . we are united to the living and to the dead. For this life of solidarity there is neither past nor present, mortality nor immortality, but life ever present."[75] In short, Bellamy's "universal identity" seems to have owed much to Comte's conception of "divine Humanity."

In light of these ideas, Bellamy's quest in the social and political realm centered upon how (to quote Thomas again) "the life of solidarity . . . could be planned and sustained by cultural habit."[76] Here, too, Comtean ideas appear to have been important among Bellamy's many influences, though in a less direct and less obvious fashion. The protagonist in "A Positive Romance" went as far as to call Comte's "fanciful schemes of new society . . . impossible and undesirable."[77] Yet such a remark should not deter one from exploring the significant similarities between the sociopolitical perspectives of the two. By no means an orthodox Comtist, Bellamy nonetheless shared many of Comte's ideological commitments.

To start with, Comte and Bellamy agreed that, although social progress toward a more advanced and rational social order was inevitable, a popular intellectual and moral revolution was the prerequisite for basic change. Indeed, as a descendant of the *philosophes*, Comte linked these two elements together. "I think it indisputable," he wrote in the *Cours*, "that the gradual development of humanity favors a growing preponderance of the noblest tendencies of our nature."[78] Perhaps an inheritance from his evangelical parents, Bellamy was fond of having his fictional characters undergo emotional moral conversions of one kind or another. The young student in "A Positive Romance" is at first embarrassed and disappointed at the plain, charmless appearance of his professor's daughter, whom he has been appointed to "worship." Upon reflection, however, he perceives her beauty as a symbol of feminine compassion and is ashamed at his initial inability to understand this higher truth.[79] Julian West, in *Looking Backward*, undergoes a conversion from selfishness

75. Ibid., 16.

76. Thomas, "Introduction," 15.

77. Bellamy, "A Positive Romance," 626.

78. Auguste Comte, in *Auguste Comte and Positivism,* ed. Gertrud Lenzer (New York: Harper, 1975), 234. Abbreviated as Lenzer, ed., *Comte* below.

79. Bellamy, "A Positive Romance," 629.

to Nationalism, just as American society had done before him. As Doctor Leete recounts, it was only after socioeconomic crisis that the hearts of the citizenry were truly won over and a system built upon better principles could be established.[80]

As for the shape of the new social order, Comte and Bellamy were both advocates of the "managed society." Comte, the great systematizer in the philosophy of science, worked from a similar impulse in drawing the outlines of his Positive Polity. In editorials for the Springfield *Union* published in the early 1870s, Bellamy was already articulating a managed, organic approach to reform. The narrow particularism of previous reform causes needed to be replaced, he argued, by a coherent, restrained, and rational plan.[81] One of the chief characteristics of Bellamy's industrial system as described in *Looking Backward* is its comprehensiveness and the high degree of control it has over its citizenry. Or, as Doctor Leete commented with regard to the place of women under the new order: "We have given them a world of their own, with its emulations, ambitions and careers, and I assure you they are very happy in it."[82] Here was a vast human construction that could reform and even mold cultural habit.

A managed, comprehensive system was sought in part for the order and efficiency it could secure. Comte's lifework was an attempt to alleviate and resolve the social flux and intellectual uncertainty of contemporary industrial society. Yet Comte's vision of order was not entirely reactionary. Comte understood that a new order must be founded upon the forces of progress and change themselves. "No real order," Comte asserted, "can be established, and still less can it last, if it is not fully compatible with progress, and no great progress can be accomplished if it does not tend to the consolidation of order."[83] From such a point of view, sudden, ill-considered revolutionary change is rejected, but then so is a mindless, antiquarian conservatism. The root, Comte always stressed, of social anarchy was mental or moral anarchy. "While stability in fundamental maxims," Comte noted, "is the first condition of genuine social order, we are suffering [today] under an utter disagreement that may be called universal." Once such basic principles were established, then "appropriate institutions will issue from them, without shock or resistance; for the causes of disorder will have been arrested by the mere fact of the agreement."[84]

80. Bellamy, *Looking Backward*, 55.
81. Thomas, Introduction, 17–18.
82. Bellamy, *Looking Backward*, 265; Bowman, *The Year 2000*, 158.
83. Lenzer, ed., *Comte*, 197.
84. Ibid., 83.

This notion of Comte's relates to Bellamy in at least two ways. First, Bellamy too saw the need for personal moral regeneration to preface social reform and thereby provide the foundation for a stable system. Second, Bellamy's own life seems to illustrate Comte's thesis regarding personal and social anarchy. Some historians have asked whether Bellamy's singular concern for social order arose from his own efforts to resolve inner conflict. Having rejected the Calvinist universe with its sovereign God, Bellamy remained concerned, in Bowman's words, with "attain[ing] once again the blissful sense of security of one who had faith."[85] Bellamy never imposed upon himself the religious "mental hygiene" of Comte, but both reformers were concerned with the causal relationship between mental confusion and social disorder.

The way to obtain social control, order, and efficiency was, Comte and Bellamy concurred, through a hierarchical division of labor. Contended Comte: "When a regular division of employments has spread through any society, the social state begins to acquire a consistency and stability that place it out of danger from particular divergencies." Under such a structure, Comte observed approvingly, "the social organization tends more and more to rest on an exact estimate of individual diversities." This "separation of functions" is as essential to "the collective organism" as "the cooperation of functions." Comte's division of labor was not simply ordered and rational, however. The structure of employment was rigidly hierarchical, modeled in fact upon the patriarchal Victorian family. For Comte, the ideal "social type" was "a reproduction, with a large extension, of the domestic organism," though requiring more artificial discipline than the latter "which nature herself ordains and administers."[86]

Comte did not favor the military model as an appropriate pattern for social reorganization; the military system had preceded the industrial and was thus a more primitive form of social organization. Nevertheless, both systems operate similarly and both are distinguished by a hierarchical division of labor. "As the ancient world," wrote Comte, "had in war its school of discipline and of government, the modern world finds these in industry . . . government springs from agreement between the natural chiefs of the various types of industry, who gather around their best representative." Just as primitive military states were founded upon martial power, so industrial societies must have governments based upon material wealth and power. Hence, government was always built upon

85. Bowman, *The Year 2000*, 26; Thomas, Introduction, 18–19. One might also interpret TBW's philosophical quest in this way.

86. Lenzer, ed., *Comte*, 272, 360, 273.

force. "Social science," Comte held, "would remain forever in the cloud land of metaphysics if we hesitated to adopt the principle of force as the basis of government. Combining this doctrine with that of Aristotle's, that society consists in the combination of efforts and the distribution of functions, we get the axioms of a sound political philosophy."[87]

Bellamy definitely shared Comte's belief in the critical need for a hierarchical division of labor in an industrial society, though (unlike Wakeman's case) it is not entirely clear where he obtained it. Thomas has called this "the pivotal principle in the new sociological perspective" of the 1880s and this "dominant theme of modernization" underlay much of *Looking Backward*.[88] As Dr. Leete explained, what Comte called "the distribution of functions" lay at the heart of the new industrial system. "The Principle," said Dr. Leete, "on which our industrial army is organized is that a man's natural endowments, mental and physical, determine what he can work at most profitably to the nation and most satisfactorily to himself." Just as in the family, the schools that trained these future laborers were "very strict" and stressed the "habits of obedience, subordination, and devotion to duty." Moreover, the "division of employments" was extended up into the political realm by means of a guild system. At the national level, individual guilds were bound together in "groups of allied trades," and it was the heads of these "divisions" that constituted the president's cabinet. Such "associations of our active lifetime," notes Dr. Leete, "retain a powerful hold on us," even after retirement.[89]

Bellamy ensured that this rigid division of labor was hierarchical by adopting a military model for his polity. Here again, Comte seems to have anticipated the basic outlines of Bellamy's Nationalism. Note, for instance, these remarks from the *Système*:

> The particular functions of each citizen [in human society], being clearly marked, throw up in each group a special government of its own, which controls and directs it on a small scale, as occasion arises. This is the germ of the wider government of society which is the product of the small combinations when their common ends are duly made general. Military activity, the only one

87. Ibid., 432, 433.

88. Thomas, *Alternative America*, 245–46. Thomas is one of the few commentators who has recognized Bellamy's concern for a hierarchical division of labor as essentially Comtean.

89. Bellamy, *Looking Backward*, 131.

fully organized at present, has a direct tendency to form lasting combinations, for it can gain no success without union.[90]

Bellamy's own "combinations" or trade guilds, under strict military discipline and under a stratified military command structure, were, in the words of Dr. Leete, "the complete solution . . . [to] the insoluble labor problem" of the Gilded Age.[91] If one valued a managed, orderly, efficient, and hierarchical industrial system, clearly, the military model was very attractive.

The implications of Bellamy's system were certainly elitist if not explicitly antidemocratic. Comte had been quite clear about the need for concentrations of capital and elite leadership in a modern industrial system. "An army can no more exist without officers than without soldiers, and this elementary truth," Comte argued, "holds good for industry as well as for war." And it was really only the great captains of industry, Comte held, that would be receptive to moral arguments regarding their larger social responsibility.[92] Judging by *Looking Backward*, Bellamy seems to have shared much of Comte's elitism. Although the state controls the means of production the industrial army does not vote for the national executive that has the primary responsibility in running the country. In fact, government itself becomes mostly executive or managerial in character, with Congress playing little more than a legitimation role. Echoing Comte's patriarchal impulse, Bellamy's managerial gerontocracy is run by materially disinterested gentlemen who have retired from active duty, but draw upon their personal experience during lengthy careers of service. Thomas has thus aptly termed Bellamy's electorate "an industrial G.A.R."[93]

Yet, as evident in this patriarchal softening of the martial element in Nationalism, Bellamy seems to have been often a reluctant militarist. Criticisms of his utopia's martial character affected Bellamy and, increasingly, he stressed that the military metaphor should not be taken too far. In responding to the criticism of Francis A. Walker, Bellamy moved from a military to a bureaucratic model for industrial organization. The precise character of the National system, he replied, would probably most closely resemble the federal civil service in Washington. As Bellamy encountered such criticism and as he grew more involved in politics (particularly with Populism), the bureaucratic, cooperative, and

90. Lenzer, ed., *Comte*, 432.
91. Bellamy, *Looking Backward*, 131.
92. Lenzer, ed., *Comte*, 360.
93. Thomas, Introduction, 59–60, 62.

egalitarian features of Nationalism were stressed in preference to its martial and authoritarian elements. The evolution of Bellamy's thought, therefore, moved his ideological position both closer to Comte with regard to its bureaucratism, and farther from Comte in its Populist rhetoric of equal rights and antimonopoly.[94]

The foregoing analysis demonstrates that Bellamy did indeed articulate illiberal political views. Huge segments of the electorate were disfranchised in Bellamy's utopia, political parties were nonexistent, and life sometimes seems monochrome and regimented. But it would appear that much of the impulse behind organized Nationalism and behind Bellamy's thought itself was genuinely humanitarian and egalitarian. Surely one must ask what Bellamy's basic intentions were. In this light, Bellamy's political philosophy bears little resemblance to a form of proto-Stalinism as one commentator seems to suggest; rather, it appears to have been an imperfectly developed reform ideology that harbored within itself both democratic and elitist elements. Emphasizing either of these elements to the exclusion of the other may serve to obscure this central ambiguity.[95]

94. This tension within Bellamyism has rarely been understood by historians. Arthur Lipow has argued that with its "despotic 'new class' ruling over a statified [sic] economy," Looking Backward foreshadowed totalitarian communism. Bellamy, Lipow observes, never used the word democracy in his first novel and had to be pulled by his political activity during the 1890s to a slightly more democratic position. Lipow admits that the book appealed both to those committed to democratic reform as well as to those who "feared democracy," but he seems not to recognize that this wide appeal may have arisen from an ambiguity within Bellamy's work. If Nationalism ever had such a "divided soul," Lipow contends that it was entirely the product of its cooperation with Populism. Lipow implies that the core of Bellamyism was always authoritarian and antidemocratic (Lipow, Authoritarian Socialism, 1–2, 6–7, 224, 288). Such an interpretation strikes me as, at the very least, one-sided. Jeffrey Lustig similarly sees Nationalism serving primarily elitist corporate interests. See R. Jeffrey Lustig, Corporate Liberalism: The Origins of Modern American Political Theory, 1890–1920 (Berkeley and Los Angeles: University of California Press, 1982), 200.

Moreover, Lipow is less clear than he might have been about the sources of Bellamy's statism and bureaucratism. Lipow goes as far as suggesting Comte as one source of the conservative reformism of leading Mugwumps but does not explicitly attach this thread to Bellamy. His passing reference to Comte along with his almost equally cryptic asides regarding Hegel and Spencer are virtually all the author says about foreign philosophical sources. Neither does Lipow examine the indigenous historical roots of "the American reform tradition" that was animated by such a "hatred of democracy" (Lipow, Authoritarian Socialism, 12–13, 13–14, 12).

95. The complex and often ambiguous ideological position exemplified by Wakeman and Bellamy was also presented in the pages of Commonwealth, a radical New York weekly published in the 1890s. Once more, the Comtean element seems to have made an important contribution. Though it has been characterized as an American Fabian organ, the publication was also a vehicle for many ex-Comtists; see Quint, Forging, 242. The

★ ★ ★

Historians have long observed the internal tensions within the radical and reform thought of the Gilded Age. These tensions produced centrifugal forces that contributed to the collapse of Populism before the turn of the century. Few analysts, however, have attempted a thorough examination of the origins and component parts of this "commonwealth" ideology that emerged during the last quarter of the nineteenth century. Though Chester Destler's interpretation of the urban antebellum roots of Gilded Age radicalism, with its emphasis upon antimonopolism and Locofocoism, is helpful, he seems less able to account for Populism's state interventionist and collectivist impulse. Destler points to Edward Kellogg's economic and monetary theory and the demands

---

Commonwealth articulated a social and political theory that sought to be simultaneously scientific, collectivist, and democratic—an endeavor in some ways comparable to Wakeman's attempted republicanization of Comte. Editor C. P. Somerby, a leading freethinker, proposed to provide "the pith" of the writings "of the abler authors of Social Science and general Reform topics" at low cost to a wide audience. Somerby contended that economic change must preface all other reforms and that it must do no less than replace competitive capitalism with a more "sane" system; see C. P. Somerby, "Aims and Objects," *Commonwealth* 1 (14 January 1893): 2. The cross-section of reform authors who appeared in the review was quite eclectic. In addition to Americans such as Bellamy, Richard Ely, Laurence Gronlund, John Swinton, Wakeman, and Ward, the *Commonwealth* also quoted from John Stuart Mill and Sidney Webb. Even the comments of European socialists such as Jules Guesde, Karl Kautsky, and Marx himself were frequently cited with approval.

And yet, while appeals to traditional democratic values often appeared in its pages, the spirit of many of the selections was more corporatist than truly egalitarian. For example, the second number featured a short piece by Bellamy that stressed the conservative and statist side of Nationalism. "Let no mistake be made here," cautioned Bellamy, "we are not revolutionists, but counterrevolutionists." The way to end the subversion of the republic by private monopoly was to implement "a plan of industrial reorganization." This new economic structure was now the only way to "guarantee to all citizens a common interest in the national concern." As defenders of this republican commonwealth, "we are [the] true conservative party," wrote Bellamy; see Edward Bellamy, "Nationalism—Principles," *Commonwealth* 1 (14 January 1893): 3.

It was this "commonwealth ideology," with its problematic blend of enthusiastic statism and equal rights rhetoric, that defined Wakeman's community of discourse during the nineties. If the *Commonwealth* is any indication, the contribution of American Comtism to this hybrid reform ideology was significant. In addition to Wakeman, many of the contributors had studied Comte and been influenced by his philosophy in varying degrees. Moreover, the list of recommended reading that appeared in the back pages of every *Commonwealth* included not only Wakeman's works, but Comtist literature by Henry Edger and David Croly (such as the latter's *Modern Thinker*). Although some of these titles were more than twenty years old, apparently the editors still deemed them worthy to offer. One may recall that the *Commonwealth* shared its offices for a time with Wakeman's Society of Humanity, ran an advertisement for the society in its pages, and even described itself as the "Official Organ" of the group for over a year. The legacy of the early New York societies was evidently a powerful one.

of Grangers and the Knights of Labor as the sources of Populism's desertion of the negative Lockean state. But Destler says little about the foreign origins of the un-Lockean statism of late nineteenth-century reform. Why was it that "unlike the earlier working class champions of equal rights, the Populists sought relief through the extension of governmental action into economic life"?[96]

One answer is suggested by Jeffrey Lustig's study of the birth of corporate liberalism in America at the turn of the century. Agreeing with Destler that industrial monopoly was the central political issue of the 1880s and 1890s, Lustig reveals how certain reformers in fact diverted the democratic collectivism of the Populists in a conservative, corporatist direction. Here, Lustig is one of the few historians to recognize the critical role of Comte. The influence of the French philosopher was "decisive," writes Lustig, in the emergence of corporate liberalism in America.[97]

But Lustig is not always so clear as he might be in showing precisely what nascent corporate liberals drew from Comte, apart from an unabashed elitism. Moreover, his case regarding Comte's influence is mainly inferential, with few explicit connections being drawn. Lustig sees Comte employed primarily by conservatives as an instrument of ideological accommodation with corporate capitalism. Drawing from Comte, corporate apologists such as Charles Francis Adams, Jr., were able to argue "that social progress depends on the rare gifts of a few businessmen, that industrial initiative must be centralized, and that hierarchy and bureaucratic rationality are inevitable in the modern world."[98] The foregoing discussion confirms the Comtean source of this approach but locates its roots firmly in the Gilded Age. Much of the statism and bureaucratic mind-set of Wakeman and Bellamy can be attributed to the persistent influence of Comtean ideas. Yet the preceding analysis does not present a monochrome portrait; some, like Wakeman, who strongly opposed private monopoly, made use of Comte for ideological ends that, while often confused, were not wholly antidemocratic. This tension would continue to characterize the social and political vision of those who worked within the American Comtean tradition.

EPILOGUE

There are few discernible changes in Wakeman's political thought between the middle 1890s and his death in 1913. After the collapse of

96. Destler, *Radicalism*, 19.
97. Lustig, *Corporate Liberalism*, 105.
98. Ibid., 105, 99.

Populism with Bryan's defeat in 1896, Wakeman became less active politically and seldom addressed political questions in his writing. What comments he did make suggest that Wakeman was drawn in an even more statist direction during the opening decades of the new century. In *Science Is Religion* (1905), Wakeman defines the state as "the social action of each people for their protection and general welfare on the earth." Such a state would be supreme in all things, including religion. "The republic," declared Wakeman, "and not the church is supreme—*Vox populi, vox Dei.*" The activist, omnicompetent, state would thus ensure that religious institutions would "pass under the control of the people."[99]

Moreover, the organicist and corporatist elements in Wakeman's ideology are especially evident in his later work. To survive, the republic must be highly unified. Explained Wakeman, "We cannot expect each for all unless all is for each, with a resultant interest and honor which will make the life and welfare of the republic that of its humblest *socius,* or member also. That such Spartan-like devotion is still possible is made manifest by the action of the Japanese people in their present Russian war. . . . Without the supreme devotion of its people" to the state and the nation, "the long continuance of a republic is not possible."[100]

The philosophical rationale for Wakeman's statism in his later writings seems, not surprisingly, to have been derived from the monism of Spencer and Haeckel. Although social evolution was "a Process of differentiation," this, Wakeman believed, was "reciprocated by a counter process of assimilation and integration, attended by a final co-operation, co-ordination and organization of both processes in the interest of, and for the welfare of the whole organization." While having many of its roots in Comte, the strong unitary and interventionist theory of the state Wakeman developed also clearly owed much to Haeckel's monism. In fact, in the same monograph, Wakeman appeared to grant Haeckel a superior place to Comte in the realm of social theory. Wakeman acknowledged that Comte had "realized and formulated" the "science of sociology" but concluded that Haeckel, in developing an evolutionary law of correlation, had himself "scientifically laid the foundation of all

99. TBW, *Science Is Religion,* 32, 15, 14. Wakeman could still sound like a Populist, however. Wrote TBW in the same monograph: "The monopolistic government of plutocratic classes must give way to that of the people sufficiently enlightened to provide for each an opportunity to do his best for himself and all; and to secure as a result, justice—'the giving to each that which may be his due' " (17). According to his grandson, TBW voted for Theodore Roosevelt in 1912 because his daughters were enamored with Roosevelt and cajoled their father into supporting him. But his reasons may well have gone deeper. Chapter 7 suggests some reasons why American Comtists were attracted to Roosevelt's "New Nationalism."

100. Ibid., 34, 35.

government, social organization and moral conduct." An "appreciation" of Haeckel's philosophy and its political implications was, for the aged Wakeman, "the condition of any successful Liberal organizing."[101]

As mentioned earlier, because of his fascination with Haeckelian monism, Wakeman traveled in 1911 to the First Monist Congress in Hamburg. Another member of the American delegation was an old acquaintance and sometime correspondent of Wakeman's, Lester Frank Ward.

101. Ibid., 37, 12.

CHAPTER FIVE

Lester F. Ward

Positivist Whig

How often I wish that from your side of the Atlantic could come some corresponding movement—or some . . . help to us here. But we must wait for the hour.
—Richard Congreve to LFW, 6 April 1893

IT IS FITTING THAT this study of the American Comtean "mind" should feature as its centerpiece the thinker whom Ernest Becker labeled perceptively "a latter-day Comte with a distinctive American modification."[1] Perhaps the most significant contribution to the development of a uniquely American Comtean tradition was made by amateur social theorist, philosopher, paleobotanist, and civil servant, Lester Frank Ward. In 1883, after several rewrites and a long struggle with reluctant publishers, Ward's *Dynamic Sociology* appeared in print—probably the most successful attempt to "republicanize" the Comtean system for Gilded Age Americans. And yet, although Ward frequently expressed

---

1. *The Structure of Evil: An Essay on the Unification of the Science of Man* (New York: George Braziller, 1968), 69.

his admiration for and debt to Comtean positivism, historians have often overlooked or underplayed Comte's influence. Frequently, Ward's intellectual milieu is described only with references to Darwin and Spencer, and, if not ignored entirely, Comte's influence is noted only in passing with no attempt to explore its larger significance for Ward's thought.[2]

This chapter examines Ward's life and work in light of his avowed positivism in order to garner a fresh understanding of his social thought and gain, en route, a more subtle appreciation of the intellectual discourse of his age. With Ward, one now moves beyond the immediate circle of New York Comtists (though, as noted in Chapter 4, he did participate in some of their ventures). Orthodox positivism had circulated among some American intellectuals since the late 1860s but, by the 1880s, a revised version was gradually moving out of the cultural margins. The case of Lester Frank Ward allows one to view Comte's profound impact on a thinker usually interpreted as an unambiguous democratic reformer. The following analysis can serve to delineate, in at least two ways, the component parts of an evolving American Comtean discourse. First, Ward's case clarifies the role of Whig political culture within this ideological mix. Furthermore, the interaction of Comtean positivism with scientific and bureaucratic thought is illuminated by Ward's civil service career in Gilded Age Washington. This chapter explores Ward's early years, describes his intellectual community in postwar Washington, explains how he encountered Comte intially, how he approached Comtean positivism critically, and, finally, how the Comtean system underlay his mature thought. Comte was enormously important to Ward because he helped him retain and update his Whiggish ideals, challenge Spencerian laissez-faire, and understand social scientists and their allies in the federal bureaucracy as "priests" of reform.

2. Richard Hofstadter, *Social Darwinism in American Thought* (Boston: Beacon, 1955), was probably one of the most influential exponents of this perspective but even more recent studies that criticize Hofstadter still accept many of his assumptions. See, for instance, Robert C. Bannister, *Social Darwinism: Science and Myth in Anglo-American Social Thought* (Philadelphia: Temple University Press, 1979), esp. 126–31. Cynthia Eagle Russett, *Darwin in America: The Intellectual Response, 1865–1912* (San Francisco: Freeman, 1976), ignores Comte entirely in her analysis of Ward's thought (102–11). Other studies that deal with Ward either observe Comte's influence without comment or overemphasize the differences between Ward and the French "father of sociology." See Ralph H. Gabriel, *The Course of American Democratic Thought: An Intellectual History Since 1815* (New York: Ronald Press, 1940), 207; Louis Hartz, *The Liberal Tradition in America: An Interpretation of American Political Thought Since the Revolution* (New York: Harcourt, Brace and World, 1955), 232–35; Alvin F. Nelson, "Lester Ward's Conception of the Nature of Science," *Journal of the History of Ideas*, 33 (1972): 633–38.

I

Lester Ward's family background and early life reveal the roots of his later thinking and can clarify how Ward was intellectually prepared for his mature encounter with Comte. Born in 1841, the tenth child of Justus and Silence Ward, Lester was raised both in Illinois and on the Iowa frontier. Justus was a humble mechanic who moved from one modest job to another; consequently, his large family never enjoyed more than a very meager existence. The few extant accounts suggest that Justus was a fiercely independent individual who had fought as a young man in the War of 1812 and was a confirmed Whig. Ward's mother reinforced his father's Whiggery with a strong dose of evangelical Protestantism. Silence Loomis Ward was the daughter of a New York parson who was an accomplished Greek scholar. She was a woman of some culture and enjoyed literature, in addition to being a fervent Christian. Hence, Silence encouraged her sons' intellectual interests but with a view to having them enter the Protestant ministry.[3]

From his parents, then, Ward seems to have inherited much that would characterize his mature thought. From his father, he received both his Whig ideology and respect for personal independence and individual effort coupled with an egalitarian commitment to social mobility. His mother seems to have instilled a genuine thirst for knowledge in her youngest; she probably also inculcated his deep-seated anti-Catholicism. A romantic short story written by a youthful Ward for the St. Charles (Illinois) *Argus*, includes denunciations of convents as ill-disguised prisons.

Emotionalism was another aspect of the evangelical faith that Mrs. Ward may have bequeathed to her son. From adolescence to old age, Ward displayed an emotional enthusiasm for the religious implications of scientific truths. Even after he had repudiated traditional Christianity, Ward continued to believe in the value of religious forms; he "prayed" regularly and was a frequent churchgoer.[4] Writing to a friend late in life, Ward reflected: "I am like a woman. . . . I attribute the warmth of my ideas to that highly emotional nature of mine."[5] It is significant Ward should have likened his sensitivity to a woman's since the image chosen by Comte to symbolize his Religion of Humanity was that of a young

3. Clifford H. Scott, *Lester Frank Ward* (Boston: G. K. Hall, 1976), 13–17.
4. Emily Cape, *Lester F. Ward: A Personal Sketch* (New York: Putnam, 1922), 111; Bernhard J. Stern, ed., *Young Ward's Diary* (New York: Putnam, 1935), 246. See also LFW, "Religious Influence of Science," *Iconoclast* 1 (15 November 1870): 1.
5. LFW, cited in Cape, *Personal Sketch*, 97–98.

mother with a child in her arms. Comte had posited a lofty place for feeling and sentiment in his system. One of his English disciples, Frederic Harrison, put it this way: "Our conceptions can only be held together and systematized by means of a harmony ultimately satisfying the deepest emotion."[6] This feature of Comtism probably appealed to Ward's emotional side.

Though he retained much of the emotionalism and sentimentalism of his evangelical roots, Ward soon broke with his parents' Protestant orthodoxy. While attending classes at Susquehanna Collegiate Institute in Pennsylvania, the youthful Ward, like so many of his contemporaries, underwent a crisis of faith. As an adolescent, he had undergone something of a conversion experience but, as a young adult at school, he was obviously experiencing doubts. Nonetheless, he continued to go to a variety of Protestant churches regularly, often several times on a Sunday. Then, when one of his professors approached him to discuss his Christian commitment, Ward became upset:

> Prof. O.S. came into my room last night and talked a long time with me concerning my duty to God. He supplicated, he admonished and he prayed. I went to church with Moody [a school friend] and we talked about the subject. My heart was very heavy, and when I sat down in church I could not suppress the tears. I wept and O how my heart felt it![7]

Ward seems to have been unable or unwilling to make the sort of spiritual confession his teachers had in mind and soon he was expressing less than orthodox sentiments regarding the authority of the Bible. At a meeting of primary school teachers, Ward supported a colleague who spoke against a resolution stressing the importance of "a profound respect for the Scriptures."[8] By the early sixties, he sounded in his writings like a moderate Unitarian in his rejection of modern-day miracles, while still affirming the existence of a "Supreme Power" that ordered the universe.[9]

The Civil War had broken out while Ward was in school and Ward's subsequent military experience would prove to strengthen his particular set of political assumptions. Ward had been raised a Whig with strong antislavery and temperance views, and thus he gravitated easily to the

6. "Mr. Lewes' Problems of Life and Mind," *Fortnightly Review* 16 (July–December 1874): 100.

7. Stern, *Young Ward*, 50.

8. Ibid., 109.

9. Scott, *Ward*, 137.

Republicans prior to the war. Looking forward to Lincoln's election, Ward hoped that the new Republican administration would move to destroy secession, slavery, and intemperance together. As an infantry-man in a Pennsylvania regiment Ward was given, in his own words, the "grand opportunity . . . for thinning out the enemies of human liberty" but was soon wounded in battle and sent back to the Washington area to recuperate. While some of his idealism regarding war was deflated by his combat experience, Ward probably came away with a greater confidence in the power of the state to effect significant socioeconomic change. Biographer Clifford Scott notes that Ward's military service was critical in confirming his "reform-oriented" (and, one could add, Whiggish) belief in "the power of a mobilized government to work good in society."[10]

When he took up residence in the nation's capital after the war, Ward remained an enthusiastic Republican. At first, even when it did not serve his own vocational interests, Ward openly opposed the Johnson administration. Evidently, service in the Union Army had made Ward an even more committed Republican. Writing to a Washington daily in 1865, Ward advocated no clemency be granted to the rebellious South and signed his letter "One Who Has Bled to Punish Traitors."[11] A

10. LFW, *Glimpses of the Cosmos,* 6 vols. (New York: Putnam, 1913–18), 1:31; Scott, *Ward,* 85. The war did, after all, have a similar legacy for many of Ward's contemporaries. Men such as John W. Draper, Francis A. Walker, and Charles Francis Adams, Jr., were all encouraged by the success of the northern war machine to view social problems as solvable when attacked by a professional scientific elite. In fact, Adams, like Ward, was powerfully influenced by Comte, and his description of his first encounter with positivism is revealing. "I was in a most recipient condition [after the war]," Adams later wrote, "and that essay of Mill's [*Auguste Comte and Positivism,* 1866] revolutionized in a single morning my whole mental attitude. I emerged from the theological state, in which I had been nurtured, and passed into the scientific"(cited in George Fredrickson, *The Inner Civil War: Northern Intellectuals and the Crisis of the Union* [New York: Harper and Row, 1965], 205). Here certainly is compelling testimony of the preparatory function that the Civil War may have played for future positivists such as Adams and Ward.

Still, the social philosophy that Ward constructed in the wake of the Civil War was far more progressive and humanitarian than the pessimistic theories formulated by George Frederick Holmes, Walker, or even his fellow positivist, Adams. These latter intellectuals, concludes George Fredrickson, were not advocating "the continuance . . . of the prewar reform impulse . . . they had all rejected this heritage"(Fredrickson, *Inner Civil War,* 215). Yet Ward's Whiggish idealism and sentimental humanitarianism appear not to have been destroyed by the war; indeed, these very elements of his personal creed may have made him more sensitive to the harsh economic realities that faced most Americans. Thus, Ward would recoil at the transparently self-serving laissez-faire economics of William Graham Sumner, while Adams readily integrated Spencerian social thought into his world-view (Fredrickson, *Inner Civil War,* 207). See also LFW, "Prof. Sumner's Social Classes," in *Glimpses,* 3:301–5.

11. LFW, *Glimpses,* 1:36–37.

supporter of Congressional radicals such as Thaddeus Stevens and Charles Sumner, Ward was an early advocate of Negro suffrage. Ward and his wife Lizzie attended debates in Congress, including those surrounding the impeachment of President Johnson. Later, however, under the retrenchment and corruption of the Grant administration, Ward became far less partisan. Still, during the sixties, by his own admission, Ward was a political "stalwart."[12]

But exactly how did Ward's Whiggish politics predispose him to accept Comte? Louis Hartz has maintained that Americans such as Ward could never be thorough Comtists because they lacked an authentic conservative tradition to supply an organic and statist foundation for their politics. Admittedly, American Whigs never held the aristocratic or feudal pedigree that characterized European conservatism, but Hartz has failed to recognize the genuinely conservative elements in antebellum Whiggery. More recently, Daniel W. Howe identifies three dominant themes in Whig rhetoric that help one understand its ideological makeup: a commitment to improvement, an emphasis upon duties rather than abstract rights, and an organic view of society.[13] All of these distinctive emphases find strong parallels in the Comtean system.

Whigs were not merely partisans of improvement but were concerned that change be managed or directed to produce progress. Whigs derived this commitment from their philosophy of history and dogged empiricism. Human history was chiefly the record of the growth and extension of political liberty. Borrowing from Scottish Common Sense philosopher Adam Ferguson, Whigs saw man's growth as a "progression" from savagery to "civilization." When public policies needed to be evaluated, the historical record had to be consulted in order to ground action upon experience and not upon abstract, rationalistic theory. Nor could one simply rely upon the march of history; self-conscious control and human intervention were seen to be essential to direct the human "experiment."[14] Whig historicism and interventionism were, then, analogous to key features of Comtean positivism.

12. Ibid., 1:36; Scott, *Ward*, 99.

13. Hartz, *Liberal Tradition*, 179–80; Daniel Walker Howe, *The Political Culture of the American Whigs* (Chicago: University of Chicago Press, 1979), 21. More recently, R. Jeffery Lustig has argued that corporate liberalism arose in late nineteenth-century America through the philosophical "marriage" of Darwinism and Lockean liberalism, with Comte serving as, in some sense, the matchmaker (*Corporate Liberalism: The Origins of Modern American Political Theory, 1890–1920* [Berkeley and Los Angeles: University of California Press, 1982]; see esp. 83–88). I hope to demonstrate here what I proposed in Chapter 1: namely, that it was antebellum Whiggery that played the role of matchmaker between Darwin and Comte on the one hand, and classical liberalism on the other, in the political thought of positivists such as Ward.

14. Howe, *Political Culture*, 73.

As in Ward's own upbringing, a strong evangelical Protestant component within Whig thought promoted a concern for purposive social improvement. The reformist post-millennialism of antebellum evangelicalism contributed much to Whig thinking about social change. Building upon an eschatology first sketched out by Jonathan Edwards, evangelical Whigs believed that man could perfect society, establish a millennium of peace and thereby hasten Christ's return. Unlike later liberal Protestants, antebellum evangelicals thus saw evangelism and social reform not as conflicting goals but as complementary means to build "heaven on earth" and ensure the Second Coming. Whig clerics stressed the need for well-to-do Christian laymen to take an activist part in promoting social betterment, for they were supposedly the sort of leaders God used to bring about both moral and material progress. It was such "men of enterprise" who stimulated both material prosperity and growth in public morality. Once the Christian supernaturalism evaporated from Whig postmillennialism, therefore, one had an activist and melioristic ideology tinged with elitism quite consistent with Comtean principles.[15]

Second, Whigs tended to emphasize the duties of individuals within a particular social context rather than individual rights based upon contractual theories. Consistent with their historicism, Whigs frequently decried the iconoclasm and rationalism of the French Revolution; meanwhile, they viewed the American Revolution as the culmination of a vast historical process with its roots in the origins of English political institutions. The relationship of individuals to the polity at large was described in a way that accepted, at least by implication, a hierarchical social structure and a paternalistic state; the duties of both leaders and led were more important than some abstractly conceived rights.[16] As Comte wrote in the *Système*, "The metaphysical theory of right" must be overshadowed by a concern for "social questions, which are to be solved for the most part through moral agencies."[17]

Finally, consistent with their hostility to the contractual formalism of the Democrats, Whigs often employed organic metaphors to describe political society. Whigs viewed the republic as a coherent natural whole and not as merely a conglomeration of separate, warring classes or interests. As with the two preceding themes, Whigs drew a parallel between the individual and society; the human being is an organic whole but with different parts or members that serve the good of the whole

15. Ibid., 151–54.
16. Ibid., 21, 70–71.
17. Gertrud Lenzer, ed., *Auguste Comte and Positivism: The Essential Writings* (New York: Harper and Row, 1975), 368.

under the direction of the brain. Whereas Democrats often pointed to conflict between haves and have-nots, Whigs extolled social consensus, contending that the various economic and occupational groups were in fact interdependent and together served the commonweal. Similarly, Comte perceived the "social organism as definitely composed of the families that are the true elements of cells; next, of the classes or castes that are its proper tissues; and last, of the cities and communes that are its real organs." All of the parts were, for Comte, interdependent and the recognition of that organic interdependence was central to social progress. "Each family," Comte explained, "when confined to a labor that directly produces only what will satisfy a small portion of its own wants, is forced to recognize the importance of other families to itself as well as its own usefulness to them."[18] Thus social progress meant further differentiation, which itself fostered altruism.

Hence, the "thematic reverberations" (to use Howe's phrase) of the antebellum Whigs did indeed echo many of Comte's characteristic emphases. The concern for social improvement and purposive planning, the stress upon moral duty and the paternalism that the latter often implied, and lastly, the organicism and commitment to functional hierarchy were all strongly paralleled in the Comtean system. Moreover, both approaches sought to link key parts of their systems in similar ways. Just as Comte's fundamental concern was to reconcile the conflicting claims of order and progress, so Whigs spoke of their desire to see "conservatism and progress . . . blend their harmonious action."[19] Indeed, Whigs invariably addressed the relationship between order and progress more explicitly than did Democrats whose attitudes toward material progress were often more ambivalent.[20] Comtean positivism could thus effec-

18. Ibid., 429–30.
19. Quoted by Howe, *Political Culture*, 210.
20. Marvin Myers, *The Jacksonian Persuasion: Politics and Belief* (New York: Random House, 1960), explores this aspect of Democratic ideology. Another perceptive discussion of this theme is contained in Fred Somkin, *Unquiet Eagle: Memory and Desire in the Idea of American Freedom, 1815–1860* (Ithaca: Cornell University Press, 1967). This shared concern is evident in the two following quotations, the first an excerpt from Comte's *Système de politique positive* and the second from a New York Whig legislature address of 1844:

> Without the theory of progress, the theory of order, even supposing that it could be formed, would be inadequate as a basis for sociology. It is essential that the two should be combined. The very fact that progress, however viewed, is nothing but the development of order, shows that order cannot be fully manifested without progress. (Cited in Kenneth Thompson, ed., *Auguste Comte: The Foundation of Sociology* [New York: John Wiley and Sons, 1975], 83)

> The whig party is devoted to progress, but it does not destroy. It seeks to establish perfect equality of political rights; but it levels upwards, not downwards, by

tively buttress a middle-class Whig belief that genuine progress came only as a result of *orderly* growth. Of course, the Whig party had collapsed by the mid-1850s and Ward's first formal political allegiance was to the Republican party of Lincoln. Republicans like Lincoln did modify Whig ideology and the young Ward was probably pleased with the rejuvenated Whiggery that thereby emerged. As Hartz suggested, the Republicans finished the democratization of an elitist Whiggery begun first by William H. Harrison in the "Log Cabin" campaign of 1840. By embracing the individualism and egalitarian spirit of the nation, the Republicans "catered openly to the acquisitive dreams of the American democrat." Ward, a man of humble Midwestern origins, was attracted to this modified Whiggery; at the same time, the persistent moralism, meliorism, and organicism of the Whig/Republican tradition retained its appeal.[21]

Ward himself seemed to recognize the larger significance of Whig principles for his politics. The mature Ward saw great moral issues, such as the battle against chattel slavery, as most suited to the realm of political debate. Before the Civil War, slavery was the most important question dividing the major parties, yet it was part of a larger philosophical edifice. Ward believed that the Democrats (and their Jeffersonian Republican predecessors) had consistently been the champions of state sovereignty and limited government. In contrast, the Republicans and their forerunners had always championed the positive, interventionist state. Note, for example, how Ward viewed the Republicans as the direct descendants of the Federalists:

> The party opposed to it [i.e., Jefferson's Republican party] was called the Federal party. Its leading representative was Alexander Hamilton, who believed in a strong central government. Later on, the Federal party took the name of Whig, borrowed from English usage, and when the slavery question arose this became the anti-slavery or free-soil party, and changed its name to Republican a short time before the Civil War.[22]

---

education and benignant legislation, not by subverting established laws or institutions. It is the party of law, of order, of enterprise, of improvement, of beneficence, of hope, and of humanity. (Cited in Rush Welter, *The Mind of America, 1820–1860* [New York: Columbia University Press, 1975], 18)

While a Democrat might well have been sympathetic with some of the principles embodied in this statement, Welter maintains (correctly, I believe) that he would have expressed them in very different terms.

21. Hartz, *Liberal Tradition*, 205; Howe, *Political Culture*, chap. 11.

22. LFW, "The Sociology of Political Parties," *American Journal of Sociology* 13 (January 1908): 445.

Ward also characterized the debate between Republican and Democrat as a battle between enlightened reform and mindless reaction. "In general," wrote Ward, "it may be said that the Whig or Republican party has constituted the party of innovation, while the Democratic party has been the party of conservation. . . . [During the 1850s and 1860s], the Republican was the progressive party and the Democratic party the conservative party."[23] On the whole, Republicans were well read and attuned to moral questions, while Democrats "read little and had no lively disinterested sympathies." After the Civil War, Ward held the situation to be "somewhat reversed." Being now the party "of the working and debtor class," the Democrats were advocates of institutional reform. Yet Ward's Whiggish elitism would not allow him to cheer the Democracy. "The Democratic party still represents," observed Ward, "the less intelligent class, and the capitalistic wing embraces the better informed portion of that party. The measures advocated by the other wing have been ill-considered and of doubtful propriety, and it is far better that they remain in abeyance until wiser measures can be framed looking to the same class of reforms."[24] Before the war, at least, the Whigs and Republicans clearly represented for Ward the party of progressive change led by men of learning and morality. For Ward, the Whigs had both the best principles *and* the best men.

Ward's family background, military service, and youthful politics clearly prepared him for his encounter with positivism. His life as a young government clerk in postwar Washington also contributed to this process of preparation. To begin with, Ward's government service bolstered his confidence in the ability of the bureaucratic state to manage society and solve problems. After months of searching, Ward landed a job in May 1865 as an accounts clerk in the Treasury Department. The new Bureau of Statistics hired him in early 1867 and Ward gradually worked his way up the bureaucratic ladder, becoming librarian of the bureau five years later. It was from this post that Ward joined the newly created Geological Survey in 1881. Through his years in government service, and especially during his tenure at the Survey, Ward saw government-sponsored scientists and bureaucrats pursuing research and offering expert advice to policymakers. Ward remarked that, for John Wesley Powell (his boss at the Survey and an important influence on Ward), the work of his employees, no matter how esoteric, "was all for science and the public good."[25]

23. Ibid., 446.
24. Ibid., 446–47.
25. Scott, *Ward,* 23, 30.

But a civil servant's life was also frustrating for a young man of ambition and ability. The thousands of government clerks constituted an exploited class of "drones" in the capital city. Worst of all, government service was far from an ideal meritocracy. Political connections were needed to advance and one had to be prepared to look the other way when it came to questions of corruption or incompetence. Isolated from the political arena where policies were hammered out, colleagues grew resentful. Ward observed indignantly in *Dynamic Sociology*: "Those who are able to tell us how things were in the remote past, how they are to be in the present [i.e., social scientists]—these must work for nothing, and meet with perpetual opposition besides."[26] The systematic analysis of social institutions "is a task," Ward lamented, "which only brave minds will undertake, and that with little hope of convincing anybody."[27] Clearly Ward would be receptive to a social philosophy that awarded tangible political power to the scientific expert and civil service technocrat. Ward's resentment was therefore different from the patrician alienation of a Charles Francis Adams, Jr. For someone who had worked as hard as Ward, Gilded Age Washington looked like a closed society. Comte's scientific meritocracy, however, held out the promise of political influence and social deference.

Ward worked hard as a young government clerk. When the Treasury Department closed up at three o'clock, Ward read at home, while in the evenings, he studied for his B.A. at Columbian College. In 1869, Ward received his bachelor's degree, having taken a wide range of courses in sciences and humanities. A Bachelor of Law followed in 1871 and, later, admission to the D.C. bar, but Ward never sought to practice law. Turning to botany, chemistry, and anatomy, Ward obtained his M.A. the next year. In short, he was the consummate Victorian "all-rounder." His tastes were catholic and his intellectual energies seemingly boundless. In a normal week, he might read Virgil in Latin, peruse a spiritualist magazine, study an English biologist, and compose an entry in his diary—in French. Typical is the following excerpt that closes his early diary: "What I need now is to read the great authors and make many scientific experiments. If I could cover the other professions of medicine and theology and learn two more languages, Hebrew and Spanish, it would help me a great deal. But perhaps that is too much."[28] For this sort of intellectual, Comte's grand synthesis would prove fascinating;

26. *Dynamic Sociology or Applied Social Science As Based Upon Statical Sociology and the Less Complex Sciences* (New York: D. Appleton, 1883), 1:78.

27. Ibid., 1:77.

28. Scott, *Ward*, 24; Stern, *Young Ward*, 318.

Ward would be able to follow the *Cours*'s many biological excursions, while the classification of the sciences could be a highly valuable organizing tool. If Comte's work appealed to the generalist, then Ward was bound to be an appreciative reader.

At about the time Ward was entering the civil service, a unique intellectual community was taking shape in the capital city. One historian of postwar Washington has described the institutional base of this emergent group as "a combination of public agencies and private scholarly and scientific societies." The community's leadership was drawn primarily from an "executive class" of chief bureaucrats but their membership lists also included many of those who held modest clerical positions. The social basis of intellectual life in Gilded Age Washington did not, therefore, reside in a university (though the community tried for some time to establish a national university in the capital), nor did it arise from groups of publishers, editors, journalists, and lawyers as was the case with the New York Comtists. Rather, this was a government-based circle. The list of government-affiliated institutions that its participants founded is a long one. These included the U.S. Geological Survey, the National Museum, the Bureau of American Ethnology, as well as bodies that later contributed to the creation of the Bureaus of Education, the Census, and Labor.[29] In these and other ways, the Washington circle of a large professional federal bureaucracy arose gradually after the Civil War.[30]

Besides their involvement in the postwar growth of the civil service, the community was also instrumental in the formation of a number of scientific societies in the capital during the 1870s and 1880s. Ward was a member of several of these bodies, including the Philosophical Society formed in 1871. The stated object of this group was "the free exchange

29. Michael J. Lacey, "The National Seminary of Learning: Washington Scientists and the Rise of the Modern State in the Late Nineteenth Century" (paper delivered at the annual meeting of the American Historical Association, Washington, D.C., 27–30 December 1982), 1, 4–5, 12–13.

30. Two new bodies created at this time are emblematic of the community's concern with collecting accurate empirical data about the nation. The Bureau of Statistics was created in 1866. Under Superintendent Francis A. Walker, the tenth U.S. Census in 1880 became a painstaking and exhaustive enterprise. In addition, the nation's physical land mass was measured and charted. In 1879 the U.S. Geological Survey was created; two years later, it was placed under the direction of Major Powell. A man, who in Morton Keller's words, "shared with Francis Walker of the census bureau a passion for the scientific collection of data," Powell turned the survey into the government's most ambitious scientific effort (Morton Keller, *Affairs of State: Public Life in Late Nineteenth Century America* [Cambridge: Harvard University Press, 1977], 104, 102). These bodies were part of the growth of a modern liberal state that, though it experienced occasional reversals, continued to expand slowly during the Gilded Age (Keller, *Affairs of State,* 101–10, 312–14).

of views and studies on subjects, and the promotion of scientific subjects, and the promotion of scientific inquiry among its members." "Philosophical" was chosen as a suitable appellation because, in the words of the founders, philosophy consisted of all "those branches of knowledge that relate to the positive facts and laws of the physical and moral universe." It was in this sense of science, broadly construed, that the society took its name. The society met usually twice a month to hear and discuss papers on a wide variety of subjects.[31] This broad, synthetic vision was typical of Washington's scientific circle.

Ward was involved in at least two other city groups, the Cosmos Club and the Anthropological Society of Washington (ASW). The former was an exclusive social club that drew together the cream of Washington's scientific community, primarily for recreational purposes. Begun in 1878, the club was partly the brainchild of Ward's boss, John Wesley Powell; not surprisingly, the Cosmos played a key role in encouraging Congress to set up the new Geological Survey in 1879. The Anthropological Society, on the other hand, was a more traditional scientific body, though it too defined its field of interest very broadly. Rather than limiting itself to archeology as initially envisioned, the ASW embraced all of human history in the New World and, like its sister societies, opened its doors to amateurs and professionals alike. The wide interests and pre-professional character of these societies attracted Gilded Age generalists such as Ward.[32]

The philosophy that underlay the Washington community blended a positivistic empiricism with a naive scientism and a bureaucratic elitism. Members of the circle were concerned with finding and collecting a mass of varied data about their society. To find out more about the republic and to collate systematically this vast body of knowledge was seen as an important civic duty. Such men viewed science as more than just an empirical method; science was a progressive and integrating worldview that implied social improvement and reform. Scientific enquiry also represented the way in which Washington's scientific bureaucracy would become an indispensable part of the policymaking process. The administrators of the new, empirically oriented bureaus would now advise Congress and the Executive Branch in their new role as scientific experts. Many in the community looked forward to forging such a close relationship with legislators and administrators.[33]

31. J. Kirkpatrick Flack, *Desideratum in Washington: The Intellectual Community in the Capital City, 1870–1900* (Cambridqe, Mass.: Schenkman, 1975), 60; Lacey, "National Seminary," 15–16.

32. Flack, *Desideratum*, 88–89, 114–15.

33. Lacey, "National Seminary," 11, 7, 13. Ward himself articulated this philosophy

Another important step in Ward's intellectual development took place more on the periphery of this intellectual circle. After he left school in Pennsylvania, Ward's freethinking on religious matters grew more advanced. In the fall of 1867, Ward was reading Voltaire and Paine's *Age of Reason*, which he described as "very bold and almost incredible, but a bit arrogant."[34] He doubtless found persuasive the two deists' attacks upon the veracity of Scripture and he was probably also attracted to their strident anticlericalism. Ward's own opposition to religious orthodoxy was itself becoming bolder in the late 1860s. Although they visited a variety of churches initially, Ward and his wife, Lizzie, became regulars at one of Washington's more liberal Unitarian congregations by the end of the decade. As with other Victorian intellectuals, the Unitarian church probably served as a sort of halfway house for Ward along the pilgrimage from Protestant orthodoxy to unbelief.[35] Ward appeared increasingly uncomfortable even with the minimal sort of theism required by Unitarianism and his anticlerical rhetoric soon became quite strident.[36]

At this stage, Ward's critique of Christianity was based upon two main

---

of bureaucratic expertise in an 1877 article in the *National Union*. Here, Ward made the seemingly self-serving argument that the Bureau of Statistics was a crucial instrument in what he termed "scientific law-making" (LFW, "The Way to Scientific Lawmaking," in *Glimpses*, 2:168). It was axiomatic to an empiricist such as Ward that, just as the physical sciences required a wealth of concrete data to progress in their understanding of nature, so the social sciences needed comprehensive statistics to explain human society. Being able to explain society "would lead to vast amelioration in the condition of the human race." But exactly how would statistical knowledge bring social betterment? Ward explained that "the primary object of statistics should be to influence and direct legislation" ("The Way," 169). Ward's vision here was not, however, simply of government attuned to scientific advice; in the waning days of the severe 1873–1877 depression, he proposed a truly planned economy. Data could be gathered by a central office and "the phenomena relating to different kinds of production should be frequently placed in juxtaposition with a view to showing which branches [of the economy] should be stimulated and which checked." Thus, government social scientists could manage and direct the burgeoning economy. Such an office would require a meritocratic elite, Ward thought: "It should take a high rank among the bureaus of the Government and the highest talent should be secured not only to direct it but also to fill the subordinate positions in it" ("The Way," 170).

34. Stern, *Young Ward*, 239.

35. David D. Hall, "The Victorian Connection," in *Victorian America*, ed. Daniel Walker Howe (Philadelphia: University of Pennsylvania Press, 1976), 83.

36. Ward's increasingly aggressive tack represented, at least in part, a response to an evangelical "offensive" of sorts. Some Protestant groups were exploring new kinds of political activity in the immediate postwar period. Evangelicals had helped form the National Association to secure an Amendment to the Constitution in 1864 that would officially recognize Christianity as the national faith. Two other bodies, the National Christian Association and the National Reform Association advocated similar measures combined with various socioeconomic reforms. Ward found such a mixture of traditional faith and progressive reform muddled and contradictory. The bouyant mood of postbellum

points. As a philosophical system, Christianity was founded not upon empirical science but upon errors and superstition. More important, as an institution, the church was a consistent opponent of social progress. Declared Ward in an address on the subject, the church had "opposed all reform tending to elevate the masses. . . . In its desperate efforts to retard civilization it has not scrupled to espouse the worst of causes and advocated the most corrupt practices."[37] As an outgrowth of these militant views and to respond to the perceived evangelical threat, Ward formed, with a few office friends, the National Liberal Reform League—a secret secularist organization dedicated to the refutation of "the leading doctrinal teachings of the so-called Catholic and Evangelical Protestant Churches."[38] The league's aim was to encourage affiliated groups in other cities, and Ward appealed to all "Liberals, Skeptics, Infidels, Secularists, Utilitarians, Socialists, Positivists, Spiritualists, Deists, Theists, Pantheists, Atheists, [and] Free-thinkers."[39] As part of its strategy of disseminating unorthodox literature, the league soon began publishing a monthly newspaper aptly titled *The Iconoclast*. Ward edited the short-lived periodical; its pages provide an insight into the basis of his objections to religious orthodoxy and the depths of his feeling on the subject.

The first issue of the *Iconoclast* began with an editorial headed "The Situation" in which Ward described the spiritual crisis of his age. Having "thoroughly examined" Christian teachings, Ward pronounced them "only the modified superstitions of barbarous ages, the natural offspring of man's primitive ignorance." Now was a time of acute "religious crisis"; the "bigots" were arrayed against "the rational element." The conflict was simple: "science versus the Church." Traditionalist clergy were the avowed enemies of science because, as Ward explained, science "teaches truth" and "theology is error." It was that simple. And, yet, Ward's argument for allowing freethinkers to assail religion was not

---

American Protestantism was also evident in the meeting of the Evangelical Alliance (an international and interdenominational body), which was held in New York in 1873. "Never since the crucifixion," declared Amherst president W. A. Stearns at the E.A. meeting, "has the religion of Christ, in its purest forms had a stronger hold on the popular heart than at this day." Such evangelical confidence alarmed the freethinker in Ward (cited in Keller, *Affairs of State*, 136). See also George M. Marsden, *Fundamentalism and American Culture: The Shaping of Twentieth-Century Evangelicalism, 1870–1925* (New York: Oxford University Press, 1980), 29, 236, notes 36, 17. Sidney Ahlstrom has characterized the 1870s as "a time of harsh interfaith contention and of controversy on the church-state question." See *A Religious History of the American People* (New Haven: Yale University Press, 1972), 765.

37. Stern, *Young Ward*, 253.
38. Scott, *Ward*, 139.
39. Stern, *Young Ward*, 314, 315.

based upon abstract notions of the right of free speech. Rather, Ward contended that only with an educational system "unfettered by theology" and a free and fearless press "can the great work of elevating and ameliorating the condition of the people be successfully prosecuted."[40] Secularism and science were both instruments of social progress and reform.

Ward frequently referred to European history to make his point. He quoted Gibbon with approval that the Dark Ages, during which the church exercised significant authority, saw "not a single discovery made to exalt the dignity or promote the happiness of mankind."[41] But one did not need to go abroad to find historical examples of Christianity's pernicious influence. In the relatively recent battle against chattel slavery, Ward pointed out that Southern evangelicals were quick to defend slavery on biblical grounds. Declared Ward with disgust, "the Bible was the 'bulwark of slavery' both in the Old and New Testaments."[42]

Like that of his acquaintance T. B. Wakeman, Ward's criticism of Christianity, especially of the church as an institution, was much harsher than Comte's had been. Comte had viewed the monolithic medieval church as a beneficent and progressive force in society. With their evangelical upbringings, Wakeman and Ward could only view the Roman Catholic church as an enemy of human progress and an agent of obscurantism and repression. Yet both Ward and Wakeman maintained a keen interest in religious subjects and a concern for the religious implications of science similar to Comte's. In an early issue of the *Iconoclast*, Ward quoted at length Mill's discussion of Comte's "religion without a God." Mill contended that true science promotes "religious culture." "Devotion to science," Mill observed, "is a tacit worship—a tacit recognition of worth in things studied, and by implication in their Cause." Not that this final "Cause" can ever truly be known; science also demarcates the proper limits of human knowledge. Thus, "while towards the traditions and authorities of men its [i.e., science's] attitude may be proud, before the impenetrable veil which hides the Absolute, its [i.e., science's] attitude is humble—a true pride and a true humility."[43]

Moreover, Ward showed some interest, in a later issue of the *Iconoclast*, in Comte's attempt to construct an atheistic religion. Again, he quoted with approval John Stuart Mill's apologetic for the Comtean Religion of Humanity. Mill had argued that religion required a creed or system of

40. LFW, "The Situation," *Iconoclast* 1 (March 1870): 1.
41. LFW, "Religion and Progress," *Iconoclast* 1 (September 1870): 2.
42. LFW, "Revealed Religion vs. Human Progress," *Iconoclast* 1 (1 November 1870): 2.
43. LFW, "Religious Influence of Science," *Iconoclast* 1 (15 November 1870): 1.

beliefs, a sentiment or dominant feeling and "a concrete object" upon which "this sentiment should crystallize." Christianity provides a personal God as its "concrete object" but another object could readily be substituted for it. Mill suggested that Comte's proposal to replace the Christian creator God with an alternate object—the Human Race—was eminently reasonable. What better way to inculcate an altruistic faith than "if the object of this [religious] attachment and of this feeling of duty, is the aggregate of our fellow-creatures." Ward was apparently as enamored with "the enabling power of this grand conception" of Comte's, as Mill had been. These and other excerpts printed in the *Iconoclast* reveal that Ward was involved, even more explicitly than many of his contemporaries, in the search for a secular surrogate for traditional Christian faith. Ward may have indulged in rather un-Comtean polemics against institutional Christianity, but he remained equally concerned with the religious implications of a synthetic, scientific philosophy.[44]

Ward retained a strong religious impulse as he advanced toward unbelief. Like many of his contemporaries, he showed a singular enthusiasm for the religious implications of scientific truths.[45] "I can scarcely utter a great truth," Ward wrote to a friend late in life, "without choking with emotion."[46] Science appeared to Ward, as it had to Spencer, "worthy of all reverence." Ward's earlier writing equated science with human progress and he was consequently attracted to both Comte's meliorism and humanism. Via scientism, then, social progress was substituted for a personal god as the object of worship. Such a substitution was natural for Ward and for many other late Victorian intellectuals because, as James Turner explains, "When progress became a purely human millennialism, reverence for progress was no longer worship of God but veneration of humanity."[47] Ward's later work moved to a much broader, more inclusive surrogate under the influence of Haeckel and other European philosophical monists. Here, not just progress or humanity, but all natural phenomena were viewed as a monistic whole; the contemplation of this cosmic unity was supposed to have a soothing effect for the individual. Thus Ward proposed near the end of his life to

44. LFW, "A Religion Without A God," *Iconoclast* 2 (June 1871): 1. The search of Gilded Age intellectuals for a secular surrogate for traditional religious faith is discussed in Paul A. Carter, *The Spiritual Crisis of the Gilded Age* (DeKalb: Northern Illinois University Press, 1971), esp. chap. 1; Hall, "Victorian Connection," 81; D. H. Meyer, "American Intellectuals and the Victorian Crisis of Faith," in *Victorian America,* ed. Howe, 59–77.

45. See, for example, Ward's article, "Religious Influence of Science," *Iconoclast* 1 (15 November 1870): 1.

46. LFW, cited in Cape, *Personal Sketch,* 97–98.

47. James Turner, *Without God, Without Creed: The Origins of Unbelief in America* (Baltimore: Johns Hopkins University Press, 1985), 250–51.

write a book entitled: "Monism the True Quietism, or the Continuity of Nature the only Faith that can satisfy the emancipated Soul."[48]

Beyond highlighting his religious quest, the *Iconoclast* also helps one to understand how Ward conceived of his own intellectual milieu by the early seventies. For the December 1870 issue, Ward wrote an editorial entitled "The Rising School" that was a paean to Victorian philosophical Radicals such as Mill, Spencer, T. H. Huxley, and Henry Thomas Buckle. Ward described the members of this "rising school of philosophy" as "Liberals in the widest sense" but he styled their philosophical system "Positivism," which "had an illustrious founder in Auguste Comte."[49] Apparently, for Ward, such English skeptics were preeminently positivists of one sort or another. Spencer, Mill, and Huxley were frequently quoted at length in the *Iconoclast*, particularly for their critical views on organized religion, which suited the paper's editorial slant. Ward subsumed these philosophers under the positivist rubric and, as seen above, when Comte was quoted, he was often taken secondhand from their works, such as Mill's *Auguste Comte and Positivism*.[50]

It was, however, an article in a French periodical, the popular *Revue des deux mondes*, that probably first introduced Ward to what he later called the "Rising School" of English positivists. Ward enjoyed reading French literature to sharpen his language skills, so it is not surprising to find him perusing the *Revue*. The weekly diary Ward kept was written in French, and in the 17 January 1869 entry he noted that he found an

48. LFW, cited in Cape, *Personal Sketch*, 121.

49. LFW, "The Rising School," *Iconoclast* 1 (December 1870): 2. Ward's description is similar to Hall's characterization of the Anglo-American intellectual network as "liberal" (Hall, "Victorian Connection," 82). See also Howe, *Political Culture*, 303.

50. The "Victorian Connection's" periodicals, in particular the *Fortnightly*, were important vehicles for English positivists either of the Comtean or more independent variety. Although Ward was probably not an early subscriber to such English journals, he was familiar with them and the positivists who contributed to their pages. In the *Fortnightly*, Ward may have read review articles by Comtists Frederic Harrison and E. S. Beesly or editorials by G. H. Lewes, one of a group of older, more critical English positivists that included Mill and Harriet Martineau. See Hall, "Victorian Connection," 84, 92; Christopher Kent, *Brains and Numbers: Elitism, Comtism, and Democracy in Mid-Victorian England* (Toronto: University of Toronto Press, 1978), 85–87, 56. For Ward's citations of books by Huxley, Lewes, and Mill, see the bibliography of his *Dynamic Sociology*, 2:634–40. If these examples are at all representative, most of what Ward read at first regarding positivism was British in origin. The handful of American periodicals that Ward and his wife subscribed to during their first five years living in Washington was an odd cross-section of heterodox religious journals, including the spiritualist *Religio-Philosophical Journal* (which points to the Wards' interest in psychic phenomena) and the *Radical*, a Boston Freethought magazine edited by radical Unitarian Sidney H. Morse. See Scott, *Ward*, 152–55; Stow Persons, *Free Religion: An American Faith* (New Haven: Yale University Press, 1947), 38.

article on positivism in the *Revue* "very interesting."[51] The article, a review essay by Louis Etienne of Buckle's positivist *History of Civilization in England*, prompted Ward to purchase and read Mill's important *Auguste Comte and Positivism* in the following year.[52] Thus Ward first garnered information about English positivism by somewhat circuitous channels.

But Ward also had direct contacts with the New York Comtists, through his role as contributor to *Evolution* in the 1870s and, later, by his occasional participation in Palmer's Nineteenth Century Club. Moreover, he corresponded with a number of English Comtists, including sectarians such as Edward Beesly and Richard Congreve (appointed by Comte himself to head the British effort), and Frederic Harrison who had disassociated himself from the sectarian group. Ward continued his correspondence with these devotees of Comte well into the 1890s. Evidently, Ward mailed complimentary copies of his own books and the Englishmen responded with warm, appreciative (though not uncritical) letters. Congreve, in fact, sent along some of his own work, while attempting to convince Ward that the *Politique Positive* and not just the *Cours* was worthy of his careful study.[53] These English Comtists seem to have found Ward's work intriguing and encouraging, but they bristled at Ward's criticisms of the "Master."

In sum, English positivists of both the orthodox and more independent varieties helped focus and define some of the concerns that Ward initially brought to his studies, while they suggested positivism as an attractive way out of the thoroughgoing skepticism that Ward and his fellow Victorians feared.

II

It was not until 1875 that Ward turned to read Comte in the original. Then, during a year in which he read Bacon's *Instauratio Magna*, John

51. Stern, *Young Ward*, 2.
52. "Le Positivisme dans l'histoire," *Revue des deux mondes* 74 (1868): 403; LFW, *Glimpses*, 1:99.
53. Letter, Richard Congreve to LFW, 4 July 1883, Brown University, Ward Papers, Autograph Letter Books, 1:32. In a later note, Congreve wrote that, in spite of his reservations, he enjoyed Ward's "publications very much." (See Letter, Richard Congreve to LFW, 21 November 1895, Brown University, Ward Papers, Autograph Letter Books, 5:170.) Ward's correspondence with Congreve and with other orthodox English Comtists reveals the frustrations of the sectarians regarding developments in America. Reflected Congreve sadly in one letter: "How often I wish that from your side of the Atlantic could come some corresponding movement—or some . . . help to us here. But we must wait for

William Draper's *History of the Conflict Between Religion and Science*, and three volumes by Spencer, Ward ordered from Paris the third French edition of the *Cours de philosophie positive* and poured over the six volumes with unabashed enthusiasm. "My habit," wrote Ward later, "was to have French works read to me by Mrs. Ward"; consequently, it took both of them several months to complete all the volumes.[54] The impact of the *Cours* upon him was profound and as a result of this and other reading he had recently done, Ward revised and rewrote the manuscript he had been working on since 1869. As Ward himself put it in characteristically emotional terms: "I fell in love with Comte's terminology." Borrowing from the *Cours* Comte's use of the term "dynamic" and the word "sociology" (which the French philosopher had coined), Ward renamed his lengthy treatise *Dynamic Sociology*.[55] Ward subsequently remarked that, at the time, he was unaware of Comte's own earlier use of the phrase. He explained:

> The problem was to combine the word dynamic with the word sociology and what more natural than simply to put them together? Comte did it in 1839, and I did it in 1876, in both cases as a simple logical process of the mind. . . . If I had found it in Comte [initially] I should certainly have cited volume and page.[56]

Furthermore, the extensive revisions of his manuscript also point to the centrality of Comte to Ward's work. A comparison between one of the early outlines for his book with one written immediately after reading the *Cours* makes this point. The former prospectus treats the sciences in a less than systematic way and employs such un-Comtean phrasings as "mental" and "moral philosophy." The latter, by contrast, uses the Comtean classification including now the word "sociology."[57]

In late 1876, Ward began this new version of his book at his government desk. Having integrated significant excerpts of the *Cours* into a large subject index he had constructed, Ward observed that the index "became my main dependence" while working on the book. Soon, he

---

the hour" (Letter, Congreve to LFW, 6 April 1893, Brown University, Ward Papers, Autograph Letter Books, 4: 54). See also: Letter, E. S. Beesly to LFW, 25 July 1883, Brown University, Ward Papers, Autograph Letter Books, 1:32–33; Letter, Frederic Harrison to LFW, 15 December 1896, Brown University Ward Papers, Autograph Letter Books, 6:129.

54. LFW, *Glimpses*, 3:171.
55. Ibid., 3:172.
56. Ibid., 3:177.
57. Ibid., 3:152, 175.

Lester Frank Ward (1841–1913) in the 1880s. Ernest
Becker called Ward "a latter-day Comte with a
distinctive American modification."

began writing at home to have the *Cours* at his fingertips.[58] In light of
these facts, it is scarcely surprising to find the imprint of Comtean
positivism upon *Dynamic Sociology*. From the first sentence of Ward's
introduction, which credits Comte as the founder of "the science of
Sociology," and throughout much of the succeeding thirteen hundred
pages, Comte's intellectual presence is inescapable.[59] Lester Ward's mature philosophical system reveals the depth of his debt to Comte, in
addition to underlining that Ward's encounter with Comtean positivism
was also critical and creative.

Although rarely presented in a direct way, Ward's epistemological assumptions are not difficult to discern in his major works. Like Comte,
Ward was an empiricist. Ward defined knowledge as "acquaintance,"

58. Ibid., 3:179.
59. LFW, *Dynamic Sociology*, 1:1. All subsequent page references cited in text will be
from this work.

available only through the senses. Thus, Ward admitted that the field of absolute or incontestable knowledge is very limited for humans. There are no intuitive truths, for "credibility [must always] rest on experience" (2:108, 513–14). The only "proper objects of knowledge," Ward explained, are "tangible facts; material objects; truths, laws and principles demonstrable either directly by the senses or deducible from such as are demonstrable." Any notion of higher, innate truths was, then, rejected by Ward. Even the most subtle human insights were simply conclusions drawn from data gathered by the senses. "Perception," Ward contended ". . . is the correlation of sensation . . . [it] consists in a comparison of sensations" (1:70, 186).

Such an empiricism had important ramifications for Ward's philosophy of science. The proper "domain" of science was strictly "the knowable [that] is the Finite, or conditioned" (1:156). If one's sole access to the Knowable is via the senses, then the scientific method must be inductive, based upon observation. Only those facts were scientific truths that could be "proved by careful and repeated examination by the senses, the only avenues of knowledge." "Close observation," Ward went on to explain, "elaborate experiment, and repeated tactual and ocular tests, would alone suffice to establish a fact so as to justify its employment as a premise" (2:201–2). Science, therefore, was defined by Ward as "a rational effort to explain phenomena," applying strictly empirical criteria and using an inductive method.

Not that empirical observation is exactly the same in each of the varied sciences. Ward noted with approval that Comte had discerned "three general classes or methods of observation applicable . . . to the lower and more complex sciences" (1:98). First, there was observation itself, narrowly construed. This method was primarily suited to astronomy. Then, there was experimentation, most useful in chemistry. And, finally, there was comparison, "the chief method applicable to all biological and sociological investigations." As will be seen below, sociology would most often employ historical research to make its comparisons. Ward drew this understanding of the nature of scientific observation entirely from Comte, concluding: "the correctness of this exposition will scarcely be questioned and its utility must be recognized by all" (1:99).

Ward also concurred with Comte that prevision or prediction "constitutes the essential quality which distinguishes all that is entitled to the name of science." With the inductive method, one is gradually able "to establish the precise laws" that in turn enable one "to predict with certainty all future results" (1:101–2). "Voir pour prevoir," Comte had written. Of course, only those sciences that have adopted a rigorously empirical and inductive method are able to make forecasts with such precision. But each science must aspire to such "positivity." Observed Ward with approval: "There is no portion of Comte's entire system which is better founded, or more absolutely sound, than this important principle of scientific foresight" (1:104).

Thus far, Ward's position paralleled that of Comte closely. Ward broke with Comtean positivism, however, over the question of causation in scientific explanation. Comte had excluded the concept of causation when explaining the relationship between phenomena and spoke instead only of "succession." Ward did agree with Comte's attempts to exclude theological arguments from science that posited a divine creator as the first or final cause. But to rule out any consideration of causation would be to hamstring science altogether. "The strict adherence," Ward reflected, "to the positivist conception [of causation] in its Comtean purity, instead of being as he [Comte] thought, the only legitimate scientific method, would be in reality the abnegation of the scientific method by substituting mere independent *succession*, assumed to be uniform, for actual *causation* among dependent terms of a series" (1:169).

One simply had to distinguish, argued Ward, final causes from immediate, efficient causes. The latter concept was "the almost indispensible postulate of science itself." In nature, "causal circumstances" prevail and it was unscientific to maintain otherwise (1:88).[60] This critical distinction allowed Ward to escape the limitations inherent in Comte's approach. Metaphysical or theological presuppositions could still be dismissed, while a highly useful explanatory tool was retained. Moreover, on a more pragmatic level, Ward believed that Comte's dim view of the use of hypotheses to direct research could seriously hamper further scientific advancement. If science was going to accomplish as much as Comte envisioned, then it would need all of its analytical tools. The reluctance to hypothesize and the "confusion of two things so wholly different" (i.e., final and efficient causes) did not serve the chief end of science: "true progress in human knowledge" (1:90–91).

Ward rejoined Comte, nevertheless, when it came to the latter's "hierarchy of the sciences." Science is not "the mere accumulation of data" in completely unrelated fields (2:246). Ward believed that the most important philosophical task of his age was the systematization of all extant scientific knowledge into a single grand structure. As Ward

60. On this point, Ward wrote of Comte: "He seems to have scarcely the remotest idea of the great principle, which even Bacon recognized, that the most important phenomena of Nature lie deep-hidden within her and are not seen by the average observer . . . , but that it is only as guided by apparent phenomena, as effects, that the true investigator is led back into the region of those deeper ones which stand to the superficial ones in the relation of efficient causes" (1:89).

phrased it, Comte's classification represented one "principal direction in which this work of unifying science is advancing." Such a hierarchy was not "mere classification," but rather a search for an organizing principle around which to arrange the sciences, or phenomena in general, and thereby, in Ward's own words, "arrive at the true order which exists in the universe" (1:7, 2). Comte had begun with mathematics as "the true basis of all the sciences," turned then to astronomy as the most general and least complex, moved down the scale through physics, chemistry, biology, and ended ultimately with the least general and most complex science, sociology (the "Queen of the Sciences"). From one science to the next, there is an increasing complexity coupled with a decreasing generality. This "filiation," as Ward preferred to speak of the hierarchy, was "by far the most important characteristic of the positive philosophy" (1:97). Indeed, Ward conceived of his *Dynamic Sociology* as part of this "great step" Comte had taken, that would distill a "heterogeneous multitude of apparently independent sciences into one homogeneous system of universal science" (1:6).

Some historians have viewed the organization of *Dynamic Sociology* as evidence of Ward's debt to Spencerian philosophy. Ward made it clear, however, in his magnum opus that he preferred the Comtean arrangement because he found it "free from all arbitrary or artificial taint, and based, as M. Comte fully believed, upon the true order of nature as revealed in the history of the evolution of the human mind and of the universe" (1:97).[61] Comte's arrangement was based directly upon natural phenomena, Ward contended, while Spencer's hierarchy was an ideal classification based upon how the human intellect interpreted the logical relationship between the various sciences. Moreover, Ward was fond of pointing out that, in his *Synthetic Philosophy*, "Spencer was compelled to adopt the Comtean series, simply because it was the order of nature" (1:148).[62] Finally, as noted above, the arrangement of topics in *Dynamic Sociology* followed the outline of the *Cours* faithfully, beginning with astronomy, progressing through chemical and biological subjects and culminating with a lengthy discussion of sociology, commensurate with its status as Queen of the Sciences. Ward therefore agreed that Comte's was the "natural arrangement" and as such "is the true order in which they [i.e., the sciences] should be studied, since the study of each furnishes the mind with that proper data for understanding the next

61. Hofstadter, *Social Darwinism*, 68.
62. See LFW, "The Place of Sociology," *American Journal of Sociology* (1 July 1895): 17–21, for an elaboration of this argument.

higher." Consequently, sociology "should perhaps be mainly post graduate."[63]

Both Ward's subscription to Comte's classification of the sciences and his rejection of Comte's teaching on causation can be viewed as outgrowths of his philosophical monism. Historians have often overlooked the fact that the implied, if not explicit, monism of Comte's writings impressed Ward no less than the "block-universe" of Spencer.[64] "Of all the philosophers that humanity has brought forth," Ward concluded, in *Dynamic Sociology*, ". . . these two [Comte and Spencer] alone have conceived and built upon the broad principle of the absolute unity of Nature and her laws throughout all her manifestations. . . . This grand monistic conception is the final crown of human thought and was required to round out philosophy into a form of symmetry, whose outlines, at least, admit no further improvement" (1:143). This "great principle of the uniformity and invariability of nature's laws, this," asserted Ward, "is the cornerstone itself of the positive philosophy, as it is of all science."[65] In this sense, to be truly scientific one had to conceive of "Nature and all her phenomena . . . as parts of one whole or unit, and bound together by an absolutely unbroken chain" (1:65–66). After all, Comte had sought higher and higher generalizations to tie together each of the different sciences. "True monism," Ward surmised, "ought to be simply the highest generalisation of known phenomena."[66]

In part to preserve this monistic naturalism, Ward felt it essential to maintain causal relationships between phenomena. In *Dynamic Sociology*, Ward affirmed "two important principles of classification" universally "recognized and avowed." One of these was "a causal dependence in all phenomena of nature," which he there termed "monism" (1:8). Ward expressed considerable optimism about the scientific "fruit" of systematic classification constructed with the aid of such grand causal laws. The great work of organizing human knowledge could go forward only after these causal "connections" had been drawn. This advance required a rigorous monism and Ward built upon what he found in the *Cours*.

What allowed Ward to accept a positivistic "block universe" while rejecting some of the deterministic extremes of Spencerian philosophy was a critical distinction he drew. There were two sorts of evolutionary development, Ward contended: one "genetic" or physical and thus haphazard, and the other "telic" or mental and thus subject to human

63. LFW, "The Place of Sociology," 26, 25.

64. Hofstadter, *Social Darwinism*, 84. The phrase was William James's characterization of Spencer's philosophy.

65. LFW, "Book Reviews," *Open Court* 9 (22 August 1895): 4613.

66. Ibid.

manipulation. "The wholly unconscious and unintelligent character of nature's processes," wrote Ward, "may be safely concluded from their genetic stamp." On the other hand, "conscious action" is "intelligent" and "teleological" in nature (2:9). Hence, the process by which a particular strain of flower evolves is genetic, whereas the process by which a unique strain is developed through cross-breeding (or other human intervention) is end-directed and telic. When one understands the natural laws that govern phenomena, then one is enabled to intervene in a self-conscious way to alter or redirect the course of natural evolution.

This important genetic/telic distinction was not, strictly speaking, Comtean. Rather, Ward referred to Kant in his discussion of the roots of such a bifurcation. Kant "perceived the true nature" of this key dualism but in his era, the agent in the teleological process was usually thought to be a divine Creator. Consequently, these two approaches, the one "empirical" and the other "dogmatic," developed as antithetical ideas. Positive science can, nonetheless, recognize telic phenomena when they are understood as the products of human or other "animate organisms" (2:19–30, 89). "Man," wrote Ward, and not God, "is the proper teleological agent." Such telic action arises from a desire on the part of the organism; it is consciously produced and involves a specific purpose or concrete end. The success in securing the desired end will depend, in part, upon the "complexity of the organism." Because humans are mainly rational (as opposed to purely reflexive) and because their "environment is so enormously complicated," they fail frequently to secure their desired ends (1:29, 2:93).

Comte did not draw such a distinction. Indeed, Ward noted that Comte was the only philosopher who "disavowed both these bases" of explanation (2:18). Comte did so as part of his revolt against philosophy in general, his attempt to transcend conventional approaches. Furthermore, the *Cours* predated Darwin; Comte believed that man's development had been anything but random. For Comte, the progressive development of mankind was a fulfillment of his original nature.[67] Comte's vision of human development seems to have been end-directed even on the natural level, whereas Ward declared that the genetic process was by its very nature haphazard and that only those processes directed by human intelligence (labeled "direct") were truly teleological.

Such important differences aside, however, it is evident that Comte (in Kenneth Thompson's words) "made the development of man's . . . intellectual capacities the predominant factor" in his analysis and Ward built upon this approach.[68] As Comte saw it, higher civilization encour-

67. L. Levy-Bruhl, *The Philosophy of Auguste Comte* (New York: Putnam, 1903), 216.
68. Thompson, *Auguste Comte*, 17.

aged the growth of "the action of man upon his environment."[69] Following and extending the Comtean argument, Ward wrote similarly that, at the present stage of intellectual development, "the principal object which man has in the study of nature is to enable him to control its forces" (2:15). Ward encountered in Comte a naturalistic and empirical philosophy that did not view man as a biological automaton but championed him as an intelligent actor. This unique emphasis of Comte's would have a decisive effect upon both Ward's biological and sociological thought.

Underlying Comte's hierarchical classification of the sciences was a distinctive philosophy of history. Ward subscribed to both of these features of the Comtean system, conceiving them to be of one piece. Ward deemed the familiar Law of the Three Stages to be the second "most important characteristic of the positive philosophy" (1:97). Like Comte before him, Ward drew upon Condorcet's progressive conception of history to bolster his exuberant optimism. In a letter to a friend, Ward once wrote: "Think of Condorcet and his faith in the future! But like all the rest he put it too early. I say a millennium. Better say ten Millenniums [sic]. . . . All mankind must [first] be in possession of all knowledge."[70] Ward expressed his faith in decidedly Comtean terms. Frequently in his early work, Ward indirectly demonstrated his acceptance of the Comtean historical model; for example, when he concurred with Comte that the theological and metaphysical states had clearly been "little conducive to progress" (1:132). More explicit was Ward's description of the "Rising School" of Positive philosophy in the Iconoclast. There, Ward placed his group of skeptical thinkers within a clearly Comtean historical framework. "The age of speculation," Ward affirmed in characteristically pompous terms, "has gone by. The age of investigation has begun. The philosophies of the past have at last culminated in a system which, while it still retains the name philosophy, is in truth, science. . . . The grand metaphysical systems of modern Europe, have all passed away."[71] Ward believed that the new scientific dispensation rendered obsolete most of the philosophies that had preceded it; this historicism also informed his approach to social reform.

Dynamic Sociology contained both explicit and implicit endorsement of the Law of the Three Stages. Ward's summary of the schema as presented in the *Cours* was laudatory. The only real point of criticism centered

69. Auguste Comte, *The Positive Philosophy of Auguste Comte,* trans. Harriet Martineau (New York: William Gowans, 1868), 516.

70. LFW, cited in Cape, *Personal Sketch,* 95–96.

71. LFW, "Rising School," 2.

upon what Ward called Comte's "most extravagant admiration" for medieval Catholicism. Otherwise, Ward concluded that Comte's "knowledge of the general trend of society and human thought is certainly wonderful, and his mode of presentation is of the highest originality and the deepest interest" (1:95–97). Even those passages in *Dynamic Sociology* that discussed the progressive development of society in language not distinctively Comtean, were often supported by references to the *Cours*. Elsewhere, Ward's criticism of historical writing was that it was unscientific, focusing on exceptional details rather than establishing overall trends.[72] The correct periodization of social and intellectual evolution for Ward clearly had to be founded upon Comte's initial outline.

Ward found Comte's insistent historical emphasis very welcome. Teachers, Ward noted, have traditionally ignored the history of the various sciences and thereby made their disciplines "dry and repugnant" to their students. Ward quoted with approval Comte's dictum regarding the centrality of history to the understanding of any science, and remarked that the French philosopher's history of mathematics contained in the *Cours* "will probably be set down among the most able and telling efforts of his life" (1:105, 107). Unable to curb his enthusiasm, Ward concluded: "I can not refrain from strongly commending this portion of the [Cours de] 'Philosophie Positive' to all who are interested in tracing the grand triumphs of the human mind and the progress of the investigation of natural truth" (1:109).[73]

III

If Ward followed Comte faithfully in his classification of the sciences, his understanding of social science was built solidly upon the Comtean definition. Ward described "the world . . . [as] greatly indebted to Comte" for his hierarchical classification and for coining the seminal term, sociology.[74] Sociology's paramount place within that classification is proved, explained Ward, "by the manner in which it comprehends all other sciences" (1:10). Holding that science is composed of "departments

72. LFW, *Applied Sociology: A Treatise on the Conscious Improvement of Society by Society,* (Boston: Ginn, 1906), 234–36. See also *Dynamic Sociology,* 2:217.

73. For Ward's agreement with Comte (contra Spencer) regarding the prominent role of human affections in history, see LFW, *Applied Sociology,* 41–43.

74. LFW, "The Place of Sociology," 16.

of phenomena . . . [all subject to] the control of invariable law," Ward argued that "science means the same in all departments or it means nothing." Sociologists must "believe that social phenomena are under the dominion of unvarying law in precisely the same sense that astronomical phenomena are" (1:457–58). The only difference is that sociological phenomena are part of an exceedingly complex system; plus, there is a widespread ignorance of the laws that govern social phenomena. Now, Ward acknowledged that social science could not be reduced to precise mathematical notation; he agreed with Comte that any attempt to do so would be a gross sort of "materialism."[75] But this limitation of sociology does not make it any less a science. It is, for instance, equally difficult to reduce some aspects of biology to precise quantification and such difficulties do not undercut its scientific claims.

If, then, sociology "can only become a science when human events are recognized as phenomena," what can be the methodology of this grand empirical science? Ward gave several different answers to this critical question but his answers are interrelated. "The method in sociology," wrote Ward, "is generalization. . . . It is essentially the process of grouping phenomena and using the groups as units."[76] Only when social phenomena are grouped or classified can comparisons be drawn, generalizations formed and these "groups brought under uniform laws and treated by exact methods." Dispassionate observation is required to arrive at such generalizations and it is here that Comte's historical method enters. Since the sociologist cannot set up controlled experiments, he must rely upon historical "observation." Ward defines this "historical perspective" as the "discovery of law in history, whether it be the history of the past or the present, and including under history social as well as political phenomena."[77] Or, as Comte had argued in the Cours, "the historical method verifies and applies, in the largest way, that chief quality of sociological science—its proceeding from the whole to the parts." Without this "chief scientific device," Comte warned, sociology would be "a mere compilation of provisional materials."[78] It was the systematic use of historical "observation" that would secure sociology's credentials as a true science.

It was important also for Ward to distinguish sociology from earlier disciplines, such as political economy, as well as from emergent social sciences such as economics. Here again, Comte was his guide. Comte

75. LFW, Pure Sociology: A Treatise on the Origin and Spontaneous Development of Society, (New York: Macmillan, 1903), 47.
76. LFW, Pure Sociology, 49.
77. Ibid., 62, 56.
78. Comte in Lenzer, ed., Auguste Comte, 248.

had made sociology "one of the great coordinate groups of his so-called hierarchy" and Ward concurred with such a conception. "We may regard sociology," wrote Ward, "as one of the great natural orders of cosmical phenomena under which we may range the next most general departments as so many genera, each with its appropriate species." Sociology embraces a number of more limited sciences but these can be pursued on their own without feeling threatened by sociologists, just as geologists do not worry that astronomers "are encroaching on their domain." Ward like Comte, then, envisioned sociology "embracing everything that pertains to man as a social being."[79]

In elaborating upon his definition of social science, Ward also adhered to the fundamental Comtean distinction between social statics and dynamics. "In all departments of nature," Ward explained, "where the statical condition is represented by structures, the dynamic condition consists in some change in the type of such structures."[80] These same principles apply to sociology as well. Wrote Ward: "The science which concerns itself with the laws of the social *order* is social statics. That which considers the conditions of social *progress* is social dynamics" (1:60). Elsewhere, Ward observed that "the social order [was] in this respect like an organism . . . made up of social structures" that are fixed in some respects but also subject to some change and development.[81] A truly scientific sociology would study both the static and the dynamic sides of social phenomena. The static would focus upon present social structures, that is, contemporary human institutions, and the dynamic would concentrate on the "the normal changes going on in society under the sole influence of natural laws" (1:60). Accordingly, institutions—their current character as well as their creation, operation, and development—"become the chief study of the sociologist."[82]

One reason for Ward's careful preservation of these Comtean categories was that they together constitute "the positive principle which underlies all considerations of order and progress." They "give," noted Ward, "to the fundamental distinction of order and progress a scientific synonymy of great propriety and value" (1:127–28). Ward found Comte's use of these twin principles intriguing and his efforts to reconcile them compelling. These "ideas," Ward remarked, "are not only exceedingly luminous and interesting, but also pre-eminently sound and philosophical." As "a true philosopher and co-ordinator of truth,"

79. LFW, "The Place of Sociology," 22, 25, 24, 22.
80. LFW, *Pure Sociology*, 221.
81. Ibid., 184.
82. Ibid., 31.

Comte drew this crucial distinction between order and progress from other sciences, chiefly biology (1:125). Consistent with his intellectual community and political culture, Ward was concerned that these rival social forces be reconciled and Comte seemed to furnish the solution to what Ward called "the great problem of human advancement" (1:126).[83] Comte's philosophy of science, and especially his understanding of social science, constituted the building blocks of Ward's sociology, as well as the foundation of his social reformism.

While the Comtean formulation was highly suggestive, Ward probed its deficiences and sought to construct a social theory sufficiently dynamic to meet the colossal needs of industrial America. Could not, Ward reasoned, social dynamics be itself divided into "passive, or negative, and active, or positive" categories? The former side, described by Comte in detail, regards society "as passive in the sense of being simply acted upon by the [natural] forces that surround it and operate within it" (1:56). But, Ward asked: what of "the power of man to modify and direct the forces of nature for his own purposes?" (1:58). This concept (i.e., "active social dynamics") Ward labels "anthropoteleology" to distinguish it from theological notions of divine teleology (1:28, 58). It entails purposeful human intervention in society to restrict, augment, or otherwise control social forces. Thus Ward believed that Comte "did not properly conceive the nature of social dynamics, although he defined it and treated it at great length."[84] Comte understood that progress was "the development of order" yet he failed to show exactly how this could be so.

In Ward's mind, then, Comte had neglected to draw a crucial distinction. If such a distinction was not drawn, Ward might well have been forced into what Hofstadter termed "the unitary assumptions of social Darwinism" typified by the sociology of Spencer or of Sumner.[85] Though he had attacked the laissez-faire doctrines of Adam Smith and the French physiocrats, Comte had not had to face the biological reductionism of social Darwinism. Ward thought it even more crucial to affirm how, through man's artificial intervention, evolution could also be teleological. Thus Ward remarked that Comte had recognized "the department of active (as distinct from purely passive) social dynamics" only "dimly . . . but his successors have thus failed to recognize it at all." This departure from Comte opened the door for Ward to what he described as "[t]he art of regulating society," named "Sociocracy."

83. See Lenzer, ed., *Auguste Comte*, 223–26 for Comte's treatment of these themes.
84. LFW, *Pure Sociology*, 223–24.
85. Hofstadter, *Social Darwinism*, 68.

Active social dynamics represent, consequently, a link between pure science and applied "art." Or, as Ward put it, this branch "necessarily connects the study of these [social] forces with the art of applying them, which is a distinctly human process" (1:137, 59–60). It is, therefore, from this vantage point that Ward wrote on political subjects and dealt with the question of socioeconomic reform.

Note, however, that Ward attempted to preserve the difference between applied sociology and the "art" of sociocracy. "Science," he wrote, "is never exactly the same thing as art. . . . Applied physics is not manufacture." Hence, Ward explained, "applied sociology is not government or politics, nor civic or social reform."[86] At best, it attempts to ascertain general sociological principles and may even suggest how they might be applied. Such unspecific generalizations could perhaps be implemented by legislators or administrators but that is not the job of the social scientist. Ward criticized Spencer and socialists (both utopian and Marxist) for failing to recognize the boundaries of science and thus concerning themselves with specific matters of public policy. Even in the realm of applied sociology, Ward was concerned that sociologists be objective, scientific experts. The sociologist observes political squabbles "as he does all social phenomena, but they only constitute data for his science."[87] To be truly scientific, social scientists must remain nonpartisan. Nor was Ward worried that such scientific objectivity might promote indifference or a do-nothing philosophy. He agreed with Comte that science was by its very nature progressive and interventionist. At even its most abstract level, the implications of Comtean social science were activist and melioristic. Once pointed to the relevant scientific analysis, governments would naturally select the correct course.

Ward's political theory, though never developed sytematically in any single work, was carefully constructed from the building blocks outlined above. Like many Gilded Age social theorists, his approach was usually historical. In the primitive state, Ward argued that some sort of association or organization gradually developed. He did not concur, however, with Comte's belief in man's "natural sociability." Ward believed that "the history of savage races" revealed mostly an individualistic spirit and intertribal struggle (1:130). This process of organization was a natural or genetic one and a more specifically governmental structure might not arise for some time. There may, therefore, be social organization of a sort without first having "rulers and laws." For Ward, society was

86. LFW, *Applied Sociology*, 8.
87. Ibid., 11.

distinct from government. The latter is a necessary and useful development, though it has most often been imposed upon the ruled by those
who desire to rule because of their own ambition and the anticipated
perquisites of holding power.[88] Such is not the way governments should
arise. They should, declared Ward, "be demanded, created, and put in
force by, and for the benefit of, those desiring to be governed," but
historically that has been rare (2:227). Might has tended to prevail,
governments being established to dominate others, though also serving
a positive, organizational role.

Historicism also colored Ward's understanding of natural rights and
their origins. Again, the rights of individual or social "organisms" are
usually determined by considerations of power or might. The "primary
law" in social evolution, as in physics, is "that in the last analysis all
results are accomplished by force" (1:32). This rule of might has always
prevailed in human society; Ward believed that to deny this demonstrable
truth was naive. Governments have always governed by force either
explicitly or implicitly. Comte had put it this way in the *Système*: "The
famous maxim of Hobbes, that government is the natural result of force,
is the principal step that till now the positive theory of power made since
Aristotle."[89] Social scientists, consequently, must discard appeals to such
artificial abstractions as "natural" individual rights or liberties. "All the
prevailing theories of human rights," Ward observed, "are but ideal
conceptions which not only have never yet been realized, but in the
nature of things never can be." Recognizing this reality would not be
detrimental to human welfare in the least but, rather, would act as a truly
liberating force. If force is the determining factor, then, under a popular,
majoritarian system, government "coercion which is now so fruitless
[would produce] a positive and increasing future benefit" (1:32). Undue
emphasis upon "natural" rights can only hamstring democratic governments from marshaling, for progressive ends, the force at their disposal.

As society develops and rudimentary government evolves, "the most
important of all human institutions"—the state—emerges. Ward insisted
once more that most theories of the state were needlessly abstract and
speculative. He contended that the state is "like all other social structures" and therefore "a spontaneous genetic product resulting . . . from
the interaction of antagonistic forces."[90] The state applies and enforces
those laws and customs that have grown up as society organized. It acts

88. LFW, "Social Genesis," *American Journal of Sociology* 3 (1897): 544. Compare with
Comte in Lenzer, *Auguste Comte*, 431.
89. Auguste Comte in Lenzer, ed., *Auguste Comte*, 433.
90. LFW, "Evolution of Social Structures," *American Journal of Sociology* 10 (1905):
595–96.

for society and "grows more and more intelligent with each step in social assimilation."[91] In order to describe social evolution, Ward used (as did Comte before him) analogies drawn from nature. "With the establishment of the state," Ward wrote, one starts to see "a differentiation of social tissues." Though Ward dismissed any discussion of abstract "natural" rights, he did describe the "most important function" of the state as "the protection of the citizen in his property rights." Property was one of the first offspring of the social organism and "was not possible until the state was established."[92] Ward's view of property and its historical role was quite positive. Along with the state and a system of laws, property "constitutes one of the leading civilizing agents." The main way it "contributed to social development" was by making private accumulation possible. In turn, private accumulation provided the basis for a complex division of labor. Moreover, it also formed the foundation for a system of exchange, trade, and commerce. The pursuit of property for its own sake gradually emerged and became a social force of considerable power. Ward conceded that such a "passion is of course sure to have its dark side," but interpreted its birth and growth as a largely beneficial development.[93] Concluded Ward in *Dynamic Sociology*: "True, indirectly and unintentionally the accumulation of wealth has advanced the race by affording leisure for a few to think out and develop natural principles, and by enabling large schemes of improvement to be carried out for which small fortunes would not have sufficed" (1:520).

From this historicist understanding of the origins of social institutions such as government, the legal system, the state, and private property, Ward turned to consider the character of the state and the question of its proper role. Ward argued that the state arose in part to check and control the natural but destructive forces of individualism and social conflict. Lacking such an institution, political society would degenerate or at least fail to progress. The advent of an institutional state apparatus was, therefore, "the most important step taken by man in the direction of controlling the social forces." The rationale behind its creation was not merely a concern for simple survival, however, but also a desire to benefit society as a whole. Here Ward quoted Gustav Ratzenhofer describing the state as embodying "the conscious sacrifice of the individual in behalf of the community."[94] Similarly, though Ward failed to cite him at this point, Comte had contended that the state was "the product

91. LFW, *Applied Sociology*, 337.
92. LFW, "Evolution," 596.
93. LFW, *Pure Sociology*, 276, 277.
94. Ibid., 551.

of the smaller [social] combinations when their common ends are duly made general."[95] Thus the state not only restrains but also unites various elements together to achieve a common cause. In this way, it actually promotes human freedom in general because it limits or redirects individual interests to serve the commonweal. Such an interpretation is scientifically sound, declared Ward, because it understands society as a natural organism. One should no more criticize how the state developed than complain about how certain creatures evolved, for as Comte understood, "we should be able in a general way to regard society as having been most frequently as well directed in all respects as the nature of things permitted."[96]

It was on these grounds that Ward mounted his attack upon both classical political economy and Spencerian laissez-faire. When one understands the state as a purely natural outgrowth, having as its "one purpose, function, or mission . . . securing the welfare of society," proscriptions of all state intervention sound abstract and illogical.[97] Ward assailed what he termed this "philosophy of despair" from several different angles.[98] For one, so-called meddling (or human interference in natural processes) is an essential part of all science and "alone constitutes man a civilized being."[99] After all, it was the advent of man's greater intellect that "repealed the biologic law or law of nature [in human affairs] and enacted in its stead the psychologic law—the law of mind."[100] If social laws are scientific, as Ward, Spencer, and Comte all agreed they were, then they are rightfully subject to human manipulation. Furthermore, Ward castigated the champions of laissez-faire for presenting only one side of the case. Intervention, even in America, has always been practiced by governments and they certainly have made mistakes in attempting to manipulate economic trends. But what of their successes? It would be absurd to suggest that intervention has never been beneficial. There is, finally, the historical record upon which generalizations are usually based. Was, in fact, this alleged "social action" of the past *social* in any meaningful sense? In many cases, explained Ward, it was mainly the policy of a tiny oligarchy; these were "the usurpations of a ruling

95. Comte in Lenzer, ed., *Auguste Comte*, 432.

96. Comte quoted by LFW in *Pure Sociology*, 533. For an instructive discussion of this theme in Ward's writings, see Sidney Fine, *Laissez-Faire and the General-Welfare State: A Study of Conflict in American Thought, 1865–1901* (Ann Arbor: University of Michigan Press, 1956), 253–64.

97. LFW, *Pure Sociology*, 555.

98. LFW, *Applied Sociology*, 14.

99. LFW, *Glimpses*, 3:304.

100. Ibid., 4:366.

class." The advent of popular governments in the West, Ward felt, therefore creates a new situation: "The fundamental error of the modern laissez-faire school has been that of confounding the present state of the world with the state of the world in the eighteenth century. The civilized world, by whatever name its governments may be called, is virtually democratic, and state action, in the long run at least, is social action in a nearly literal sense."[101]

Ward readily admitted that, in the past, a "deep-seated dread and detestation of government has been salutary in the extreme." Such a well-founded fear spawned the liberation of most of Europe from oppressive or despotic governments. The industrial West thus enjoys majoritarian democracies at present. Nor do popular majorities threaten to become the new despots. In a revealing aside, Ward dismissed a potential "tyranny of the majority." There is a "popular sense of justice," said Ward, that would prohibit such oppression and the government must take care "to refrain from shocking this public sense of justice."[102] Also, the rule of law prevents arbitrary, tyrannical actions by a particular government and its popular constituency. Unfortunately, many still harbor their old fears of government, in spite of these important developments. Ward observed incredulously: "The most representative forms of government are still feared, watched, and suspected as if they were self-constituted despotisms."[103]

Far from being beneficial, these atavistic attitudes serve "to produce a thoroughly false and perverted idea of what government really is."[104] Such views have a host of negative ramifications for the polity. Good men avoid government service; public offices are viewed as the rightful property of the victors; and elected officials are presumed to exercise more power that they actually do. By far, the most serious consequence of this archaic view, however, is that it restricts the legitimate positive and protective powers of government. A much more menacing despotism was arising—concentrations of private capital—"far more dangerous" to the commonwealth than the circumscribed activities of the state. Yet, because of outmoded popular prejudices, that same state was being prevented from protecting its citizens from "organized aggrandizement [and] the abuse of wealth."[105] Governments are restrained from responding by obsolete notions that would have expired long ago had they not been fed and encouraged by self-interested apologists for the established

101. LFW, *Applied Sociology,* 16, 15.
102. LFW, "False Notions of Government," in *Glimpses,* 4:65.
103. Ibid., 4:66.
104. Ibid.
105. Ibid., 4:68.

economic order. The answer to this alarming and inequitable situation was fairly simple for Ward: popular education and mass mobilization: "They [the working people] need no revolutionary schemes of socialism, communism, or anarchy. The present machinery of government, especially in this country, is all they could wish. They have only to take possession of it and operate it in their own interest."[106]

If these, then, are the common, false views of the state and its role, how did Ward conceive of the state's correct functioning? What was his vision of "ideal government"? (1:35). While Ward's organic and historicist conception of civil society owed much to Comte, other aspects of his critique of laissez-faire economics echo traditional American "equal rights" or antimonoply rhetoric. Ward clearly drew upon an indigenous egalitarian tradition coupled with an emergent interventionist radicalism to attack both Spencer and classical political economy. Nevertheless, he needed Comte to provide the scientific foundation upon which to draw together these disparate parts of American political culture. With Comte, Ward was able to advocate state-led reform with greater certainty and coherence than if he had relied solely upon older, indigenous reform ideals. Ward's unique blend attracted many of those who sought such a scientific rationale for the positive state.

Instead of being formed to serve the interests of the ambitious few who seek to rule, "a true government" for Ward would be the product of public demand. Consequently, government officers would be truly public servants, not arrogant masters. "Society," Ward predicted, "would be the source of authority, and the government its agent" (1:52). The state, then, having as its primary object "the good of society as a whole," proceeds with concerted efforts to control the social forces and thereby secure the greatest good for the greatest number.[107] Such self-conscious action is no different than the telic control or intervention of the individual, though in a democratic polity such action is truly "collective telesis." The "effects [of such intelligent efforts] do not," Ward explained, "belong to evolution" per se. They are rather "the products of social or collective telesis and may be called *institution*."[108] Humans have long built institutions; under a popularly controlled state, institutions would now be genuinely social. To quote Comte: "the preponderating social forces, of necessity, at last become the directing ones."[109] Ward, too, saw the rise of collectivism as a necessary and beneficial

106. Ibid., 4:71.

107. LFW, *Pure Sociology*, 551.

108. Ibid., 545. Ward used the word "institution" hardly at all in *Dynamic Sociology*, but it appears more frequently in his later work, perhaps because of his having read Veblen.

109. Comte cited in Lenzer, ed., *Auguste Comte*, 38.

development. Noting its spread in Europe and elsewhere, Ward observed: "this universal growth of collectivism *pari passu* with the growth of intelligence is simply the natural and normal integration of functions with the development of social structure."[110] Both Ward and Comte saw an interventionist state dictated by the very laws of social science.

Ward was concerned, as Comte had been, with reconciling the previously conflicting claims of order and progress in society. Under Ward's ideal system, the Positive state would contribute to this important reconciliation. In the past, Ward reflected, civilization had progressed but often "without producing any improvement in the condition of the human race." "Human achievement" (or institutions) must be "socialized" in order "to harmonize achievement with improvement." Once institutions were reformed to serve only the commonwealth, Comte's coveted reconciliation of order and progress would also be accomplished. Ward therefore shared Comte's concern; albeit he changed the terminology slightly when articulating it. This harmonizing of achievement and improvement is, concluded Ward, echoing his French predecessor, "the purpose of applied sociology."[111]

Having established that state interventionism was sanctioned by the immutable laws of social science, Ward himself then posed the next question: "How can it [i.e., social reform] be brought about? This is the problem of sociology."[112] If the state will inexorably intervene in the economy and society, then, in a democratic system, it will seek reforms that will benefit the popular majority. Ward's conception of the democratic state was melioristic at its core. Yet Ward reflected that, as popular revolts toppled autocratic regimes "and nations grew more and more democratic, the telic element declined, and the most democratic governments have proved the most stupid."[113] It was essential to the growth and prosperity of the polity that the telic element be reintroduced in a way consistent with democratic principles. In his attempts to do so, the friction within Ward's system between radical egalitarian values and a Whiggish / Comtean elitism becomes most apparent.

Ward rejected Comte's positive priesthood as "a chimera." He argued that "spiritual" and "temporal" powers "can not be divorced" so neatly. Rather, society had a single voice in the realm of policymaking and that should be the popularly elected legislature. It is the legislators then who will attempt "the desirable modification of social structures," which

110. LFW, *Pure Sociology*, 564.
111. LFW, *Applied Sociology*, 21.
112. LFW, "Collective Telesis," *American Journal of Sociology* 2 (1897): 813.
113. Ibid., 811.

Ward termed reform.[114] Representative systems constitute a problem in this regard, however. For "nothing . . . worthy of the name of scientific legislation," Ward contended, ". . . is possible except in a democracy in which all the people are intelligent, so that the representatives of the people are persons of considerable mental development."[115] One solution was to create a highly educated electorate, but another part of Ward's answer sounded more elitist.

The increasing importance of the committee system in Congress and the growth of the power of the executive were both viewed by Ward as salutary developments. "Committee work is," Ward enthused, ". . . the nearest approach we have to the scientific investigation of social questions." Committees could truly deliberate because they could investigate, "hear testimony . . . and weigh evidence for and against every proposed measure." This process thus approximates the scientific method in a modest way. A more powerful executive with greater discretionary powers would also facilitate a more scientific system. Administrative officers deal directly with the public or particular affected industries and therefore see what laws need to be changed or new laws drafted. They are best acquainted with "the needs of the public and with the best means of supplying them."[116]

In developing this argument for a new system of "scientific legislation," Ward appears to have reintroduced under a different guise Comte's positive priesthood. "Attractive legislation" (as Ward called state intervention) would not be produced "to any considerable extent in the open sessions of legislative bodies."[117] "A public assembly," Ward contended, "governed by parliamentary rules is as inadequate a method as could well be conceived of for anything like scientific legislation."[118] Legislatures will, of course, continue to play a key role but their proceedings "will become a merely formal way of putting the final sanction of society on decisions that have been carefully worked out in what may be called the sociological laboratory."[119] The social scientist here enters the policymaking process, for only empirical investigation can tell the activist state where and how to intervene. Indeed, Ward stipulated that "any attempt to do this [i.e., implement reform] must be based on a full knowledge of the nature of such [social] structures, otherwise its failure

114. LFW, *Applied Sociology*, 4.
115. Ibid., 338.
116. LFW, *Psychic Factors of Civilization* (Boston: Ginn, 1897), 310–11.
117. LFW, *Applied Sociology*, 338.
118. LFW, *Psychic Factors*, 309.
119. LFW, *Applied Sociology*, 338–39.

is certain."[120] Real policy options must be evaluated and selected by the civil service technocrat in a suitably neutral scientific environment. Such nonpartisan experts would work "on the problems of social physics from the practical point of view."[121]

One of the most striking, and characteristically Comtean, features of Ward's model here is its apolitical color. Ward frequently assailed Gilded Age politics as wasteful, artificial, and self-indulgent. "The real interests of society are, temporarily at least, lost sight of, clouded and obscured" when party hacks govern. For Ward, elections had become "the factitious excitement of partisan struggles where professional politicians and demagogues on the one hand, and the agents of plutocracy on the other, are shouting discordantly in ears of the people."[122] Ward implied that most contemporary policy questions could actually be resolved quickly "in a business way without favor, or bias," if social scientists were given a decisive role in the legislative process. When the citizenry realized that the present partisan system is "child's play," then "the social consciousness will banish it and substitute something more business-like."[123] The latter system recognized that society is ruled by certain natural laws and discards the misplaced confidence in the traditional parties' power to effect substantial change without an adequate knowledge of such laws. As Comte had phrased it, society must reject its old "faith in the unlimited power of its political combinations to perfect social order."[124] In effect, Ward's description of a movement away from partisan politics to "scientific lawmaking" followed Comte's earlier advocacy of an empirical politics in the positive state—as Comte conceived it, a system based upon "observation" rather than "imagination."[125]

On the other hand, although his championing of a sort of sociological technocracy was strongly Comtean, Ward obviously had a personal stake in such a system. He was part of a nascent national bureaucracy that aspired to influence policymakers. Moreover, ideas about an administrative elite were not exclusively Comtean; most advocates of the new social science championed such views and similar ideas were deeply rooted in Whig political culture. Ward also borrowed equal rights rhetoric in constructing his political critique. Often (as evident in the excerpt just quoted), Ward not only denounced demagogic politicians

120. Ibid., 4.
121. Ibid., 339.
122. LFW, *Psychic Factors*, 326.
123. Ibid., 325.
124. Comte in Lenzer, ed., *Auguste Comte*, 35.
125. Ibid., 34–36.

for their pandering to popular fancies but also dismissed them as "the agents of plutocracy." His work blended egalitarian liberal and social-scientific languages. He argued, for instance, that scientific expertise must assume a greater role because dispassionate science cannot be so easily bought or "managed by the shrewd representatives of wealth."[126] A genuinely scientific state would ensure an egalitarian polity because it would seek rationally, and would alone be capable of delivering, the greatest good for the greatest number. If parties had become agents for minority elements that imposed their individualistic and unscientific interest upon the commonwealth, then partisan politics were dispensable.

Ward held that the Positive polity needed both a technocratic bureaucracy and an educated voting public to carry out social telesis. Though Ward commented that Comte's fragmentary thoughts on education should have been included in "their natural place in the chapter on social dynamics," he deemed Comte's educational theory to have been "the vital part of his whole theory of human progress" and "among the most eminently sound of all doctrines contained in" his work. The Comtean vision of positive education was praised by Ward because its author was among the first Europeans to advocate that advanced education no longer be restricted to members of a social elite. "The first essential condition of positive education, at once intellectual and moral, considered as a necessary basis of a true social reorganization, must certainly consist in its rigorous universality," Comte had written (quoted by Ward, 1:133).

Yet a number of Comte's scattered comments on the reorganization of education in the *Cours* were rather elitist in character, and one is led to inquire why Ward would have stressed only Comte's liberal position on mass education. More to the point, why did Comte not place his discussion of education in his section on social dynamics? And why would Ward have thought it naturally belonged there?

The answer to these latter two questions discloses a key difference between Ward's social theory and that of Comte. No matter how progressive Comte sounded regarding education for all elements of society, never in the *Cours* did he argue for mass education as a vehicle for upward social mobility. Nor did this fact escape Ward's attention. Near the end of volume 2 of *Dynamic Sociology*, Ward conceded that Comte "nowhere clearly indicates the evils of inequality as a reason for it [universal education]" (2:606). Ward, on the other hand, consistently saw education as the "Great Panacea"—the title to the first version of what later became *Dynamic Sociology*, composed before Ward had read

126. LFW, *Psychic Factors*, 326.

Comte in earnest—a means not only to expand knowledge but also to implement scientific reform and overcome social inequality.[127] Against "socialists" and others, Ward maintained that it was "the unequal distribution of knowledge" that caused "the present unequal distribution of wealth":

> Knowledge is power, and power has ever been wielded for self-aggrandizement, and must ever be so wielded. To prevent inequality of advantages there must be equality of power, i.e., equality of knowledge. (2:602)

Since Ward believed there to be no "great inequality in the natural capacity of the human mind," a uniform system of universal education would allow "the great bulk of humanity" to raise itself "if afforded an opportunity." What distinguished the self-made man was his singular energy and drive, not his intellectual genius. All of which shows, Ward concluded, that present distinctions dividing society "are for the most part differences of position, of education, of opportunity—artificial differences—and that real, or intellectual differences are comparatively slight" (2:601).

Ward was surely a Whig in the Lincoln mold. The Algeresque theme of the self-made man that runs through Lincoln's life and thought seems to have been equally part of Ward's. "Those who seek opportunities and create circumstances," Ward contended, "do so by virtue of emotional forces which usually accompany only average talents."[128] Given an equal opportunity by means of a universal system of education, most individuals could presumably make something of themselves, just as Ward had himself escaped his humble beginnings through night classes and an ambitious program of self-education.[129]

After his enthusiastic partisanship of the late 1860s Ward grew to become virtually apolitical. He took few public stands on specific contemporary issues and was not affiliated with any political party. Perhaps his rising status in government service discouraged such activity. Certainly his understanding of the role of the social scientist precluded partisan advocacy. Yet science as conceived by Ward was profoundly practical and inherently action-oriented. The conflicting demands of

---

127. LFW, *Glimpses*, 3:150.

128. Richard Hofstadter, "Abraham Lincoln and the Self-Made Myth," in *The American Political Tradition and the Men Who Made It* (New York: Random House, 1973), esp. 126–36. See also: LFW, "Broadening the Way to Success," in *Glimpses*, 4:34–43.

129. Scott, *Ward*, 20–28.

these two different impulses constitutes another revealing tension in Ward's work. For example, in a closing section of *Psychic Factors*, later deleted from the book when published, Ward argued forcefully for a large public sector in the economy. Nationalized industries, Ward believed, should compete with private firms, even in "supplying public consumption," and this would "greatly improve the condition of the laboring classes . . . [and foster] the political independence of the voter." After advocating such bold measures, however, Ward quickly retreated to a dispassionate scientific posture: "Such are some of the problems of applied social science to be investigated in the dry light of science, as little influenced by feeling as though it were the inhabitants of Jupiter's moons instead of those of this planet that were in the field of the intellectual telescope."[130]

Despite the strictures of scientific sociology, Ward did articulate a general position on several major issues of his era. On the tariff, Ward, like Wakeman, argued for protectionism upon "sociological" grounds. Ward held that, as with other "attractive legislation," a protective tariff could be demonstrated empirically to benefit the majority of the populace.[131] Ward also supported civil service reform, while taking pains to argue that accusations of widespread bureaucratic corruption were false. Genuine reform, declared Ward, would dismantle the system of party patronage appointments and establish a true meritocracy, not simply pursue isolated individual offenders.[132] Ward was equally alarmed about industrial concentration and the concomitant maldistribution of wealth in the nation. In response, Ward called somewhat vaguely for significant state ownership and regulation in the area of transportation, fossil fuels, and banking.[133] Moreover, Ward deemed the grievances of organized labor to be, on the whole, just and argued that workers should share more fully in the fruits of their labor.[134] Finally, Ward praised the urban social work of the turn of the century as "very useful" and "often of a high order," though noting its differences from scientific sociology.[135] Still, Ward usually took care to maintain a dispassionate scientific tone in discussing his general proposals and protrayed them as specific reforms demanded by science and not as planks in a party

130. Manuscript fragment, LFW Papers, Library of Congress, Box 5, pp. 854–55. Compare with LFW, *Psychic Factors*, 331.

131. LFW, "The Sociological Position on Protection and Free Trade," in *Glimpses*, 4:180–89.

132. LFW, "True and False Civil Service Reform," in *Glimpses*, 4:106–13.

133. LFW, "Plutocracy and Paternalism," in *Glimpses*, 5:231–40.

134. LFW, "Some Social and Economic Paradoxes," in *Glimpses*, 4:158.

135. LFW, "Contemporary Sociology, *American Journal of Sociology* 7 (1902): 478.

platform. He concluded in another context: "Each of these reforms the people have a right to demand as something affecting their personal interests as well as the safety of the country, and it is in this direction, and not in that of any political party, that they should resolutely move."[136]

The preceding discussion has shown the significant ways in which Ward's philosophy was distinctively Comtean, as well as explored the ways in which Ward "Americanized" the Comtean system. In general, both thinkers, in keeping with much of nineteenth-century thought, were scientistic and historicist. Like Comte, Ward's philosophy of science was simultaneously empirical, naturalistic, and monistic. Unlike Comte, Ward upheld the legitimacy, indeed the necessity, of causal explanation. Ward's fundamental understanding of science in general and social science in particular was built upon the Comtean definition and classification; consequently, it shared Comte's interventionist ethic, meliorism, and reformism.[137]

Moreover, Ward viewed the contemporary crisis of industrial democratic societies in much the same way Comte had done. Ward consistently held that the reconciliation of order and progress (or "achievement" and "improvement," as Ward phrased it) was the central problem of advanced societies. These hitherto antagonistic forces could be reconciled and social reconstruction advanced by what Ward termed "the socialization of achievement."[138] Comte too had called for a scientific restructuring of institutions to serve human needs better but when his blueprint was laid out fully in the Système it made no provision for the conventional state. Instead, Comte called for the extension of the power of industrialists to the political realm, coupled with the exercise of the spiritual and educative function by a Positive priesthood. Economic and scientific elites would, therefore, rule their separate social spheres, appropriating the state's traditional functions. Freed of some of Comte's elitism and rooted in an American egalitarian tradition, Ward was, by contrast, able to push his social theory in the direction of a democratic collectivism.

There remained, nonetheless, a significant illiberal element in Ward's system. The apolitical and bureaucratic thrust of some of Ward's writings clearly owed much to Comte, as well as to Ward's own brand of statist Whiggery.[139] Comtean positivism was central to Ward's system because

---

136. LFW, "True and False," 113.
137. Becker, Structure, 68–69.
138. LFW, Applied Sociology, 21.
139. For a development of this theme, see Richard Vernon, "Auguste Comte and the Withering Away of the State," Journal of the History of Ideas 45 (1984): 549–66. Lustig, Corporate Liberalism, esp. 255–60.

it allowed him to unite his democratic impulses with the more elitist and organicist American Whig tradition on an apparently scientific basis. This synthesis that characterized Ward's thought is akin to the ideological amalgam that produced corporate liberalism in America around the turn of the century. Jeffery Lustig describes twentieth-century American liberalism as a problematic grafting of a conservative corporatist vine onto a Lockean stem.[140] Both syntheses joined potentially conflicting elements and both received a significant Comtean contribution.

Grand theorists and their monistic systems were decidedly unfashionable in American sociological circles by the early twentieth century. Nevertheless, Ward's critique of Spencerian political economy was adopted by many of his contemporaries and had a profound influence upon a generation of reform-minded social scientists. Beyond academia, Ward's thought also had a significant impact.[141] Ward came to have a sizable following among Progressives. Reformer Frederic C. Howe put it this way to an aging Ward in 1912:

> You took the heritage which I received from the old school of thought and gave it a new organizing central thought that has been as it were a core about which other things arranged themselves. And I think you have done that for all of us. . . . Certainly the whole social philosophy of the present day is a formative expression of what you have said to be true.[142]

In short, if "Ward's philosophy . . . is," in the words of David Noble, "indispensible . . . to an understanding of the philosophy of social planning that flowered in America during the Progressive Era," then the Comtean origins of the Progressive mind also warrant recognition.[143]

---

140. Lustig, *Corporate Liberalism,* 255–60.

141. Becker, *Structure,* 72, 74; Commager, ed., *Lester Ward,* xxxvii.

142. Letter, Frederic C. Howe to LFW, 27 July 1912, Brown University, LFW Papers, Autograph Letters, 12:59–60.

143. David W. Noble, introduction to *Dynamic Sociology* (New York: Johnson Reprint, 1968 [1883]), 1:xiii.

CHAPTER SIX

Positivist as Academic

Albion Small and E. A. Ross

Think how completely Comte is ignored in this country! I am now prepared to take him up thoroughly and show his significance.

—LFW to E. A. Ross, 7 August 1896

BEYOND THE SOCIAL THEORY of Lester Ward, Comte's significance for American sociology becomes more difficult to assess. Between 1890 and 1914, academic sociologists in the United States moved slowly away from some of the Comtean ideas that had framed the discourse of the amateur social theorists who had preceded them. By the 1890s (and in some circles earlier), the grand systems of Spencer and Comte were increasingly dismissed as crude and outdated. Historians have advanced a variety of explanations for this shift away from the kind of evolutionary positivism that had dominated social-scientific discourse since the 1860s. Perhaps the interpretive rubric "professionalization" can best integrate the various factors suggested by different analyses, while situating these intellectual changes in their proper social context. It does not matter whether one focuses on a "revolt against positivism," a fundamental shift in historical consciousness, or the Mendel–Weisman revolution in biology (that destroyed Lamarckian evolutionary theories); all these factors were tied to economic and political realities.[1] Thomas Haskell contends that several broad, societal developments contributed to an increased recognition of social interdependence that was central to the rise of a new social science mentality and to a departure from the amateur musings of the recent past.[2] Haskell highlights the intrusion of the capitalist market into the lives of average Americans, the transportation revolution that knit together the nation's "island communities," and the more defined, specialized divison of labor as all contributing to the advance of professionalization.[3] The first academic sociologists, though many had been introduced to the "science of society" through Comte and Ward, gradually turned away from attempts at grand synthesis and eschewed Comtean historicism and reformism. In order to be taken seriously as professionals, the new generation of sociologists who entered academia during the 1890s required, in Haskell's words, "a style of explanation that would acknowledge the interdependent quality of human affairs, being neither as voluntaristic as nineteenth-century idealism had been, nor as reductionistic as positivism."[4]

Historians of American social thought have long recognized this development (even if they failed to see the centrality of Comte in the process), but they have exaggerated its speed and overlooked the persistent influence of Comtean themes in early American sociology.[5] Because

1. See H. Stuart Hughes, *Consciousness and Society: The Reorientation of European Social Thought, 1890–1930* (New York: Random House, 1958), chap. 2.; James T. Kloppenberg, *Uncertain Victory: Social Democracy and Progressivism in European and American Thought, 1870–1920* (New York: Oxford University Press, 1986), esp. 23–26. Kloppenberg observes in an aside that "the United States never produced a systematic positivist like Comte or Haeckel"(23). Surely Ward and Wakeman are good examples of such positivists.

2. *The Emergence of Professional Social Science: The American Social Science Association and the Nineteenth-Century Crisis of Authority* (Urbana: University of Illinois Press, 1977), preface.

3. The phrase is Robert Wiebe's. See *The Search for Order, 1877–1920* (New York: Hill and Wang, 1967), 44f.

4. *Emergence*, 162.

5. A partial listing of the literature on this subject would include Robert C. Bannister, *Sociology and Scientism: The American Quest for Objectivity, 1880–1940* (Chapel Hill: University of North Carolina Press, 1987); Leon Bramson, *The Political Context of Sociology* (Princeton: Princeton University Press, 1961), chap. 4; Hamilton Cravens, "The Abandonment of Evolutionary Social Theory in America: The Impact of Academic Professionalization Upon American Sociological Theory, 1890–1920," *American Studies* 12 (1971): 5–20; Mary Furner, *Advocacy and Objectivity: A Crisis in the Professionalization of American Social Science, 1865–1905* (Lexington: University of Kentucky Press, 1975); Roscoe C. Hinkle, *Founding Theory of American Sociology, 1881–1915* (London: Routledge and Kegan Paul,

the Comtean system was a complex amalgam in which different (even opposed) elements were held together as in solution, the movement away from Comte can be understood in at least two different (though not mutually exclusive) ways. In one sense, American sociology's desertion of Comte's explicit utopianism clearly made it less Comtean in character. This repudiation of the interventionist, reformist element (especially as developed by Ward) enabled some sociologists to assume a more conservative position regarding the social and economic status quo. Thus the evolution of the discipline in the United States may have made it less Comtean (as Ernest Becker has argued) but its resurgent elitism and political conservatism also represent a genuine Comtean echo.[6] Key

1980); Floyd N. House, *The Development of Sociology* (Chicago: University of Chicago Press, 1936); Donald Martindale, "The Roles of Humanism and Scientism in the Evolution of Sociology," in *Social Change: Explorations, Diagnoses, and Conjectures*, ed. G. Zollschan and W. Hirsch (New York: Wiley, 1976), 628–51; Dorothy Ross, *The Origins of American Social Science* (Cambridge: Cambridge University Press, 1991). Bramson describes "a liberal sociology of change and process" that arose at the end of the nineteenth century but does not show clearly where its common assumptions came from (*Political Context*, 85). Cravens's important article shows how the first academic sociologists rejected Spencer, and emphasized "psychic factors" but eventually embraced a kind of cultural analysis of society that eschewed biology altogether. Although I have followed some of Cravens's approach here, he ignores Comte entirely and pays scant attention to Ward's influence on the first generation of academic sociologists. Hinkle, meanwhile, describes briefly the three tenets of "evolutionary naturalism" shared by early sociologists but does not explore the historical origins of these beliefs in any depth (*Founding Theory*, 16–17). By far the most helpful and sophisticated analyses of this general subject are those of Bannister and Ross. Bannister asserts the emergence of a scientistic "objectivism" among American sociologists during the 1907–1917 period and views this as a movement away from some key themes of late nineteenth-century social science. Though he does not focus on Comtean thought within this movement, Bannister does describe the two main variants of objectivism ("nominalist" and "realist") as "in effect split[ting] the legacy of Comtean positivism: the one adopting the emphasis on quantification as the route to positive knowledge, and the other, Comte's utopian program, without the mumbo jumbo of the Religion of Humanity" (*Sociology*, 6). Dorothy Ross shows how Ward's positivism and sometimes radical rhetoric kept him out of academia during the 1880s and 1890s, while disciples Albion Small and E. A. Ross were pushed by similar political and professional forces away from Ward's reformist brand of Comtean social thought (see *Origins*, chaps. 3, 4, 7). Haskell does recognize implicitly the persistent influence of positivism, since he understands the emergent social science of the turn of the century as a "synthesis" of nineteenth-century idealism and positivism (*Emergence*, 5).

6. Becker appears to recognize only one side of the picture here. While the rejection of the Comtean model of social science meant a concomitant repudiation of Ward's pragmatic reformism, Becker gives short shrift to the profoundly conservative core of the Comtean system. He fails to recognize that by becoming more elitist and socially disengaged, American sociologists remained loyal to another part of Comte's complex vision. Despite this limitation, I have found Becker's treatment of Albion Small most illuminating. See Ernest Becker, *The Lost Science of Man* (New York: George Braziller, 1971).

parts of the Comtean vision dovetailed neatly with the new professional ethos of academic sociology. While American sociologists sought to be more specialized, more truly "scientific," and less crude in how they applied biological laws to society, many nevertheless retained the technocratic elitism and antidemocratic assumptions of the Comtean tradition.

This transition did not, therefore, represent a simple or clean break for the founding generation of American sociology. For Albion Small and Edward A. Ross, the main subjects of this chapter, the process was difficult; their struggle, however, can tell us much about the emergence of academic sociology in the United States, the transformation of American liberalism at the turn of the century, and the significance of Comtean thought for both developments.

Like so many of his early colleagues, Albion Woodbury Small was the son of an evangelical Protestant minister. Born and raised in a small town in Maine, Small attended Colby College, graduating in 1876, before proceeding to Newton Seminary to obtain ministerial training. But instead of following his father's path, the younger Small went to study in Germany for two years. Soon after he returned to Maine in 1881, he accepted a position teaching history at his alma mater. Colby could not hold his interest for long, however, and in 1888 Small went to pursue a doctorate in history at Johns Hopkins. Small served briefly as president of Colby after finishing his graduate work in Baltimore. It was as president that Small received an invitation to chair the sociology department at the newly founded University of Chicago in 1892. Though his training made him appear more suited to teach history, Small now headed the first bona fide American sociology department.

The formative influences on Small during his graduate years were a blend of European and American elements. Positivism's impact on Small was significant but much of Comte troubled the young Baptist. Small encountered the works of Comte and those of Spencer and Schaffle while studying in Germany. Years later, he commented regarding Comte's writings that he had then "been more impressed by their absurdities in detail than by the saving remnant of wisdom."[7] Part of the problem in assessing Comte's initial effect is that Small clearly revised negatively his opinion in later years.[8] Thus some of Small's later assessments of Comte

7. Vernon K. Dibble, *The Legacy of Albion Small* (Chicago: University of Chicago Press, 1975), 31.

8. Becker notes this transition: "In his [i.e., Small's] early references to Comte, for example, he gave Comte prominent place as the direct precursor of modern sociology, whereas at the end of his life he [changed his interpretation considerably]." Becker refers here in his notes to chapter 1 of Small and Vincent's textbook, *An Introduction to the Study of Sociology* (New York: American Book, 1894). See *Lost Science*, 49.

sound almost dismissive.[9] Yet, even in the restrictive atmosphere of Colby, Small openly acknowledged that he had adopted Comte's "conceptions of scientific method."[10] This admission came in a defensive preamble to a lengthy sociology syllabus Small had printed for seniors at Colby. Moreover, Small admitted decades later that Comte's call for a science of society and his view of sociology's dominant place in the hierarchy of the sciences had "helped" him in the late 1880s "to articulate vague feelings for which no adequate expression of his own had been found."[11]

One can infer from some of Small's later comments on the subject and from his personal background wherein lay the chief difficulty with Comte. Small wrote in the 1920s that in "one or two more years [after his initial encounter] Comte ceased to be edifying."[12] Apparently, Comte's uncompromising positivism was bracing to the young Small but some features made much of the mixture finally unpalatable. Perhaps Small's subsequent reflections on the cultural barriers to Comtean positivism in nineteenth-century America can provide some clues here. In a short anonymous contribution to mark the centennial of Comte's 1822 appeal for a science of society, Small proposed that a "more searching" explanation for Comte's lack of American admirers lay in important cultural factors. For Americans steeped in the pious orthodoxy of evangelical Protestantism, the stark naturalism of the *Cours* was deeply disturbing and, for many, simply unacceptable. "To every one in England, Germany, and America with a reserve of religious or ethical tradition, however, positivism meant simply the blatant atheism of the Robespierre cult of 'reason,' with slightly bettered manners. To this day the scientific substance of positivism has been largely discounted because of this association of ideas. If Comte had carried none of this handicap he might have been more convincing."[13] Certainly the young Albion Small had more than a modest "reserve of religious or ethical tradition" when he first encountered Comte in the 1880s. What Small (and, by extension, American social scientists in general) needed, then, was a genuinely American reading of Comte that recast the atheist Frenchman's ideas into the more familiar Whiggish and reformist terms of American evangelicalism. This is precisely what Small found in the work of Lester Frank Ward.

Small rarely belittled his debt to "the founder of American sociol-

9. AS, *Origins of Sociology* (New York: Russell and Russell, 1967 [1924]), 317.
10. Ibid., 316.
11. Ibid., 317.
12. Ibid., 317.
13. AS, "A Comtean Centenary," *American Journal of Sociology* 27 (1921–1922): 513.

ogy."[14] Indeed, Small remarked about his first encounter with *Dynamic Sociology* that he remembered being "aware of feeling as the alchemists might have felt two or three centuries earlier if they had stumbled across the 'philosopher's stone.' "[15] Small appears to have read Ward's two-volume tour de force in 1888, just prior to his graduate studies at Johns Hopkins. His reaction, as described in a eulogy of Ward penned in 1913, is most revealing: "The epithet 'materialistic' stood then for the most inexorable taboo in my ritual. After finishing the first reading, I wrote to the author: 'I was well along in the book before I found reason to question my classification of you as a materialist. If that is what you call yourself, I must admit that materialism ceased to seem to me a very terrible foe to the spirit, when I found you ending the book with an exhortation."[16] Like Ward, a product of nineteenth-century evangelicalism, Small was reassured by the moral earnestness of Ward's rhetoric. Moreover, in Ward's Whiggish reformism, Small found a social theory that was committed to improving actual social conditions; by contrast, Comte's social vision had seemed separated from the real world. "American sociology," he concluded in a revealing personal aside in 1922, "came into existence in response more directly to the appeal of sympathy than to that of science. At the beginning, American sociologists were more interested in real people and their life-problems, than in academic abstractions. [But] Comte's propositions affected them as more of the head than of the heart."[17] Comte's method, his understanding of the nature of science, and his view of sociology's place among the other sciences clearly appealed to Small's head. But much of Comte's actual social blueprint had struck Small as strange and foreign; it failed to appeal to his heart. For a while at least, Ward's sociology brought these two important halves together for Small.

That Ward mediated Comtean positivism for Small is confirmed by a survey of his early work, especially his contributions as editor of the *American Journal of Sociology* (which he founded at the University of Chicago in 1895). In the inaugural issue of the *Journal*, Small laid out a grand blueprint for American sociology that was at once synthetic, rigorously scientistic, and reformist. Here, and elsewhere in these initial issues, it is clear that Small's attempts to define the founding discourse of American sociology were constructed largely on Wardian and Comtean foundations. Although Small spent considerable space explaining how

14. AS, "The Evolution of a Social Standard," *American Journal of Sociology* 20 (1914–1915): 10.
15. AS, "Lester Frank Ward," *American Journal of Sociology* 19 (1913–1914): 76.
16. Ibid., 76.
17. AS, "Centenary," 512–13.

he would modify or expand upon Ward's system, it is clear that, for Small, Ward's work had framed the discussion. "My own work in studying and teaching societary relations," declared Small, "was guided at the outset by Comte's classification."[18] Thus, Small began his editorial introduction to the *Journal* by asserting that no one could now doubt that human society was an organic whole. Advanced industrial society in the United States has made it clear, argued Small, that "[w]hatever modern men's theory of the social bond, no men have ever had more conclusive evidence that the bond exists."[19] Small, like both Comte and Ward before him, had no doubt that society was an integrated, natural organism. This organicism was, of course, common to many Gilded Age social theorists (as Morton White and many others have subsequently shown). But Small's early understanding of sociology drew upon Comte, via Ward, in more concrete and specific ways as well. For one, Small echoed their concern that the sociological method be strictly Baconian. All assumptions, all institutions needed to be subjected to an unrelenting questioning. Careful, scientific study must precede any political efforts to introduce change, but such scientific study should not be abstract, specialized research in narrow, obscure fields. Rather, the approach of sociology must be synthetic, holistic, and practical. Specialized inquiry had now to give way to the integrative work of the new social science. "That which has been unconscious and accidental hitherto," contended Small, "will be methodically undertaken hereafter. Analytic and microscopic scholarship is abortive without the complementary work of the synthetic scholar who builds minute details into comprehensive structures."[20] Hence, sociology needed to meet the demands of rigorous science without giving up entirely the grand, systematic view of Comte or Ward. As Ernest Becker and Dorothy Ross (among others) have stressed, methodological questions carried weighty political implications for the founding generation of American sociologists.[21]

Closely tied to Small's synthetic view of sociology (as it had been to Comte's vision and, especially, to Ward's) was a practical, reformist, or

18. AS, "Static and Dynamic Sociology," *American Journal of Sociology* 1 (1895): 199.
19. AS, "The Era of Sociology," *American Journal of Sociology* 1 (1895): 2.
20. Ibid., 8–9.
21. See, for example, Dorothy Ross's treatment of the acceptance of marginalist methodology by American economists (*Origins*, chap. 6). Becker has framed the problem this way: "But now we see the terrible bind that sociology was in: on the one hand, it had to forge a methodology of the social problem, i.e., a socially critical body of knowledge that would attack the ravages of laissez-faire capitalism. On the other hand, it had to do this 'scientifically' and 'objectively'; it had to justify itself vis-à-vis those other disciplines that were scornful of its sentimentalism and ideology"(*Lost Science*, 7).

interventionist impulse. Small was committed to a sociology that would enable society to improve and reform itself in a thoughtful, measured way. Yes, he conceded, it was essential that a scientific understanding of a social question come before political action, but the objective consideration of the latter was also a proper part of any sociology. In what sounded like a close paraphrase of Comte, Small wrote: "The institutions which our generation inherits may be very crude, but they are the deposit of all the wisdom and goodness of the ages, in reaction with the ignorance and the evil. He who would reorder them should first understand them."[22] What Small bemoaned was that many "American scholars, especially in the social sciences" stopped at this point in their analysis. "Within the scope of scholarship," Small argued, "there is first science, and second something better than science. That something better is first prevision by means of science, and second intelligent direction of endeavor to realize the vision."[23] Like Ward, Small envisaged a sociology that had broken completely with what he called the "do-nothing traditions" of the past.[24]

In fact, if Small disagreed with Ward at all during this early period, it arose over whether his mentor's system was sufficiently interventionist, or (to use Ward's language) "dynamic." One of Small's first contributions to the *American Journal of Sociology* was a careful critique of Ward's understanding of the proper spheres of statical and dynamic sociology. Ward had argued that only the latter field within sociology addressed the amelioration of social conditions; Small believed, however, that one could not exclude entirely such considerations from the statical sphere. Declared Small: "I regard the discovery of the outline of an improved social order as the most important concern of the statical division of sociology."[25] While Small's dissent remained polite and measured, he concluded forcefully: "I not only believe with Professor Ward that sociology should aim 'at the organization of happiness,' but I contend that scientific conceptions of what the [statical] conditions of happiness would be are necessarily involved in the pursuit of this aim."[26]

Yet, if Small adopted Ward's meliorist vision (and, indeed, pressed it at first even further than had his predecessor), he also retained a strong, characteristically Comtean elitism in his sociology. As Chapter 5 has shown, this elitist or technocratic strand was certainly present in Ward's social thought, though it was often overshadowed by Ward's own

22. Ibid., 7.
23. AS, "Scholarship and Social Agitation," *American Journal of Sociology* 1 (1895): 564.
24. Ibid., 564.
25. AS, "Static," 207.
26. Ibid., 208

egalitarian ethos. Small also sent mixed signals in his early work, sometimes using language that could be construed as antidemocratic.[27] Because Comtean social science so celebrated intervention and control, the question invariably surfaced: Who would exercise this social control? Who would administer the positive state? Concerned, among other things, with establishing the scientific credentials of his new discipline, Small asserted in the first number of the *AJS* that sociologists would provide a needed corrective to the unscientific demands for reform emanating from the masses.[28]

Small began by observing that even those of humble station now recognized the increasing interdependence of society's component parts. With the development of the printing press and the general decline in illiteracy, every citizen, regardless of his station, had an opinion on the "social question" and some inchoate ideas about the proper way forward. But these popular demands for reform were not built upon a truly scientific understanding of society, that is, how it was constituted and how it functioned. Commented Small: "A little learning is a dangerous thing, jeopardy from that source is today universal. The millions have fragmentary knowledge of societary relations, and they are trying to transmute that meagre knowledge into social doctrine and policy. . . . Popular judgement is just now intoxicated with the splendid half truth that society is what men choose to make it." Reforms were being proposed, warned Small, "without due estimate of human limitations."[29] To address this alarming situation, sociologists had to assert their own scientific expertise and assume their proper leadership role. "The relation of popular sociology to would-be scientific sociology should be settled in the minds of scholars before more confusion results," Small cautioned.[30] Popular social theory had been developing outside the walls of the academy, beyond its sober influence. The new discipline could, therefore, play a vital role in present circumstances. "The doctrines of professional sociologists are attempts," Small explained in patronizing tones, "to substitute revised second thought for the hasty first thoughts composing the popular sociologies in which busy men outside the schools utter their impressions."[31] Moreover, as social conflict worsened, social scientists would rightly be called upon to act as neutral mediators. Small wrote elsewhere that "there is ground course

27. Much of what follows is based upon Dorothy Ross's interpretation of Small. See Ross, *Origins*, 122–40, 219–27.
28. See AS, "Era," 3.
29. Ibid., 3.
30. Ibid., 5.
31. Ibid., 6.

work for scholars in strengthening the rational basis for settlement of disturbed or threatened social relations. . . . [R]eferee work by scholars is in demand."[32] Only the "dispassionate" social scientist both understood the underlying social forces at work in particular crises and could see through the naive assumptions of the general public. Small believed that "it is the business of scholars to rise above the superstitions which forbid inquiry into the rightfulness of the traditional."[33] True to his Comtean assumptions, Small stressed that social change had to be guided and directed by a kind of academic priesthood.

Such scientifically crafted reform, Small underlined, would avoid the anarchic, destabilizing character of contemporary reform movements. Like Comte and most of his American following, Small held that genuine social progress would only arise from reforms that were grounded upon the fundamental principles of social order; as Comte had believed, the relationship between order and progress was symbiotic. Too many popular reformers were addressing only superficial questions. "Large and satisfying improvement of present social order must wait," argued Small, "upon deepening and broadening of the foundations of order."[34] The concern was for orderly change and, for Small (even more than for Ward), social reform was an expression of technocratic control. As we shall see, such an approach was only a short step away from the social control envisaged by E. A. Ross.

The preceding discussion has focused primarily on Small's early work, as exemplified by his initial contributions to the *American Journal of Sociology*. Most treatments of Small's career agree, however, that his thought underwent considerable change during his many years at Chicago. Though there is less agreement about exactly when the critical shifts took place, some historians have noted crippling tensions within Small's sociology almost from the beginning and several highlight a crucial transformation said to have occurred around the turn of the century.[35] Although other factors were also certainly at work, it is clear that a good part of Small's struggle was wrapped up in his halting,

32. AS, "Scholarship," 570.
33. Ibid., 570.
34. Ibid., 571.
35. Becker evidently believes this change occurred sometime before 1913 (see *Lost Science*, 19). Bannister holds that it began with the Bemis case in the mid-1890s but notes that Small published work that reflected the older reformist approach in 1910 and again in 1913 (see *Sociology*, 34). Dorothy Ross contends that Small started to turn away from Ward's original vision with the Bemis incident and settled into a more conservative position in the wake of Bryan's defeat in 1896, though she also observes that Small was not always consistent in this regard (see *Origins*, 134–35). As Ross notes, there is little recognition of any of this development in Dibble's study of Small.

ambivalent movement away from the sociological vision of Comte and Ward. Pursuing an uneven and sometimes contradictory course, Small came, by the advent of the First World War, to repudiate much of the grand, synthetic view of Comtean social science, along with its reformist thrust.[36]

Simply stated, Albion Small sought at first to retain the reform concerns he admired in Ward, while rejecting the amateur social theory of the reformers and clerics who had dominated the discourse before the 1890s.[37] The emergence of sociology as a distinct discipline in American universities at this time, and the professionalization of social science in general, made Small's project a difficult balancing act. Although Ward had probably felt this tension less (since he did not obtain an academic teaching position until 1906), both Small and Ward definitely wrestled with it. In this regard, their shared reformist concerns and common theoretical roots were actually part of the problem. As Ernest Becker succinctly puts it, "the very heroes they championed [Comte in particular] were the baggage that hindered them most" in their fight to gain academic legitimacy for sociology.[38] Because of differences in background, temperaments and position, Small felt the tension most acutely. In Becker's words, "Ward offered the world a superordinate sociology along Comtean lines, and that was that. And in this sense, his failure [to influence American sociology after his death in 1913] and rapid eclipse were much like Comte's."[39] But things were different for Small and, consequently, the evolution of his sociology was more anguished.

Many of Small's early contributions to the *AJS* were written during a much-publicized controversy at Chicago involving one of Small's colleagues. Edward W. Bemis had been appointed by President Harper to teach economics at Chicago, but by 1893 the university's chief executive was beginning to regret having made the appointment. Bemis's immediate superior, J. Laurence Laughlin, had opposed Bemis from the start and Bemis's outspoken liberal views on various social questions were alarming the university's conservative supporters and bolstering Laughlin's case against the young lecturer.[40] Small managed at first to stand clear of the imbroglio, but when he did take sides, it was with President Harper and against Bemis. The Bemis affair seems to suggest that, despite his rhetoric, when push came to shove, Small's understand-

36. See Becker, *Lost Science*, 19.
37. Ross, *Origins*, 122–23.
38. Becker, *Lost Science*, 17.
39. Ibid, 24.
40. Bannister, *Sociology*, 41.

ing of the role of professional social science was not Lester Ward's. It was Bemis's uncircumspect public statements, said Small, regarding the Pullman strike and other controversial issues of the day that made him unfit for his job. The "untimely and immature" remarks of his colleague were undermining Small's concerted efforts to establish Chicago as a bastion of "objective" social science, high above the political fray of the turbulent 1890s.[41]

Yet Small continued to struggle with the larger question of sociology and social reform. While helping to ease out his radical colleague, Small simultaneously attacked conservatives in his discipline in an uncharacteristically direct article, "Scholarship and Social Agitation."[42] Although he avoided actually naming his targets, he denounced "that type of scholarship [exemplified by Franklin Giddings at Columbia] which assumes superiority because it deals only with facts."[43] Practitioners of the new discipline must be willing to get their hands dirty if they are going to exercise any moral authority in society. In words that Bemis probably found sadly ironic, Small declared: "Scholarship must either abandon its claims to the function of leadership, and accept the purely clerical role of recording and classifying the facts of the past, or scholarship must accept the responsibility of prevision [a favorite term of Comte and Ward] and prophecy and progress."[44] Other articles contributed by Small to the *AJS* at about this time expressed similar views regarding the role of academic sociology and even included strong criticism of specific abuses of corporate business.[45]

Small's words and actions during this period do, then, appear contradictory. Perhaps the best explanation for his vigorous rhetoric in these articles was a guilty conscience.[46] After all, Small had learned from Ward that sociology must take a critical stance and that social scientists should be active participants in the political process; perhaps Small was seeking to atone for his reactionary tack in the Bemis case. In any event, Small soon returned to a much less activist or interventionist position, from which he rarely strayed in subsequent years. This final reversal (as Dorothy Ross characterizes it) may well have been brought on by the collapse of Populism in the wake of the 1896 presidential contest and the concomitant transformation of Gilded Age reform through the rise of the Progressive movement. Reformers and reform were changing and

41. AS quoted by Bannister, *Sociology*, 41.
42. See Ross, *Origins*, 134.
43. AS, "Scholarship," 564. This passage is also quoted by Ross; see *Origins*, 134.
44. AS, "Scholarship," 567.
45. See, for example, AS, "Private Business Is a Public Trust," *AJS* 1 (1895): 276–89.
46. Ross, *Origins*, 133.

Small appears to have accepted the core of the "professional compromise" that characterized Progressive social science.[47] Like many Progressives, Small came to accept a highly concentrated corporate economy and a high degree of economic inequality as unavoidable.[48]

The exact boundaries of this compromise and the extent of Small's departure from the perspective of Comte and Ward are both apparent in Small's 1905 text, *General Sociology*. Here, Small turned away from the biological analogy that had so dominated social theory since the early work of Sumner and Ward. Instead, Small posited a set of six "interests" that together constituted the foundation of human society. Small tried to keep some of Ward's psychological emphasis by identifying these "interests" with common human "desires." These "interests" were, therefore, both subjective desires and the objects actually desired. But this marriage was not entirely successful and there was much more of Gustav Ratzenhofer's theory of conflicting social interests in *General Sociology* than there was the sociology of Comte or of Ward.[49] Furthermore, Small's analysis placed a new emphasis on what he termed the "social process"; sociologists needed now to focus upon *how* societies actually functioned and changed and to leave normative judgments about ideal reforms to a later time and place.[50] This new abstract and dispassionate approach, this concern for process over intervention strategies represented an important movement away from the normative interventionism of Comtean sociology. Such a method would be well suited to the kind of quietest scholarship that Small had earlier decried. Robert Bannister has summed it up well: "Process theory, in stressing how over why, thus marked a step on the road to transactional analysis and political behaviorism. . . . The theory of interests likewise supplied a theoretical basis for the image of university scholars as a class-above-class. . . . In practice, this formulation effectively removed the sociologist from the public arena."[51] It appears that sociologists like Small were beginning to understand their social role differently, as purveyors of abstract, academic knowledge, rather than as participants in the process of social reform. In the interest of "objective" science, Comte's positive priesthood and Ward's scientific legislators had been transformed into

47. Ross, *Origins*, 221.
48. Dorothy Ross, "Liberalism," in *Encyclopedia of American Political History*, ed. Jack P. Greene (New York: Scribner, 1984), 2:757. Comtean thought appears to have helped some reconcile themselves to the concentration of power and social inequality inherent in the emerging economic order.
49. Bannister, *Sociology*, 48–49; Ross, *Origins*, 224–25.
50. Ross, *Origins*, 224–26, 136–37, 237.
51. Bannister, *Sociology*, 49.

ivory-tower academics, too heavenly minded (or "objective") to be any earthly good.

And yet, though Small laid the groundwork in *General Sociology* for a wholesale rejection of the Comtean system, the book also contained examples of Ward's continuing importance for Small and Small's acceptance of assumptions central to Comte. In his analysis of Ward's sociology, for instance, Small praises Ward for breaking with the Spencerian school, stressing that, with the knowledge gained through social science, "we may eventually make human progress a scientific program." Ward had emphasized, Small wrote, "deliberate telic application," and this alone has earned Ward "a secure place" in the discipline. Moreover, Small observed, "it is Comte, to be sure, from whom Ward takes his cue" in this regard. While he characterized Comte's scientific foundation as weak, Small acknowledged that, especially in comparison to Spencer, Comte's contribution had been central and salutary.[52]

Small also took pains to caution that the new weight placed by modern society on the impersonal market and on contract as opposed to status should not lead sociologists to neglect the enduring influence of tradition, of considerations of social status. "If it [social status] should be eliminated in any case," Small warned, "there would at once be confusion and danger, if not anarchy. The social end is not abolition of status, but, first, security of status, and, second, flexibility or exchangeability of status." As Small concluded in more explicitly Comtean language, "Comte, Le Play, Schäffle, De Greff, and indeed, all the modern sociologists, have either expressly or by implication insisted on the function of order in the achievement of progress."[53] By the first decade of the twentieth century, then, Small had begun to attach to his sociology non-Comtean elements (especially components of German *Sozialpolitik*) that undermined his Wardian system. At the same time, however, many of the categories and much of the rhetoric of the Comtean tradition remained.[54]

There was less of this ambivalence in Small's later work, as Small's rejection of Ward, and of the Comtean perspective in general, became

52. AS, *General Sociology* (Chicago: University of Chicago Press, 1905), 84. The preceding quotations are also from this source.

53. Ibid., 607.

54. Becker, *Lost Science*, 49. This ambivalence within Small's thought surfaces again, even more strikingly, in his *Meaning of Social Science* (1910). For example, his interest in Comte's integrative, holistic approach to social science apparently died hard. As he wrote in *Meaning*, social science's "knowledge of human experience cannot at last be many; in the degree in which it approaches reality it must be one knowledge. . . . The thing to be known is one connected whole"(9–10). See also Becker, *Lost Science*, 41–42; Bannister, *Sociology*, 53–54.

Albion Woodbury Small (1854–1926), founder of the
American Journal of Sociology. Small's work laid the
groundwork for a break with the Comtean tradition.

more explicit. Admittedly, Small's eulogy for Ward printed in the *AJS*
in 1913, did seem to reflect Small's earlier, more positive evaluation.
Here, Small declared that Ward's "fame will grow as the years pass,"
and that he "would rather have written *Dynamic Sociology* than any other
book that has ever appeared in America."[55] Yet, only three years later,
Small's assessment of Ward's work had become far more negative. In a
lengthy overview of the emergence of sociology in America for the
Journal, Small recognized Ward's importance but criticized what was
most Comtean in Ward's sociology. "No one," contended Small, "has
approached him [i.e., Ward] in grasp of the relations between cosmic
evolution in general and the evolution of human associatings."[56] This
characteristic of Ward's thought was no longer considered a virtue,

55. AS, "Ward," 67, 77.
56. AS, "Fifty Years of Sociology in the United States, 1865–1915," *American Journal of
Sociology* 21 (1916): 752.

however. Those who came after Ward did not share his encyclopedic vision, but Small now argued that "this contrast with Ward was also greatly to the advantage of his successors"; their work was consequently distinguished by a "comparative openmindedness." In light of Small's early writings, one cannot but be startled by his conclusion: "Not one of them [i.e., Ward's successors] has even yet arrived at an answer as complete in form as Ward's was in the beginning. For myself, I think we have arrived at something better. The human lot is not reducible to as simple formulas as Ward supposed. Discovery and acceptance of this fact are long steps beyond satisfaction with a version of the human lot which makes it simpler than it is."[57] Small continued to note Comte's formative influence upon Ward and celebrated Ward's emphasis upon "psychic forces," but his praise of Ward was now considerably more measured, and much of it sounded simply defensive. "His historical importance does not stand or fall with the validity of his psychology," Small explained. His "exposition [of how human thought directed social development] has never been accepted in detail by sociologists who were scrupulous about their psychology. Because of its central contention, however, it fairly ranks as the foundation of American sociology. It has furnished a basis on which sociology has flourished for a generation in this country."[58] Ward remained for Small an important historical figure in the emergence of American sociology but his grand, synthetic system had become something of an embarrassment.

As Bannister and others have chronicled, the years from American entry into World War I until his death in 1926 were difficult for Small. For personal and professional reasons, German militarism and his own country's crusade against everything German troubled Small deeply. In addition, trends within his department at Chicago seemed to be running against Small's original vision for sociology in the academy. Newer faculty, like Robert Park, appointed in 1914, pursued narrow, monographic studies, concerned with applying a dispassionate, objective, scientific method. As graduate student Edwin Sutherland observed at the time, Small was "certainly losing ground here as a sociologist [vis-à-vis Park] and from the reports of the students, I judge that he is beginning to realize it."[59]

These pressures are evident, once again, in Small's assessment of Ward's significance for contemporary sociology and of the relevance of the Comtean stream in general. Reflecting on the centennial of Comte's

57. Ibid., 753.
58. Ibid., 755–56.
59. Quoted by Bannister, *Sociology*, 61.

first significant publication, Small wrote: "It will be one of the tasks of future historians of sociology to account for the fact that, in spite of Lester F. Ward's long primacy among American sociologists, and in spite of Ward's avowed discipleship of Comte, the sociological movement in the United States did not show credible signs of ability to sustain its life until it was actuated by influences among which the unprompted observer might easily overlook the Comtean factor."[60] Despite Comte's formative influence, then, Small held that academic sociology was only "sustained" by other influences whose impact had proved to be longer-lasting. "When the demand [for a sociological discipline] came," Small reflected, "it was actuated by impulses among which the Comtean tradition was not the most powerful."[61]

Small developed these ideas further in his last book, *Origins of Sociology*, published in 1924. Here, Small's revised view is presented most forcefully. Small opens a chapter that is primarily an examination of German social theory with the following: "The present writer feels bound to emphasize the conviction that Ward improvised an entirely mistaken interpretation of cause and effect when he led Americans to believe that they owe sociology to Comte. This myth, which Ward started into circulation, has ever since been accepted as self-evident truth. . . . The present contention is that the evolutionary process in American sociology actually found little use for Comtean elements, and that the efficient cross-fertilization came from the German tradition." The concerns of contemporary sociologists served to confirm for Small that German political scientists, not Comte nor Ward, anticipated the subject matter and methodology of American academic sociology.[62] "It came about," said Small, "that by 1890 the academic atmosphere of the United States was thick with germs of ideas which came from or through this German tradition" (*Origins*, 328). Small continued to note Ward's debt to Comte but, perhaps as a consequence of his argument, treated Ward now as an exceptional case. He conceded, for example, after focusing upon German influences almost exclusively: "We must specify that Lester F. Ward, whose influence was for a long time the most evident factor in American sociology, avowedly represented the Comtean succession" (329).[63] It was almost as though, in his revised view of sociology, Small needed now to read Ward out of its history. Having virtually removed Ward and "the Comtean succession" from the

60. AS, "Comtean," 512.
61. Ibid., 513.
62. AS, *Origins*, 323.
63. Note, in particular, Small's telling phrase, "always excepting Ward's system," on 335.

mainstream of his discipline, Small was finally free to reject the grand, synthetic vision that had once animated his own sociology. Accordingly, sociology became for Small a neutral, empirical *method* employed by academics to study certain, narrowly defined, social problems. As he put it in *Origins*: "Sociology in the United States has come to be, first and chiefest, one of the numerous independent techniques by means of which research into the facts and the meanings of human experience is now conducted" (334). Small now extolled the new, objective study of "group processes" and suggested tellingly that a good title for the rise of sociology in the previous fifty years would be "Up from Amateurism" (347).

But Small's last book also contained an uncharacteristically candid admission regarding his changed outlook. At one point in the narrative, Small paused to explain one way that Ward's work had been unique. With *Dynamic Sociology*, Small reflected, an obscure Washington bureau- crat had "launched a rounded and complete system of doctrine" that Ward exposited in subsequent work but did not fundamentally alter for the next thirty years (341). Although it did attract its adherents, its strong influence was comparatively brief. Commented Small: "*Dynamic Sociology* affected the few who valued it most highly, and the present writer was of the number, as a pillar of fire. But the currents of the world's thought were already moving so fast that its leadership was bound presently to be overtaken and passed" (342).

When exactly had Ward's system been eclipsed by others? Small was uncertain: "It is impossible to assign a date for this readjustment of sociological values. The present writer had not formed the judgement just expressed at the time of Ward's death (1913), or at least he had not advanced it from his subconsciousness into verbal expression. He has no means of knowing how many of the many American sociologists at that time were aware that the high spots of their thought-world were no longer identical with those of Ward's" (342).[64] Small clearly understood his movement (and that of his discipline) away from Wardian social thought as evidence of a theoretical and methodological maturation. In the end, Small was left with a sociology that contented itself with the "objective" study of social processes and discarded as naive the reformist,

64. Dorothy Ross suggests that several early academic social scientists did not so much discard as sublimate their reformist impulse into this ideal of scientific control through the "objective" observation of social processes (see her treatment of sociologist William F. Ogburn in *Origins*, 394). Perhaps Small's mind also worked this way, but I do not think the sources allow one, in his case, to advance such a psychological interpretation with confidence.

interventionist impulse and the integrative, holistic view of social science that had typified "the Comtean succession" in America.

The case of E. A. Ross (1866–1951) also provides substantive insights into this broader transition within American sociology. As the discipline left the political debates of the 1880s and 1890s behind it, Ross gradually relinquished the reformist, potentially radical position of his mentors, Lester Ward and historical economist Richard T. Ely. But, by discarding the kind of engaged social theory of Comteans like Thaddeus Wakeman and Ward, Ross actually arrived at a conservative posture that shared some of the elitism and emphasis on *controlled* change that had typified the perspectives of Gilded Age Comtists such as David Croly, Henry Edger, and of Comte himself.

Like Ward, Ross was born in the American Midwest, the son of evangelical parents with Republican political loyalties. In fact, the parallels with Ward's early career are striking. Ross attended a pious provincial college, showed an early interest in teaching, and through encountering the writings of Darwin and Spencer, quickly came to reject the religious orthodoxy of his upbringing.[65]

But, because of Ross's relative affluence and changes in American higher education since the Civil War, his graduate studies and subsequent academic career contrast with Ward's experience. After a brief, abortive foray in philosophy at Berlin, Ross enroled in the Ph.D. program in political economy at Johns Hopkins in early 1890. There, Ross was under the tutelage of Richard T. Ely and, having completed a technical study of sinking funds for his dissertation, he received his doctorate in 1891. Ross taught economics and sociology for brief periods at Indiana University and Cornell before accepting a lucrative offer from President David Jordan to join the faculty at recently founded Stanford. Ross's outspoken Populist sympathies, however, soon got him into trouble with Stanford's board of trustees and, especially with the widow of its founder, Jane Lothrop Stanford. Although President Jordan defended Ross at first, he eventually bowed to pressure and dismissed the brash sociologist in 1900.[66] Ross quickly found other employment, teaching at Nebraska for nearly six years and then, in 1906, happily accepting a position at the University of Wisconsin that he held for more than three decades.[67]

65. J. Weinberg, G. J. Hinkle, and R. C. Hinkle, introduction to *Social Control: A Survey of the Foundations of Order,* by Edward Alsworth Ross (Cleveland: Case Western Reserve University Press, 1969 [1901]), x–xiii; Edward Alsworth Ross, *Seventy Years of It: An Autobiography* (New York: Arno, 1977 [1936]), chaps. 2, 3.

66. See full account in Furner, *Advocacy,* 233–59. See also Weinberg et al., Introduction, xv–xvi; EAR, *Seventy Years,* chap. 7.

67. EAR, *Seventy Years,* chaps. 8, 9.

It was during his graduate days at Johns Hopkins that Ross encountered Ward's *Dynamic Sociology* and began a long personal relationship with its author. Intellectually, Ross had been prepared for Ward during his studies in Europe. "I had become a positivist," he later wrote about his philosophical position in 1889, "giving up all attempt to ascertain the cause or 'ground of being' of things."[68] He met Ward at professional meetings in 1890 and drew together "a little band of Wardians" back at Hopkins.[69] In his initial years as a college professor, Ross's sociology was definitely within the Comtean stream. Ross later described his first classes at Stanford thus: "I offered 'Statical Sociology' based on Spencer and 'Dynamic Sociology' based on Comte and Ward. In these courses what we did was first to read two volumes of Spencer's *Principles* and then to read the two volumes of Ward's *Dynamic Sociology*. My job was to stress, interpret and organize."[70] Ross also appears at this time to have understood his own personal, philosophical journey in Comtean terms. Writing to Ward in 1891 he commented: "I find as you suggest, the escape from religion and theological problems a great saving of time and effort. I am now so free from theology that I do not even feel resentment toward it. . . . I am through the *anti-theological* period as well as the *theological* period and can study the old system with as much calmness and interest as if I were examining a Devonian fossil."[71]

The Comtean premises of Ross's early sociology are apparent in his most famous contribution to the discipline, *Social Control*, published in 1901. Much of *Social Control* had, in fact, appeared in preliminary form in several articles in Small's *American Journal of Sociology*. In both the articles and subsequent book, Ross's analysis clearly owed much to Comtean social thought, especially as developed by Ward. In effect, his examination of how social control functioned in human society represented a new way to reconcile the competing claims of order and progress. Ross was chiefly worried that the potentially anarchic individual would undermine the kind of social order without which there could be no authentic social progress. "In an aggressive race," Ross observed, "order is perpetually endangered by the unruliness of the individual, and can be maintained only through the unremitting operation of certain

68. Ibid., 32.
69. Quoted by Robert Bierstedt in *American Sociological Theory: A Critical History* (New York: Academic Press, 1981), 133.
70. MS letter, EAR to L. L. Bernard, in L. L. Bernard Papers at the Pennsylvania State University. In the same letter, Ross referred to "the tremendous stimulus [I] received from Ward."
71. EAR to Lester F. Ward, *American Sociological Review* 3 (1938): 365. Emphasis in original.

social forces."[72] Developing a racial theory not found in Comte (but not entirely absent from Ward's writings), Ross sought to explain how a people as individualistic and nondeferrential as northern Europeans could have attained any degree of social harmony or cohesion.[73] Part of the explanation for Ross lay in human nature. Some aspects of human nature were constant, independent of social influence and one needed to understand these (and how they produced social control), before examining external, social factors (viii).[74] In his discussion of human nature, Ross therefore identified sympathy, sociability, and the senses of justice and resentment as foundational (6). Sympathy, argued Ross, knitted together the family and promoted harmony in society. Moreover, Ross echoed Comte's language in treating sympathy as synonymous with "the services of spontaneous altruism" (11). But such social altruism, although essential, was not a sufficient base upon which to build a society, especially an advanced, industrial society, like fin de siècle America. Ross explained: "A differentiating society produces and consecrates stupendous inequalities of condition; so that, did it trust itself to spontaneous feelings apart from law and morality, it would be ground to powder between compassion and envy, as between the upper and nether millstones. It is obedience that articulates the solid, bony framework of social order; sympathy is but the connective tissue" (12).

Perhaps the most demonstrably Wardian (and, indirectly, Comtean) part of Ross's analysis is his understanding of social order (or human civilization) as an artificial product of human "telesis." The kind of order evident in modern societies could only be the manipulated creation of intellect. Ross contended that "the essence of the process [of social development] consists in the replacement of instinct by reason. . . . The great social expansions have occurred, not in the most gregarious varie-

72. EAR, *Social Control: A Survey of the Foundations of Order*, ed. J. Weinberg, G. J. Hinkle, and R. C. Hinkle (Cleveland: Case Western Reserve University Press, 1969 [1901]), 3. Subsequent page references in text are, unless otherwise indicated, from this work.

73. Ross had long been more concerned than the egalitarian Ward about social order and the disruptive effect of the headstrong individual. In a letter to Ward penned in 1892, Ross admitted that his "philosophy [was] diverging from yours [i.e., Ward's] at one important point." Ward had argued that progress was due solely to "the better utilization of the forces and materials of nature." Such improved "utilization" could be achieved through education, Ward's "Great Panacea." But Ross asserted that "there is another great source of progress in [social] happiness, viz., illumination [elimination?] of internal friction, wrong, struggle, war, and evil, etc. . . . Should there not, then, along with developing intelligence to give us command over natural and social forces, go increasingly a developing sympathy to prevent the (socially) costly pursuit of individual gain?" (EAR to Lester F. Ward, *American Sociological Review* 3 [1938]: 368). In one sense, this brings Ross closer to Comte and the latter's concern for the corporate welfare.

74. See also Bierstedt, *American Sociological Theory*, 139.

ties of mankind, but in those races that have sense enough to perceive
the advantages of association, and wit enough to construct a good social
framework" (17).[75] There is, Ross believed, a "collective mind" that
envisages and secures social order and thus directs social progress. "The
thesis of this book is that from the interactions of individuals and
generations there emerges a kind of collective mind evincing itself in
living ideals, conventions, dogmas, institutions, and religious sentiments
which are more or less happily adapted to the task of safeguarding the
collective welfare from the ravages of egoism" (293).

Ross therefore adopted a variant of Comte's "holy humanity" as part
of his social vision and, with it, much of Comte's paternalism and
elitism. "This public," Ross commented revealingly, "composed of
living and dead is, if you will, a despot, but still a paternal, benevolent
despot" (293). Ross was well aware of the threat to individual rights that
society represented and, like many of his fellow Progressives, he stressed
that those who administered the social state had to be representative of
the mass. "The more distinct," he cautioned, "those who apply social
pressure from those who must bear it, the more likely is regulation to
be laid on more lavishly in obedience to some [narrow] class ideal,"
rather than out of concern for the commonweal (84). Ross settled, then,
for the pluralist avenue chosen by many liberals at the turn of the
century; expert elites should administer the state but they must be
representative of the majority. Yet Ross could not escape the odor of
elitism that easily. "Society can dispense with the guidance of the elite
and the genius," he wrote, "only when the way is straight and the path
is clear. A people creeping gradually across a vast and empty land, as we
Americans have been doing this century, may safely belittle leadership
and deify the spirit of self-reliance. But when population thickens,
interests clash, and the difficult problems of mutual adjustment become
pressing, it is foolish and dangerous not to follow the lead of superior
men" (83–84).[76] Ross left little doubt in *Social Control* (and in his earlier
writings during the 1890s) that he believed the United States had reached
such a point of crisis. Natural order no longer prevailed in American

75. Weinberg et al. put it this way: "He [Ross] was well aware that progress was in
conflict with order. He would not, however, halt the march of progress. As a disciple of
Lester Ward, the first of the American sociologists to denounce the determinism of Spencer
and Sumner, Ross proposed precise measures to minimize human unhappiness and social
disorganization. *Social Control* may best be understood as the response of a melioristic
sociologist to Sumner's essay on 'The Absurd Effort to Make the World Over.' Along
with Ward, Ross would supplant blind, wasteful, and irrational social change with social
measures intended to make the evolution of society purposive, constructive, and intelligent." See Weinberg et al., Introduction, xxxviii.

76. Ibid., 83–84. Also quoted by Bierstedt, *American Sociological Theory*, 147.

society as it once had and planned intervention was now required if anarchy was to be avoided.[77]

Furthermore, Ross's acute concern for order and control also prompted him to value highly the kind of *internal* control afforded by organized religion. Again, Ross's priorities and even his language echoed Comtean conservatives of the Gilded Age. Although Ross gently criticized Comte's blueprint, his conclusion was identical to that of an Edger or a David Croly: "The best guarantee of a stable control from within is something that reaches at once feeling, reason, and will. To be widely effective for righteousness a religion should strike the chord of feeling, but not so exclusively as Quakerism, or Shinto, or Neo-Catholicism, or the Religion of Humanity, or the Salvationists. . . . A social religion succeeds best when it strikes all these chords, and the limited habitat of certain sects is undoubtedly due to a narrowness of appeal that restricts them to certain temperaments of certain social layers" (429–30). Such had, of course, been the original purpose of the Comtean system, which had been designed to appeal to the total person in a way that unscientific faith and atheistic science could not.[78]

Although, like Small's, Ross's later work clearly diverged from Ward's perspective, the imprint of Comtism is still very evident in his 1905 text, *Foundations of Sociology*. Though Ross eschewed Ward's view of sociology as grand synthesis, the language he used in *Foundations* still betrayed a belief in the preeminence of the "Queen of the Sciences." "The relation of the trunk of a tree to its branches is, I believe, a fit symbol of the relation of Sociology to the special social sciences." Though Ross conceded that some branches also had independent roots, others, he alleged, did not and these "having no source of life other than the main trunk, must be termed departments of special sociology."[79] In addition, Ross spoke of "social forces" in terms very similar to Ward, especially in the stress he placed upon what both sociologists called the "psychic factors." "Undoubtedly

77. Weinberg et al., Introduction, xix.

78. Both Ward and Small had high praise for *Social Control* when it appeared. Small wrote in the *AJS* that the book could only become obsolete "through the passing of our present Zeitgeist." Quoted by Weinberg et al., Introduction, xxxv. See also *American Journal of Sociology* 9 (1903/1904): 578.

79. EAR, *Foundations of Sociology* (New York: MacMillan, 1905), 27–28. Also quoted by Bierstedt, *American Sociological Theory*, 159. Ross had certainly subscribed to the Comtean view earlier in his career. As he wrote to Ward in 1892 about a course he hoped to offer at Cornell: "If I realize my plans, I will put up a course on Theoretical Sociology next year that will be an eye-opener. Sociology is the queen of the sciences, and a one hour a week course of lectures on it will draw a big audience" (*American Sociological Review* 3 [1938]: 375).

E. A. Ross (1866–1951). Ross relinquished the
reformism of his mentors, Lester Ward and Richard
T. Ely, but his concern for order and control echoed
Gilded Age Comtean conservatives.

men's choices are conditioned," Ross observed, "and their projects
limited by the physical framework they live in. . . . Still, since the
external facts are foreseen and taken into account in intelligent telic
action, it is necessary to regard social phenomena as essentially
psychic, and to look for their immediate causes in mind" (152).[80]

But, as in the case of Small, the seeds of a different kind of sociology
(the sort that would come to dominate the discipline in the twentieth
century) were also apparent in Ross's early work. In *Foundations*, Ross
broke with Ward's characteristic emphasis upon the evolution of human
institutions (what Ward termed "achievement") as the proper object of
sociological study. Instead, Ross paralleled Small's increasing emphasis

80. Quoted by Bierstedt who notes Ward's influence here. See *American Sociological
Theory*, 163–64. The following two quotations are also cited by Bierstedt, 158, 165.

upon process, and stressed that sociology should focus upon objective "social phenomena." To do so, sociologists needed to flee from normative judgements. "Sociology," Ross declared, "does not venture beyond the causes and laws of the phenomena it considers" (17). Moreover, while Ross accepted Ward's bifurcation of the discipline into social statics and social dynamics, he argued that sociologists must examine social change from a purely "objective" perspective and discard the loaded notion of "progress" which implied subjective judgment (185–89). Finally, Ross's predictions regarding the future of the discipline underlined his own movement toward an "objective" social science of the kind championed by behaviorism. As Ross commented revealingly in *Foundations*: "The statistical method, which enables us to measure social phenomena exactly and to substitute quantitative truths for qualitative, constitutes an instrument of precision, which certainly is destined to be applied to sociological problems in ways yet undreamed of" (81).[81] The ethical science of man was, in short, becoming for Ross the dispassionate academic discipline of the behaviorists.[82]

Understanding E. A. Ross as part of an American Comtean succession serves, then, to highlight how Ross came to reject the potentially radical, interventionist position of Ward, while accepting a more conservative attitude toward the social and economic order. Of course, in the United States, conservatism meant seeking to conserve *liberal* capitalist economic structures, rather than resuscitate some traditional system. But then Comte himself had never been a simple reactionary; he had always championed a "prospective conservatism." Ross's path to such a position was different from that followed earlier by David Croly or Courtlandt Palmer but he, too, came to accept the prevailing relations of production under American capitalism as a given and acquiesced in the high degree of inequality produced by such a system. As Dorothy Ross succinctly puts it, "Ross's *Social Control* was an argument for a new liberalism. It accepted as inevitable

81. See also Bierstedt, *American Sociological Theory*, 168 n. 119.

82. Gisela and Roscoe Hinkle have observed (correctly, I think) that "after World War I, the conception of social control diverged substantially from Ross's views in some instances and became unqualifiedly and unapologetically instrumentalist and objectivist (i.e., behaviorist)" (see Weinberg et al., Introduction, xlviii). I am simply making the modest point here that there were "objectivist" seeds in Ross's work as early as *Social Control*.

Though Comte rejected introspective psychology, it would be wrong to characterize his position as protobehaviorist. Comte dismissed psychology because, in his day at least, it was insufficiently grounded on empirical science and thus smacked of metaphysics; he certainly did not eschew moral judgments in his sociology nor rule out the idea of progress. Later, Ward tried to place his discussion of the "psychic factors" upon a solidly empirical foundation, even tinkering briefly with the pseudoscience of phrenology.

the inequality and conflict generated by capitalism, and sought to counter them with an enlarged vision of social control."[83] Thus, while E. A. Ross broke with the revisionist Comtism of Wakeman and Ward, he retained some of the conservatism and emphasis upon elite control characteristic of Comte and his first American disciples.

There were certainly other forces at work in this important shift within American social science and within American liberalism in general. In graduate school, Ross had been profoundly influenced by marginalist economics, its quantitative methodology, and its implicit acceptance of economic disparity. And Ross was always enough of a liberal individualist to worry about how the collective could overwhelm the independent individual. But a social and economic conservatism did prevail in the new liberalism of Ross and others. Ross's focus on social control contributed to a growing commitment within his discipline to the dispassionate study of "social process," isolated from anything that smacked of ideological concerns.[84]

Thus, both Ross and Small came to believe that "the direction of industrial society was toward liberal harmony: an increasingly peaceable, rational, and ethical adjustment of interests."[85] A "liberal harmony" perhaps, but a harmony that bore a not incidental resemblance to the rigid, hierarchical harmony of the New York Comtists and of Comte himself. "Social control," to again quote Dorothy Ross, "expressed . . . [the] professional ambitions [of Small, Ross, and others], ambitions that already showed signs of moving in the direction of a technocratic science of prediction and control." Like Comte, and some of his early American followers who sought to create a kind of positive priesthood, Small and Ross envisaged a benign bureaucracy administered by a class of experts, probably themselves.[86]

Of course, as Comte had understood, such elite management carried with it awesome responsibilities. And, despite previous paeans to scientific objectivity, Ross appeared to understand that the new technocratic priesthood could not avoid normative judgments entirely. "The secret of [social] order," E. A. Ross reflected revealingly in the final pages of Social Control, "is not to be bawled from every housetop. The wise sociologist will show religion a consideration it has barely met with from the naturalist. He will venerate a moral system too much to uncover its nakedness. . . . He will address himself to those who

83. Ross, Origins, 233.
84. Ibid., 236–37.
85. Ibid., 254.
86. "Imagining themselves at the controls, they imagined a wholly beneficent exercise of social control" (Ross, Origins, 254). The preceding quotations are also from this source.

administer the moral capital of society—to teachers, clergymen, editors, law-makers, and judges, who wield the instruments of control. . . . In this way he will make himself an accomplice of all good men for the undoing of all bad men."[87]

87. EAR, *Social Control*, 441. One of the few American sociologists in the twentieth century whose theory and method remained explicitly Comtean was Dartmouth's McQuilkin DeGrange (1880–1953). After receiving his M.A. at Columbia, DeGrange earned his doctorate in France and much of his subsequent work represented a (largely unsuccessful) attempt to rehabilitate Comte among his American colleagues. See, especially *The Curve of Societal Movement* (Hanover, N.H.: Sociological Press, 1930) and *The Nature and Elements of Sociology* (New Haven: Yale University Press, 1953). A reviewer in the *American Journal of Sociology* described the latter volume as "Neo-Comtean" (see *AJS* 59 [1953–1954]: 593).

CHAPTER SEVEN

Herbert Croly

Positivist Progressive

While I was at college I was surrounded by other influences, and while retaining everything that was positive and constructive in his [i.e., David Croly's] teaching, I dropped the negative cloth in which it was shrouded . . . his disappointment must have been all the more severe because he exaggerated the differences that existed between us. It was his opinion that his negative opinions were necessarily connected with those which were positive; and that it was impossible truly to hold the one without the other.

—Herbert D. Croly, 1889

HERBERT CROLY HAS SUFFERED at the hands of intellectual historians a fate in some respects similar to that which befell his predecessor Lester Ward. Until recently, Croly lacked a biographer and, though he figures in many studies of the Progressive Era, there are precious few systematic analyses of his political theory. With the notable exception of David Levy's more recent study, most works dealing with Croly's thought invariably mention the influence of his parents' Comtism but fail to explore this key dimension at any length. Indeed, nearly all historians downplay the long-term influence of orthodox positivism upon Croly, contending that it had only a vague and amorphous legacy.[1]

1. See, for example Charles Forcey, *The Crossroads of Liberalism: Croly, Weyl, Lippman, and the Progressive Era, 1900–1925* (New York: Oxford University Press, 1961), 16; Henry F. May, *End of American Innocence: A Study of the First Years of our Own Time, 1912–1917*

By contrast, my discussion concentrates upon Croly's Comtism as perhaps the best way to understand his often difficult work. Moreover, I argue that it was through Ward and Croly that American Progressivism was able to draw directly upon Comtean social thought. By way of these two seminal social theorists, the transformation of American liberalism received its most significant Comtean contribution. Nor did the systems constructed by Ward and Croly only demonstrate, in Hartz's phrase, "a pathetic clinging to 'Americanism.' "[2] Although often hobbled by tensions, the work of these two thinkers represented, rather, a creative attempt to apply Comtean insights to uniquely American circumstances. The end product was a sometimes contradictory blend that has continued to typify American liberalism in the decades since the First World War.

I

Herbert Croly was born into a remarkable family. His mother, Jane Cunningham Croly ("Jennie June") was a prominent feminist journalist and frequently referred to as the first American newspaper woman. The daughter of an English clergyman, she came as a young girl to the United States. Jane married Herbert's father, David Goodman Croly, in 1857 and eventually became the mother of five children while continuing her career in journalism. In fact, the combination of newspaper work and a demanding social life may have meant that young Herbert enjoyed little of his mother's attention. Such a conclusion seems corroborated by Herbert Croly's failure to make any mention of his mother in the first

---

(New York: Knopf, 1959), 317; David W. Noble, *The Paradox of Progressive Thought* (Minneapolis: University of Minnesota Press, 1958), 56; Arthur Schlesinger, Jr., has gone so far as to assert that "it is neither possible nor especially profitable to try and identify particular influences" upon Croly. See his Introduction in Herbert Croly, *The Promise of American Life* (Cambridge: Belknap Press, Harvard University Press, 1965), xii; John Chamberlain, *Farewell to Reform: The Rise, Life and Decay of the Progressive Mind in America* (New York: John Day, 1933), 222–27; David W. Levy, *Herbert Croly of the New Republic: The Life and Thought of An American Progressive* (Princeton: Princeton University Press, 1985). Chamberlain was one of the few (before Levy) to recognize the significance of Comtean thought for Croly. (See *Farewell*, 224–25.) Though Levy recognizes the importance of Comte, he views the latter's thought as an anomaly and not as part of a larger American Comtean tradition with strong affinities to nineteenth-century American culture.

2. Louis Hartz, *The Liberal Tradition in America: An Interpretation of American Political Thought Since the Revolution* (New York: Harcourt, Brace and World, 1955), 233. Hartz here characterizes Croly's rhetoric as "practically unintelligible."

chapter of his unfinished autobiography.[3] Nonetheless, her reformism and genteel feminism apparently had some impact upon the young Croly. On the other hand, the influence of David Croly on his son was undeniably profound. The elder Croly was a New York newspaperman of Irish extraction who became a leader of the city's positivist circle in the 1860s and 1870s. Together, Herbert's parents "turned their home," in Eric Goldman's phrase, "into the country's best-known salon on Positivism."[4] Though neither the first nor probably the last American child to receive the distinction, Herbert was baptized into the orthodox Comtean faith. Sounding still rather embarrassed by his parents' exuberant sectarianism, Croly reflected later in life that his baptism "may not be an important educational birthmark, but ill-favored as it is, it is unmistakably mine own."[5]

David Croly, too, may well have neglected his son's upbringing until his resignation as editor of the *New York Daily Graphic* in 1878, when his son was nine years old. From that point up to his death in 1889, the elder Croly lavished attention upon his son. His primary concern seems to have been to encourage young Herbert's thinking along certain moral and philosophical lines. As an adult, Herbert Croly attributed his interest in the world of ideas to his father's attention. "He was himself a running brook of ideas," Croly remembered, "on every subject in which a citizen of the world ought to be interested, and he literally poured a part of this flood into my little mental receptacles without noticing or caring how much of it overflowed." In his "Memoirs," Croly recalled the lofty tone of his father's didactic monologues; "words such as humanity, progress, social aspiration and the like" impressed Croly as a boy and their power "endured" as he matured. "Unless I am very much mistaken," he observed, "my regular immersion in this shower of humanitarian ideas and aspirations was the most important single influence in my education" (319).

But the young Croly did not come away with only a vague recollection of idealistic rhetoric. "My father's preaching," he noted, "was not only assiduous and ardent; it was after a fashion coherent." As recorded in Croly's "Memoirs," Croly's father "pro-claimed allegiance to Auguste Comte and his religion of humanity." Herbert remembered his father's

3. Charles Hirschfeld, ed., "The Memoirs of Herbert Croly: An Unpublished Document," *New York History* 58 (July 1977), 315; Forcey, *Crossroads*, 13; see also Levy, *Herbert Croly*, 1–11.

4. Eric F. Goldman, *Rendez-Vous With Destiny: A History of Modern American Reform* (New York: Knopf, 1963), 191. Hirschfeld concludes that David Croly's influence upon his son was "pervasive and enduring" ("Memoir," 315).

5. Croly in Hirschfeld, ed., "Memoirs," 320. See also Levy, *Herbert Croly*, 11–18.

Comtism as "a philosophy which was also a religion" (320). It seemed to him that

> Comte was trying, like so many other thinkers of the early nineteenth century, to envisage the conversion of scientific truth into steady progress in the arts of secular life, but unlike his contemporaries, he considered that the new liberated society no less than the old would need authoritative religious conviction and guidance. . . . In spite of the crochets and pedantry of its founder, it [Comtism] deliberately renounced the chief weakness of liberalism, which was precisely its lack of positivism. (321)

Thus, far from being a sterile or corrosive rationalism, Comtean positivism for Herbert Croly represented an ambitious, though not entirely successful effort to grapple with the great scientific and religious questions the nineteenth century had posed. In his "Memoirs," he described his father as having all the "ardor and elan of a religious convert"; he convinced Herbert "of the impossibility of carrying on the work of human emancipation without a religious clue and a religious fortification" (322).

The positivism of his father did not, therefore, leave Herbert Croly with a closed scientific determinism, as indoctrination in Spencerian positivism might have done. David Croly's Comtism exhibited a robust faith in man as an active agent, using positive science to improve his environment. Croly wrote that he emerged from his father's tutelage with a strong sense of the central role of ideas in human development and with a conviction that individuals were able to save themselves. The young Croly concluded "that ideation was constructive" and "human beings were . . . masters of their own destiny" ("Memoirs," 320, 322). Like Ward before him, Croly found a melioristic voluntarism in Comte that differed from much of the scientistic determinism of his age. As he phrased it, social betterment "could be effected only by effort, propagated conviction and the expert use of every available instrument." This set of assumptions, in a distinctively Comtean blend, constituted, said Croly, "the point of departure of my own future work" ("Memoirs," 322–23).

Such an upbringing also formed a peculiar personality, however. Croly always found interaction with others, especially with strangers, extremely difficult. Acquaintances often remarked at his cold, awkward, and nervous manner in casual conversation. In part because of this painful shyness, he had few intimate friends and spent long periods in isolation. Then there was his intense relationship with his father, which continued almost without abatement until the latter's death in 1889. Croly often seemed to exist in a detached world of ideas, a world dominated by his father's teachings.[6]

In 1886, the seventeen-year-old Croly enrolled in Harvard University as a freshman. Croly attended classes at Harvard off and on for the following eleven years. In fact, he did not receive his bachelor's degree until 1910 when the college awarded him a degree for *The Promise of American Life*. Though his studies were frequently interrupted, Harvard had a profound influence upon the young New Yorker. By the 1880s, the college was well advanced along the path of change begun by President Charles W. Eliot. Assuming the presidency in 1869, Eliot had enlarged the faculty severalfold by the time he retired in 1909. Eliot's vision for Harvard was a prestigious university that would turn out young leaders with a strong sense of civic duty and a solid scientific background. The president did not understand science as an abstract esoteric discipline; rather, he wanted Harvard, in the words of historian Bruce Kuklick, "to be 'scientific' in the sense of welding theory and practice."[7] Hence, Croly found an altruistic elitism and practical scientism at Harvard that was quite congenial with the "Positive Priesthood" cherished by his father. One of President Eliot's most celebrated reforms, the introduction of the elective system, allowed Croly the freedom to pursue single-mindedly the fascination with ideas that his father had instilled in him. With greater specialization, more advanced courses could be offered and Croly enrolled in some of the college's most demanding philosophy offerings. Indeed, Croly concentrated in philosophy, with fully half of his twenty-six courses taken between 1886 and 1897 being in either philosophy or religion. Eliot had helped to transform philosophy at Harvard by the 1880s. He drew the philosophy department away from Francis Bowen and Unitarian orthodoxy to a more speculative and experimental position. William James was hired in 1873 and in 1877 was moved to the philosophy department to teach a new course now called "Psychology." Five years later, James persuaded Eliot to hire a young idealist, Josiah Royce. At about the time Croly arrived as a freshman, George Santayana was working to complete a Harvard doctorate in philosophy and was appointed an instructor in 1889.[8] The triumvirate of James, Royce, and Santayana dominated Harvard philosophy in the 1880s and 1890s. All three had been steeped

6. Forcey, *Crossroads*, 6–8.

7. Bruce Kuklick, *The Rise of American Philosophy, 1860–1930* (Cambridge: Harvard University Press, 1977), 131.

8. Ibid., 134–35, 253; Forcey, *Crossroads*, 18.

in German idealism and sought to apply its insights to the study of the individual psyche. As Kuklick observes, this broad "idealistic consensus and the interest in psychology molded" the department.[9] Though critical differences developed among them, particularly between James and Royce, the Harvard philosophers accepted key features of neo-Kantian idealism as a way to resolve the conflict between religion and science that had dominated the 1860s and 1870s. James came to articulate what he described as a "pragmatic-economical interpretation of science," which argued that by employing strictly empirical observation, "the human mind . . . could not pretend to a knowledge of the ultimate nature of reality; that, on the contrary, it was only an instrument which selectively ordered its experience according to its own interest in simplicity, coherence, and predictability."[10] Comte had not constructed his attempted reconciliation of faith and empirical science upon such idealist foundations and, as Herbert's father quickly recognized, the Harvard approach ran counter to the Comtean position.

During the last quarter of the nineteenth century, the narrow positivist conception of the scientific method as entailing only empirical observation was being challenged. Not only Comte but Mill and other positivists were being attacked and their traditional empiricism was increasingly criticized as too restrictive. New emphasis was now placed upon what Mandelbaum has called, "the creative, constructive aspects of scientific imagination in the formulation of hypotheses and intellectual models."[11] Comte had, of course, profoundly distrusted the use of grand hypotheses in scientific research since, for him, they smacked too much of theological or metaphysical speculation. Comte had characterized as "vain . . . any research into what are called Causes, whether first or final."[12] Ward, as noted above, had softened this unbending inductive empiricism of Comte somewhat. Yet, by the 1880s, Europeans such as Ernst Mach and especially Heinrich Hertz and Henri Poincaré, as well as Americans such as James, were already moving far beyond Ward's limited criticism. These philosophers were laying new stress upon the active, organizing role of the individual mind. They now saw science as limited in its method, restricted to "selectively ordering experiences in such a way that further experiences could be predicted." For Comtists, this new approach seemed to open the door to metaphysics because it viewed

9. Kuklick, *Rise*, 138.

10. Maurice Mandelbaum, *History, Man and Reason: A Study in Nineteenth-Century Thought* (Baltimore: Johns Hopkins University Press, 1971), 19.

11. Ibid.

12. Auguste Comte, *The Positive Philosophy of Auguste Comte*, trans. Harriet Martineau (New York: Blanchard, 1855), 28.

the human mind only as "an instrument which selectively ordered experience"; science "could [thus] not pretend to a knowledge of the ultimate nature of reality." Yet that is precisely what positivists such as Wakeman and Ward claimed for science.[13]

Linked to this new emphasis upon the independent and innovative role of the individual mind was a new openness on the part of James and others to accept sources of knowledge beyond empirical science, such as individual intuition or emotion. A neo-Kantian revival of the sort that underlay the rise of the Harvard philosophy department during the 1880s and 1890s would alarm an orthodox Comtist and be a source of some distress even for a more independent positivist such as Ward. Mandelbaum summarizes these developments this way: "at the end of the nineteenth century . . . the earlier systematic form of positivism had to all intents and purposes lost its hold upon the major streams of thought. What had once seemed to be the philosophic import of the physical sciences no longer carried the same conviction."[14]

David Croly became alarmed as early as October of Herbert's first year at Harvard. Responding to Herbert's observation about "the divergence between" his father's Comtism and the philosophical works being studied, David Croly encouraged his son "to form your own judgement on all the higher themes." Yet this advice was a little disingenuous, followed as it was by a lengthy list of recommended reading dominated by Comte's works and those of his more loyal English disciples. Although he admonished his son with the scriptural injunction, "prove all things and hold fast to that which is good," David Croly clearly hoped that the philosophical idealism of the Harvard department would be tested by the Comtean canon and found deficient.[15]

Later letters contained such cautions as "beware of metaphysics," avoid "antiquated theological arguments," and "life is too short to master the unfruitful thinkers such as Hegel and the lesser lights."[16] It seemed to the elder Croly that he was fighting a losing battle. When David Croly died in 1889, he despaired that he had lost his son to an outmoded Germanic idealism. Herbert himself admitted, in fact, that "for the moment" he had "abandoned . . . the phenomenalism [empiricism?] of my positivist inheritance" and even became "a warm adherent to Hegelianism." By his own admission, he had been most influenced at college by Josiah Royce, and, in exploring Royce's brand of idealism, he said he had "revolted against his [father's] instructions."[17]

13. Mandelbaum, *History, Man*, 19.
14. Ibid., 20.
15. *Memories of Jane Cunningham Croly—"Jenny June"* (New York: Putnam, 1904), 64–65.
16. Levy, *Herbert Croly*, 58, 64, 59.
17. HDC in Hirschfeld, ed., "Memoir," 324.

It would be easy to overdraw the threat that Harvard philosophy posed to Herbert Croly's Comtean indoctrination.[18] Croly himself conceded that "before long [I] cease[d] to find my own revolt [against positivism] entirely convincing." "As a matter of fact," he observed, "I soon abandoned Hegelianism." Croly described his return to a philosophical position closer to that of his father's as altogether "natural."[19] Indeed, he lamented soon after his father's death that it was unfortunate that the elder Croly, "exaggerated the differences that existed between us."[20] Moreover, significant features of James's pragmatism and of Royce's idealism were completely consistent with Comtean positivism. Like Ward and several of Comte's later students, James came to be a thorough-going critic of Spencer and of his monolithic system. James's chief objection to Spencer arose, as did Ward's critique, from the way in which the Englishman's philosophy appeared to deny that independent human effort could effect significant change. Spencerian naturalistic determinism seemed to rule out self-conscious improvement altogether.[21] The interventionist impulse in both James and Ward was, in fact, derived (though in rather different ways) from Kant. James's "rebellion against all 'block-universe' philosophies" had been anticipated to some degree by Comte, if not by Wakeman and Ward. Comte had not always been consistent in this regard and there were undoubtedly monistic germs in the master's systematic approach. But a loyal son of David Croly (and, by extension, of Auguste Comte) would probably have found James's emphasis upon human effort and his consistent empiricism quite appealing. The philosophy of Josiah Royce, though opposed to Jamesian pragmatism, also shared a positivist's "respect for empirical evidence."[22]

A more important common theme in the work of James and Royce was that of personal religious faith. Here again, the attitudes of the two

18. According to Schlesinger, for instance, Croly's "Positivism as an ideological commitment quickly evaporated upon exposure to Harvard yard" (Introduction, vii). David Noble similarly describes the young Croly "rejecting Comte's technical social philosophy" during his university days (*Paradox*, 56). Even David Levy concludes that Herbert's father's "Religion of Humanity was plainly defeated at Harvard" (*Croly*, 67). Herbert certainly discarded the cultic or sectarian elements of Comtism but then there is evidence that his father may also have done so by the mid-1880s. As I hope to show in this chapter, Herbert Croly continued to cling to several key features of the Religion of Humanity.

19. HDC in Hirschfeld, ed., "Memoirs," 324. Even Levy seems to overdraw Croly's rebellion somewhat (see Levy, *Herbert Croly*, 67).

20. *Real Estate Record and Builder's Guide* 20 (4 May 1889): 7.

21. Mandelbaum, *History, Man*, 400–401.

22. Levy, *Herbert Croly*, 67. See also Leszek Kolakowski, *The Alienation of Reason: A History of Positivist Thought*, trans. Norman Guterman (Garden City, N.Y.: Doubleday, 1968), 101.

Harvard philosophers were in some ways closer to Comte's original intent than were the views of emphatic secularists like Wakeman or Ward. Although James and Royce were theists of a sort, like their French predecessor, they both recognized the importance of religious forms and greatly admired men of faith in history. "Religion," declared James, "is the greatest interest of my life."[23] This religious theme was even more central to the philosophy of Josiah Royce, who recalled that it was religious questions that initially "drove the author to philosophy."[24] As for David Croly, he seems to have preserved the Comtean stress upon religious conviction and the benefits of religious forms. Herbert Croly testified in his unfinished memoir to this characteristic of his father. David Croly, observed his son, was endowed "not with religious scepticism and nihilism but with a genuinely religious aspiration and faith. . . . He communicated to me a sense of the importance of religion, of its necessary association with a valid body of knowledge."[25] The elder Croly thus wrote to his freshman son: "Do cultivate all the religious emotions, reverence, awe and aspiration. . . . Go to Catholic and Episcopal churches and surrender yourself to the inspiration of soul-inspiring religious music."[26] What alarmed his father most, therefore, in the teaching of James and Royce was not their acceptance of the validity of religious experience but, rather, their theistic assumptions and their arguments that religious faith could be built upon a foundation that transcended empirical science. Herbert Croly implied that his father's concerns arose at this point when he later commented that he had torn back at college "the negative cloth in which it [his father's philosophy] was shrouded."[27] Religious emotion was one thing, metaphysical arguments were quite another.

Still, the young Croly's exposure to the Pragmatism and Idealism of the Harvard department need not have done permanent damage to his Comtean outlook: part of what Croly was taught very much complemented his father's teachings. The philosophy courses Croly took at Harvard by no means extinguished his Comtism; once his youthful rebellion against his father's creed evaporated, Croly returned to a position very close to that of his father.

The Harvard economists were, however, clearly opposed to the state

23. Paul F. Boller, Jr., *American Thought in Transition: The Impact of Evolutionary Naturalism, 1865–1900* (Chicago: Rand McNally, 1969), 141.

24. Ralph Barton Perry, "Josiah Royce," *Dictionary of American Biography* (New York: Scribner, 1934), 8:208.

25. HDC in Hirschfeld, ed., "Memoirs," 322.

26. *Memories of Jane Cunningham Croly*, 65.

27. Supplement to *Real Estate Record and Builder's Guide*, 7.

interventionism and organicism of the Comtists. Perhaps because of this clear opposition, Harvard political economy seems to have had a much less significant and lasting impact upon Croly than did James, Royce, and Santayana. David Croly certainly had every reason to be concerned by the teaching of Charles F. Dunbar, J. Laurence Laughlin, Francis G. Peabody, and Frank W. Taussig.[28] The elder Croly quickly recognized their classical, laissez-faire assumptions. "The theories that prevail there [i.e., at Harvard]," David Croly wrote to his son, "are, I apprehend, a quarter of a century behind the age." Herbert's father took pains to counter the negative-state philosophy of the Harvard professors. As he explained in one letter: "The tendency all over the civilized world is for the great corporation of the nation to do what has so far been relegated to the irresponsible corporations."[29] He also took care to counter the biological arguments of social Darwinism. In sentences that are practically paraphrases of Ward's arguments, David Croly explained to his son that "to properly serve man, the brutal and blind forces of Nature must be manipulated." In one letter, David begged Herbert "to read what Comte says of it [i.e., English political economy] in Miss Martineau's translation of his philosophy."[30] David Croly's concerns were certainly well founded but he would probably have been put at ease if he had lived to read Herbert's mature writings on social and economic subjects. Herbert's later divergence from classical political economy is quite clear, as is his continued loyalty to Comtean ideals as interpreted by his father.

In sum, Croly emerged from Harvard with a reformed and eclectic sort of positivism. The lengthy and emotional correspondence with his father and his prolonged and unfinished studies suggest that these were difficult years for Croly. He struggled earnestly with what he encountered, and perhaps for a time the outcome was uncertain. Much later, friends still observed what one described as his "anguished seriousness."[31] Nonetheless, Croly's mature work would still show the indelible imprint of his father's mind.

II

Upon leaving Harvard in 1893, Croly reentered the working world at a time when American society was undergoing rapid change. It was a

28. Levy, *Herbert Croly*, 67.
29. Ibid., 60.
30. Ibid., 63.
31. Quoted by Forcey in *Crossroads*, 7.

period during which Populism was making significant inroads in the South and West only to fall apart at the moment of its greatest opportunity in the presidential election of 1896. And, at about the same time, an urban, more affluent (though more disparate and complex) movement historians have labeled "Progressivism" was beginning. It was with this latter movement that Croly soon identified, though he would also prove to become one of its most incisive critics. Most important for this discussion, however, are the significant ways in which Progressive ideology harmonized with key features of Comtean social thought. Political scientist R. Jeffery Lustig has referred to what he terms "the positivism of the Progressives"; the case of Herbert Croly can help to clarify in what meaningful ways American Progressives echoed Comte.[32]

Robert H. Wiebe understands the central organizing principle of Progressive social and political thought to be bureaucratic in nature. Out of this fundamental bureaucratic principle, Wiebe draws several of the distinctive emphases of the Progressive movement.[33] The bureaucratic rhetoric of the Progressives was part of a larger organizational impulse that sought to bring the social and political life of the nation under national institutions, just as the American economy was undergoing a process of economic concentration and national integration. Like Comte in early nineteenth-century France, Progressives were concerned about socioeconomic instability caused by the rapid advance of capitalism and the persistence of outdated formalistic social theories. This Progressive concern, was in some respects, therefore, a reincarnation of Comte's animating interest in resolving the perceived conflict of order and progress.

The Comtean answer furnished by many Progressives was organization on a national scale. Progressives hoped to build national institutions upon a naturally harmonious national community. Many Progressives assumed that interdependence and cultural consensus was basic to the social organism. This singular emphasis upon community and the harmony purportedly inherent in human society was entirely consistent with Comte's solidarism and organicism. Like good Comtists, many Progressives, especially the "group theorists," stressed social functions or duties over individual rights. For example, social-group-work theorists such as Mary Parker Follett believed that "genuine democracy meant discovering the natural unity which bound all men." Though not necessarily antidemocratic, such a perspective could readily be drawn

32. *Corporate Liberalism: The Origins of Modern American Political Theory: 1890–1920* (Berkeley and Los Angeles: University of California Press, 1982), 262.

33. *The Search for Order, 1877–1920* (New York: Hill and Wang, 1967), see esp. 159–63.

in a conservative direction. Progressive assumptions regarding social harmony proved unrealistic but most Progressives followed Comte in accepting much of the prevailing economic system.[34] Accordingly, some Progressives were as enthusiastic champions of economic concentration as Henry Edger and the early sectarian Comtists had been. In short, some kinds of Progressive thought were akin to Comtism in their bureaucratic or organizational thrust, in their paramount concern for social order and in their belief in underlying social consensus.

Two other subsidiary themes are suggested by the preceding analysis. One is an inherent elitism. Government bureaucracy, just like Bellamy's industrial army, was a hierarchical structure, though, it was hoped, a meritocratic one. Progressivism's characteristic emphasis upon executive authority could be (and often was) turned in an explicitly elitist direction. Furthermore, Progressives conceived of the scientific expert in terms very similar to Comte's description of the "Positive priesthood" and virtually identical to Ward's vision of the civil service technocrat. Such a system may indeed have "trod . . . close to elitist rule," but most Progressives were not openly, intentionally authoritarian. Like most nonsectarian American Comtists of the 1880s, Progressives, in Wiebe's words, "believed they were only modernizing, not destroying democracy." Several of the key components of the Progressive system—as Wiebe puts it, "the philosopher-kings, the rational public, the social consensus"—were strongly reminiscent of both Ward and Comte.[35]

American Progressivism, then, constituted the broad milieu in which Croly wrote. Croly's more immediate intellectual context comprised chiefly those men who would later help Croly edit the *New Republic*. The degree to which these figures influenced Croly is difficult to determine. Croly was surrounded by several Progressive intellectuals of note at the *New Republic* who together made up an informal community of discourse. Perhaps most important in Croly's circle in the early teens were Walter Weyl and Walter Lippmann, who had arrived at rather similar positions on public issues by about 1912. Weyl and Lippmann had moved away from earlier flirtations with socialism and had become, with Croly, "convinced that middle-class liberalism held the key to America's future."[36]

34. Lustig, *Liberalism*, 125–26, 132, 149; William Graebner, "The Unstable World of Benjamin Spock: Social Engineering in a Democratic Culture, 1917–1950," *Journal of American History* 67 (1980): 625. When Follett established in 1922 what came to be called "the Inquiry," its membership included Croly and John Dewey (Graebner, "Unstable World," 626).

35. Wiebe, *Search*, 161, 162.

36. Forcey, *Crossroads*, 169.

They did, however, arrive at their tentative consensus from very different directions. Neither Weyl nor Lippmann were positivists in any Comtean sense. On the whole, Weyl was less elitist and more democratic in his politics than was Croly. Also, Weyl evinced less interest in culture than did Croly and a greater interest in quantifying social phenomena. Lippmann, because of his abrupt change of course between *A Preface to Politics* and *Drift and Mastery* is more difficult to characterize than Croly, but he had clearly imbibed more of the antipositivistic irrationalism of Freud, Bergson, and Nietzsche.[37] The editors of the *New Republic* were, as Lustig describes them, Comtean "in their vision and cultural emphasis."[38] The three shared an important set of assumptions that were generally consistent with the positivism of Croly and Ward. All three were strongly critical both of Marxian socialism and classical liberalism. Most often, their criticism of the latter tradition centered upon the dangers of an unrestrained individualism. In the American context, the most common target was the Jeffersonian school of limited government, especially as developed by the Jacksonians and the nineteenth-century Democracy. Not unlike Comte before them, Croly and Lippmann were criticized, especially in their early work, for being elitist and antidemocratic. As spokesmen for a middle way between socialism and Manchester liberalism, these Progressives were also champions of the middle class and believers in its reform potential. All were committed to an active, interventionist state and a large public sector in the national economy. As Forcey has pointed out, Progressives were echoing Ward's earlier calls for "attractive legislation" when they criticized the negative state.[39] Finally, Croly, Weyl, and Lippmann agreed with Comte about the powerful directive role ideas had played in human history. Thus the Progressivism of the three formed a rough philosophical consensus consistent with Croly's Comtism.

III

If elements of Progressive thought dovetailed rather neatly with positivism, it remains to be seen how in his mature work Croly creatively applied Comte to early twentieth-century American conditions. Such an examination can reveal how Croly followed (knowingly or not) the trails

37. Ibid., chaps. 2, 3.
38. Lustig, *Liberalism*, 208.
39. Forcey, *Crossroads*, 111.

blazed by his American Comtist predecessors and in what ways he explored new intellectual territory. Although Croly's social thought did undergo a certain development between the 1890s and 1930, the Comtean element, which is the primary concern here, changed little. Prior to the publication of *The Promise of American Life* in 1909, Croly composed editorials for the *Architectural Record* on a wide variety of subjects. It was *The Promise*, however, which established Croly's reputation as an astute social commentator and political analyst. While it was not a popular success, the book landed Croly the job of editing the *New Republic*, founded in 1914 with the financial support of Willard Straight.[40] Croly's second book, a companion piece to *The Promise*, also appeared in 1914. *Progressive Democracy* revealed a more optimistic and democratic spirit than had its predecessor. Under the influence of John Dewey and (notably) sociologist Albion Small, Croly deemphasized organic nationalism in America and stressed instead the importance of participatory democracy. Croly continued to edit the *New Republic* until his death in 1930 but produced little published work in these later years. In addition to two books on architecture, Croly also wrote two biographies, one of Marcus Hanna (1912) and one of benefactor Willard Straight (1924).[41]

Croly's overall social theory was avowedly organicist. This organicism was founded (as Comte's had been) upon a thoroughgoing critique of classical economics and Enlightenment liberalism. The contractual, constitutional limits that eighteenth-century theorists imposed upon themselves were especially odious to Croly. Nations should not be limited by such strictures. "Every popular government," Croly declared in *The Promise of American Life*, "should in the end, and after a necessarily prolonged deliberation, possess the power of taking any action, which, in the opinion of a decisive majority of the people, is demanded by the public welfare. Such is not the case with the government organized under the Federal constitution."[42] Croly contended, in fact, that one of the ways in which Hamilton's political philosophy was to be preferred to Jefferson's was the former's transcendence of abstract constitutional formalism. Hamilton "realized," said Croly, "that genuine liberty was not merely a matter of a constitutional declaration of rights. It could be protected only by an energetic and clear-sighted national government, and it could be fertilized only by the efficient national organization of American activities." Similarly, Croly saw the abolitionists as "tearing

40. D. G. Villard, "Herbert D. Croly," *Dictionary of American Biography*, suppl. 1 (New York: Scribner, 1944), 11:209–10.

41. Forcey, *Crossroads*, 155–57.

42. HDC, *The Promise of American Life* (New York: Macmillan, 1909), 35–36. All subsequent page references in text will be to this edition.

Herbert Croly (1869–1930), son of
David Croly and founding editor
of the *New Republic.* Through
Croly and Lester Ward, American
Progressivism received its most
significant Comtean contribution.

at the fabric of American nationality" because they were "applying a
narrow and perverted political theory to a complicated and delicate set
of economic and social conditions" (44, 80–81).

To correct the United States's "erroneous democratic theory" and
address its concomitant problems, Croly articulated an answer in *The
Promise* that also betrayed his organicism (26). Croly proposed a spirit of
democratic nationalism as "the road whereby alone the American people
can obtain political salvation." For Croly, a nation was defined both by
"its habits and traditions of historical association [which] constitute an
indispensable bond" and by its loyalty to a particular formative political
idea. In the case of the American nation, that central principle or idea is
democracy. Croly hoped that, by joining political democracy with a
strong sense of nationalism, he could forge a powerful instrument to
secure American greatness. Devotion to democratic politics was not
enough by itself, however. Observed Croly, "The American nation, no
matter how much (or how little) it may be devoted to democratic
political and social ideas, cannot uproot any essential element in its
national tradition without severe penalties—as the American people
discovered when they decided to cut negro slavery out of their national
composition" (267, 268).

Thus democracy was dependent upon community and vice versa. Too often in the past, these twin principles had been viewed as necessarily in conflict but Croly argued that the one could not be fully realized without the other. Croly's social organicism prompted him to go as far as to argue that "[t]he less confidence the American people have in a national organization, the less they are willing to surrender themselves to the national spirit, the worse democrats they will be. . . . The American people are not prepared for a higher form of democracy, because they are not prepared for a more coherent and intense national life" (271).[43]

Croly's nationalism thus rested on his organic ideal. The classical liberalism of traditional American political theory only exacerbated "the chaotic individualism" that was producing a deeply divided society (23). Declared Croly in the *Architectural Record* (which he edited briefly at the turn of the century): "In its deepest aspect the social problem is the problem of preventing such divisions from dissolving . . . society—of keeping such a highly differentiated society fundamentally whole and sound."[44] If traditional negative liberalism had not resolved this central social problem (indeed, it appeared to have fostered these very divisions), then there was a need for a constructive, nationalistic liberalism that would again bind together the polity just as classical Greece or Renaissance Italy had been bound together by a unified culture. Croly believed that genuine democracy flourished only where real community existed. Consequently, Croly concluded that "American democracy can be advanced only by an increasing nationalization of the American people in ideas, in institutions, and in spirit."[45]

Beyond the Comtean organicism, Croly's approach to social and political analysis was also broadly historicist. Croly's method in much of *The Promise*, as well in the later *Progressive Democracy*, was historical. Nearly a quarter of the former book was made up of Croly's survey of the American past and much of the remainder of the book dealt with current problems historically. Though the latter study was less dominated by historical analysis, it too opened with lengthy historical reflections. *The Promise* in particular was, as Byron Dexter has called it, "a theoretical answer in American terms to the question of what had happened to America."[46] It was through an understanding of the nation's history that Croly hoped to construct that "theoretical answer."

Croly began with the ideological debate that emerged in Washington's

43. See Lustig, *Liberalism*, 132.
44. HDC quoted by Forcey, *Crossroads*, 27.
45. Ibid., 24; HDC, *Promise*, 271.
46. Byron Dexter, "Herbert Croly and the Promise of American Life," *Political Science Quarterly* 70 (1955): 198.

first cabinet between Hamilton and Jefferson. This argument between Hamiltonian activism and nationalism and Jeffersonian laissez-faire and state particularism had characterized American political discourse from its inception, Croly contended. The Jeffersonians and their descendants had, however, usually prevailed. Thus Jacksonian Democrats showed their lineage by their war on the Second National Bank and their enthusiastic support for the spoils system. Equally, the abolitionists proved to be a destructive force in the way they applied abstract Jeffersonian rights in an ahistorical manner. Only the Civil War, Croly believed, "began to emancipate the American national idea from an obscurantist individualism and provincialism." Then, in the post–Civil War era, the development of the nation's economy demonstrated clearly the contradictions within the Jeffersonian / Jacksonian school. The rise of big business made apparent to most, Croly wrote, that "the two primary interests of American life, . . . the interest of the individual business man and the interest of the body politic . . . [could not] substantially coincide" (86, 117). Having sketched the historical roots of the modern American dilemma, Croly went on in *The Promise* to chastise his fellow countrymen for not having reassessed their abstract political principles in light of their actual history. "The truth is," said Croly, "that Americans have not readjusted their political ideas to the teaching of their political and economic experience." At first, the contradictions inherent in the Jeffersonian equal rights school were not readily apparent. But as the society developed, "the demands of the 'Higher Law' began to diverge from the results of the actual legal system." Better students of history could recognize that "with the advent of comparative economic and social maturity, the exercise of certain legal rights became substantially equivalent to the exercise of privilege." Study of such Enlightenment ideas in their historical context demonstrated to Croly their serious limitations, indeed their danger, if applied uncritically to present circumstances. "Belief in the principle of equal rights," Croly argued, "does not bind, heal, and unify public opinion. Its effect rather is confusing, distracting, and at worst, disintegrating" (182, 183, 185).

Yet, like Comte, Croly's historical perspective was joined to a robust faith in science and a sincere commitment to a truly scientific but practical sociology. This abiding scientism of Croly is most evident in his lesser writings. For example, after World War I, Croly wrote an article to promote the establishment of a school of social research along the lines of the Ecole Libre des Sciences Politiques in Paris. The piece, which appeared in the *New Republic*, largely echoed Comte and Ward's philosophy of social science. Social research, Croly held, "must contrive and use experimental methods just as they have been used in physical laboratories."[47] In fact, this very theme was the main thrust of Croly's introduction to Eduard C. Lindeman's 1924 *Social Discovery*. Lindeman, a pioneer of adult education, had joined the editorial staff of the *New Republic* after the war and would become one of Croly's closest friends during the 1920s.[48] His book suggested how a social theory might be based upon purely empirical foundations, and it served to establish his reputation in social work circles. Croly's introduction defended the scientific pretensions of Lindeman's social theory. "Hazardous as the claim [to empirical certainty] may be," Croly reflected, "it is inseparable from knowing as distinguished from merely believing something about social processes."[49] One of the problems connected with a social theory that made scientific claims was that such pretensions had been discredited by the claims made by earlier pseudoscientific thinkers such as Ricardo, Marx, and Spencer. Such theorists merely used scientific jargon "to hide a dogma or an interest behind a screen of scientific authority." Their main failing, Croly explained, was that their "formulas were not . . . being satisfactorily verified in experience."[50] Significantly, Croly then noted Ward's *Dynamic Sociology* as one of the first key works to break with the scientistic determinism of its predecessors. Although the work of Ward and others "was a substantial improvement . . . [it] still lacked the skeptical modesty of science." Yet again, the main deficiency was "inadequate verification." In light of these previous failures, it is significant to note that Croly continued to trust that social theory could rightly aspire to the certainty of the natural sciences. Indeed, Croly saw with Lindeman "the need of performing for the social sciences a task analogous to that which Francis Bacon proposed to perform for the physical sciences in publishing the *Novum Organum*."[51]

Croly believed that this new social science would thus be truly empirical and "trustworthy" but also eminently practical.[52] Croly was

47. HDC, "A School for Social Research," *New Republic* (8 June 1918): 168. Croly's vision would ultimately become the New School for Social Research, though by then Croly had fallen out with its organizers. See also Levy, *Croly*, 269–71.

48. Levy describes Croly as "captivated by his sincerity and his earnest attempts to apply religious insights to social problems." Croly himself once wrote of Lindeman: "He and I are more closely allied intellectually than I have been with any previous friend" (Levy, *Croly*, 281).

49. HDC, Introduction to *Social Discovery: An Approach to the Study of Functional Groups*, by Eduard C. Lindeman (New York: Republic, 1924), x; Clarke A. Chambers, "Eduard Christian Lindeman," *Dictionary of American Biography*, suppl. 5 (New York: Scribner, 1977), 5:430–32.

50. HDC, Introduction, xi. Notably, Croly did not mention Comte in this context (see x–xi).

51. Ibid., xi–xiv.

52. Ibid., xv.

faithful to Comte's characteristic emphasis upon the pragmatic nature of science in general and on social science in particular. Rigorously scientific thinking about social problems was not enough; Croly concurred with Ward that every true science had its applied as well as its pure side. The test of all social science was its practical application. Declared Croly in the *New Republic*: "The work of understanding social processes is entangled inextricably with the effort to modify them." Social science had now to concern itself with "practical experimentation" and leave behind the academic ivory tower. Croly's vision for social science is neatly summarized in his proposal for a school of social research. There, he argued that such a school would "contribute to the social education of the American people . . . [and foster] more serviceable social disciplines."[53]

Croly's understanding of social science was thoroughly Comtean in two other respects. For one, he clearly viewed the contemporary crisis as in some sense a product of intellectual chaos or philosophical uncertainty. He described "the faith" upon which his social research school would "be founded" as the belief "that science can give back to mankind some of the security and integrity which its own capture by individual, national and class particularism has jeopardized." Croly retained the Comtean conception of science as a potentially integrating, unifying force in modern society; a worthy replacement for the theological or metaphysical faiths that had cemented past civilizations. As Croly put it, the new school would "anticipate by education the birth of the new faith"—a faith that would undergird a new social unity. Consequently, social science had a key role within Croly's organic social vision.[54]

The second additional echo of Comte in Croly's philosophy of science and in his understanding of the role of social science within the polity is slightly more ambiguous. In some ways, Croly sounds as though he shared Comte's notion of a scientific elite that would educate society and otherwise spearhead social reform. Croly, for example, called for scientists and "social evangelists" to popularize and apply the latest findings of the new social science. The school of social research he envisaged would train a new generation of managers and social "engineers." Labor arbitrators and managers attuned to promoting social consensus would seek cooperation and not confrontation between management and labor. But in the same article, Croly reflected (with disappointment?) that the "American democratic tradition and organization is hostile to the expert, whether he be a state official or a social worker."[55] Perhaps because of this prejudice, or because of past charges

53. HDC, "School," 169, 171, 167.
54. Ibid., 168, 171.
55. Ibid., 171, 169, 170.

of elitism leveled at him, Croly's remarks on this subject were more circumspect in his later work. In his introduction to Lindeman's book, Croly took care to distinguish his ideas from the utopian elitism of many nineteenth-century social theorists. His model for the social scientist, Croly explained, was that of the participant observer: "The trustworthy [i.e., empirical] knowledge of social processes would never as the result of future growth assume a form which would justify the social scientist in calling himself a law-giver. He would remain an observer who imaginatively or actually participated in the activities which he observed."[56]

Thus the technocrat would be dispassionate and objective because his method was scientific but he would also be intimately involved in society because science must be practically oriented. Previous social theorists failed to appreciate these subtleties. "Their social and psychological theories," wrote Croly, "were arrogant and imperious because the people themselves were not disinterested. . . . Their anthropological or social science was the rationalization of special interests or particular projects."[57] Croly appears to have been struggling with some of the same tensions that had characterized Ward's social theory. The social scientist was to be deeply concerned with the practical implications of his investigations and yet remain wholly objective and nonpartisan.

Moreover, because of the influence of thinkers such as James and Dewey, Croly's thought diverged from the Comtean system (and much of Victorian philosophy) in its more tentative, open-ended character. Croly often stressed the *process* of reform rather than an ideal blueprint. Although Ward may have been slightly more explicit about the character of his envisaged "sociocracy," Croly again seemed to echo him in his description of the proper role of the social scientist: "The primary function of the social discoverer is to understand. In relation to action it must always be expressed in alternatives rather than in some absolute objective."[58] The social scientist "is never seeking or expecting a consummation," he explained. Such an approach on Croly's part, though not entirely absent from Ward's work, does certainly underline Croly's break with the Comtean tendency toward comprehensive systems. Another feature of Croly's understanding of the nature and role of social science was an echo of Comte as well as of James and Royce. Croly believed that religious fervor was an essential part of any movement for systematic reform. A popular moral or spiritual conversion had to

56. HDC, Introduction, xvi.
57. Ibid., xviii–xix.
58. Ibid., xviii.

precede social reconstruction, Croly contended. As he explained in *The Promise*, "the laborious work of individual and social fulfilment may eventually be transfigured by an outburst of enthusiasm, . . . the finer flower of an achieved experience" (453). Yet, though he argued that some sort of "suffering and repentance" had to come before reform would blossom, Croly was less clear about whether spiritual revival had actually to precede social renewal, as Comte had insisted.[59] Croly argued, for example that the eagerly anticipated cooperation between empirical science and pragmatic reform "will not go very far until it receives an impulse from the restoration of religion to a worthier place in human life, but the religious revival, if it comes, must come when and where it pleases."[60] Regardless of the exact sequence, Croly saw the social function of religious awakening in terms similar to both those of Comte and of his Harvard mentors.

If Croly's social and political theory was organic, historicist, and scientistic, it was also statist and interventionist. The connection between scientism and statism was a natural one for Croly, as it had been for Ward. After all, the state represented to Croly one of "the most important agencies of social experimentation."[61] Not that such experimentation had always been or would be successful. Croly readily conceded that the state would sometimes "make serious and perhaps enduring mistakes." But, he added, "if a selective policy is pursued in good faith and with sufficient intelligence, the nation will at least be learning from its mistakes" (*Promise*, 190–91). The state was, accordingly, the primary agent in carrying out the sort of experimentation that alone would make social science truly scientific.

Croly asserted that "the national public interest has to be affirmed by positive and aggressive action." Again, the logical vehicle to spearhead such action was the state apparatus. Here, the question for Croly was not whether such interventionism violated certain abstract principles but, rather, whether it worked. Objections about the selectivity of such intervention were illegitimate. "The practice of non-interference," argued Croly, "is just as selective in its effects as the practice of state interference." Therefore, Croly's theory of the state was mostly pragmatic and historical. Indeed, in *The Promise*, Croly spent nearly fifty pages describing the origins and growth of the nation state in Europe from the Dark Ages to the present. The point of "this long digression" was to understand the state through its history and "to exhibit the European nations as a group of historic individuals" (190, 263).

59. HDC, Introduction, xx.
60. HDC, "School," 171.
61. Ibid., 169.

Emblematic of Croly's interventionist and melioristic ethic was the stress he laid upon public education. The argument was reminiscent of Ward's approach and the common denominator was again probably Comte, though Dewey's influence was also important for Croly, particularly in his later writing. While he cautioned against the popular American "superstition" that education could accomplish anything, Croly maintained a robust faith in the power of the educative process: "It is by education that the American is trained for such democracy as he possesses. . . . Men are uplifted by education much more surely than they are by any tinkering with laws and institutions, . . . even bad institutions and laws can be made vehicles of grace [through education]." "That faith [in education]," observed Croly, "is the immediate and necessary issue of the logic of our national moral situation" (400, 402).

Croly believed that the problem was not faith in education itself but that Americans had too narrow and limited a conception of what education involved. "The proposed means of education," he wrote in *The Promise*, "are too conscious, too direct, and too superficial" (404). It is one's entire lifetime experience that is most critical in one's personal growth. Formal education can illuminate that experience but is no real substitute for the "school of life." This broad, pragmatic view of education Croly also sought to apply to the corporate or collective level: "National education in its deeper aspect does not differ from individual education. . . . The fundamental process of American education consists and must continue to consist precisely in the risks and experiments which the American nation will make in the service of its national ideal." No genuine social progress will be attained, however, "if the American people balk at the sacrifices demanded by their experiments, or if they attach finality to any particular experiment" (405).

Croly's view of the role of social science in a progressive society, with its typically Comtean emphasis upon a technocratic elite, was mirrored in his discussion of industrial and governmental leadership in America. It appeared important for Croly to disassociate himself both from those Progressives who saw the great trusts as inherently evil, as well as from those who viewed affluent entrepreneurs as a uniformly malevolent lot. As he reflected in a revealing point in *The Promise*: "I am far from believing that this concentration of economic power is wholly an undesirable thing, and I am also far from believing that the men in whose hands this power is concentrated deserve, on the whole, any exceptional moral reprobation for the manner in which it has been used. In certain respects they have served their country well." Croly continued, then, the Comtean tradition's approval of the "captains of industry," as long as the underlying principle—"the subordination of the individual to the demand of a dominant and constructive national purpose"—was first understood. Powerful individuals within the economic system were not the problem. Problems arose instead when such individuals acted irresponsibly on account of "the chaotic individualism of our political and economic organization" (23). These elites needed, therefore, to be given national direction, not thoughtless popular censure.

In the governmental realm, Croly portrayed political leaders in elitist terms strongly reminiscent of earlier American Comtists. Croly's portrait of Lincoln, for example, broke with the traditional image of a simple, backwoods "man of the people" whose virtues were only those of his fellow countrymen writ large. In *The Promise*, Croly took pains to show that Lincoln's greatness arose from those characteristics that distinguished him from most of his contemporaries. The average American voter of the mid-nineteenth century was, Croly contended, "wholly incapable either of disinterested or of concentrated intellectual exertion." Yet Lincoln was a great president in part because he was "an example of high and disinterested intellectual culture" (90, 91). Unlike his contemporaries, he was "morally humane, magnanimous and humble." An appreciation of these rare qualities involved "an implicit criticism" of traditional democratic values in America (98, 99).

Not that democratic values and principles should be scorned; Croly believed that most deserved to be cherished. Croly praised Theodore Roosevelt for the way in which he "revived the Hamiltonian ideal of constructive national legislation" without resurrecting Hamilton's antidemocratic biases. Hamilton's opposition to democratic principles Croly termed his one "fatal error." The challenge was to construct a truly democratic polity where unique individuals would be encouraged to rise to the top. Such figures "must not only be permitted, they must be encouraged to earn distinction." In fact, Croly believed that "Individual distinction, resulting from the efficient performance of special work, is not only the foundation of all genuine individuality, but is usually of the utmost social value." Or, as he summed up his perspective in less ambiguous terms: "The essential wholeness of the community depends absolutely on the ceaseless creation of a political, economic, and social aristocracy and their equally incessant replacement" (168–69, 196).

This characteristically Comtean assertion of the important role played by social elites had significant implications for Croly's constitutional views. Not unlike Ward, Croly was concerned that federal and state legislatures had ceased being truly deliberative bodies; that instead, members now voted along strictly partisan lines. Originally, representatives were not merely party automatons but were community leaders who were uniquely informed and could therefore provide distinctive insights on a whole range of policy questions. "Representatives," noted Croly, "were often selected [in the past], who were capable of adding something to the candid and serious consideration of a question of public policy. The need helped to develop men capable of meeting it." By contrast, the role of congressmen today was "at worst that of mercenaries" (326). Whereas they had once been individuals of independent judgment, Croly concurred with his fellow Progressives that representatives were now too often only the pawns of party machines or special interests.

One solution, particularly on the local level, was to create executive positions within government with real authority and considerable discretionary power. Croly proposed a quasi-presidential system for municipalities where the chief executive would wield broad legislative and appointive powers. This system Croly described as designed to "concentrate power and responsibility" in a single elected official (338). Just as Croly's predecessors had seen economic concentration as an unavoidable and beneficial outgrowth of socioeconomic evolution, so now Croly saw concentrated governmental power as beneficial when properly directed. As Croly explained in a revealing passage: "The chief executive, when supported by public opinion, would become a veritable 'Boss'; and he would inevitably be the sworn enemy of unofficial 'Bosses' who now dominate local parties. . . . The real 'Boss' would destroy the sham 'Bosses' " (340). With the appropriate controls, the political boss was no more inherently evil than the industrial boss; but both had to be forced to conform their actions to a coherent national purpose.

Possibly the strongest echo of Comte came in Croly's vision of political leaders as secular "saints." Just as he stressed the critical role for elites in a democratic system, so Croly envisaged such leaders as modern surrogates for the medieval saints. Lincoln was a great leader because, as Croly explained revealingly, he "differed as essentially from the ordinary Western American of the Middle Period as St. Francis of Assisi differed from the ordinary Benedictine monk of the thirteenth century" (90). As for the average member of the polity, he "can become something of a saint and something of a hero . . . by the sincere and enthusiastic imitation or heroes and saints." It is incumbent upon "his exceptional fellow-countrymen to offer him [such] acceptable examples of heroism and saintliness." Much depends, therefore, on elite leadership, on the "work of some democratic St. Francis." This note—so strange to American ears—has been observed by earlier historians and wrongly attributed to Hegelianism. It is, rather, an authentic Comtean echo (454, 453).[62]

62. Noble, *Paradox*, 64–65. Unlike Noble, Forcey appears to recognize the Comtean roots of this part of Croly's thought (see *Crossroads*, 46).

Which brings one, finally, to consider the role religious ideas played in Croly's mature work. His concern that elites represent saintly models for the general public represented an effort to rehabilitate Comte's Religion of Humanity purged of its nineteenth-century sectarian character, and put to organic use. Croly sought to resurrect social homogeneity and a defined sense of national purpose not with a "positivized" Catholic church but with a strong, purposive nationalism. "In this country," Croly argued, "the solution of the social problem demands the substitution of a conscious social ideal for the earlier instinctive homogeneity of the American nation. . . . A democracy cannot dispense with the solidarity which it imparted to American life, and in one way or another such solidarity must be restored" (139). Consistent with his organicism, Croly held that national solidarity was the only avenue whereby liberal democracies could transcend the old, abstract opposition of liberty and equality. "Such a [new] democracy," declared Croly, "would not be dedicated either to liberty or to equality in their abstract expressions, but to liberty and equality, in so far as they made for human brotherhood" (207). Croly hoped that a strong nationalistic spirit when joined to a venerable democratic tradition would constitute the sort of fervent humanism that Comte had sought to institutionalize in the positivist church.

Hence, religion was a persistent theme in Croly's work but primarily in a pragmatic or functional sense. That is, Croly hoped to extract and employ the emotional component from religious commitment (which was virtually all either Comtism or idealism had left him). While he eschewed Comte's particular attempt to institutionalize religiosity without dogma, Croly's approach was still essentially Comtean. He recognized religious sentiment as a powerful force both within the individual and within society. The religious impulse, Croly believed, could be used to integrate and galvanize the nation.[63] Whether Croly's "religion" ever went beyond this narrow functional approach to embrace beliefs distinct from empirical science, is more difficult to say.[64]

Although Croly did (as noted above) continue to express faith in a science of society during the 1920s, it is clear that he was considerably

63. Noble, *Paradox*, 75–77.

64. In his last years, Croly did become interested in the mysticism of Russian guru Gustave Gurdjieff. See Dexter, "Croly," 217. Edmund Wilson wrote of Croly shortly after his death: "I believe that Croly's later writings represented an attempt on his own part to explain to his own rational intelligence this mysterious spring of spiritual power. He was attempting to assign it somehow to a God of more vitality and majesty than Comte's Supreme Being, to that God in whom he had been taught not to believe" ("H.C.," *New Republic* [16 July 1930]: 268).

chastened by the Great War and its immediate aftermath. Partly because of a personal faith in President Wilson, Croly and his fellow editors at the *New Republic* supported U.S. intervention in 1917. Randolph Bourne, one of the few insiders to break with the magazine's editorial policy, charged that Croly and associates were so taken with technocratic management and social control that they had allowed themselves to be co-opted by the war machine and its irrational and reactionary allies. Croly never formally replied to Bourne's challenge, but the *New Republic's* decision to oppose the ratification of the League treaty did represent a kind of mea culpa. Croly conceded to Louis Brandeis in 1919 that the magazine's opposition was "practically a confession of failure, so far as our work during the last few years is concerned."[65] Nor, after the war, was Croly so confident in the ability of the state to solve social problems. Progressives, he concluded in an unfinished manuscript begun in 1920, "The Breach in Civilization," should not "fall back uncritically on the state as the conscious agency of individual and social liberation."[66]

And yet, as Croly became more skeptical about the omnicompetence of expert administrators, he returned to some decidedly Comtean ideas about religion and its significance for the individual and for society. Although "The Breach in Civilization" did not make an explicit defense of Comte's Religion of Humanity, Croly's understanding of the Protestant Reformation and of its social and cultural legacy was thoroughly Comtean. It was the Reformation that had, in Croly's mind, smashed the social and philosophical oneness of Catholic Christendom. Croly called upon his readers "to resurrect the mediaeval vision of a single catholic community." Following Comte, Croly underlined the baleful effects of dividing or fragmenting "authoritative knowledge," be it religious, philosophical, or scientific. Without a rebirth of the unified medieval vision, "civilization will remain divided against itself and will drift helplessly to its own destruction." Hence, Croly's postwar disillusionment undermined his faith in the interventionist state that the "Comtean succession" in America had celebrated, while it simultaneously prompted him to return to Comte's original cultural and religious diagnosis.[67]

65. Cited in Levy, *Croly*, 265. See 260–62 for preceding material.
66. Cited in Levy, *Croly*, 292.
67. Quoted in Levy, *Croly*, 291. Levy contends that Croly's views in *Breach* did not represent a return to the Religion of Humanity as practiced by his father (see 292–94). Croly certainly did not advocate adopting the organization and ritual of the Comtean sect but I think Levy exaggerates here the differences between Croly's position and that of Comte. Yes, Croly did speak now about emulating Christ, but that sort of rhetoric was not uncommon in Comte's writings, despite the latter's atheism (see *Croly*, 293–94).

On the whole, therefore, Croly's mature work is best understood as part of a larger American Comtean tradition. Croly was, of course, indebted to other thinkers besides his father. Never a sectarian, Croly's thought did show the imprint of other philosophical and political traditions. His exposure to Hegelianism is clearly evident in the emphasis Croly placed upon ideals as important motivating principles. The personal faith in abstract ideals that Croly described verged on a quite un-Comtean fideism. Nor was his championing of a revivified nationalism as the salvation of the American system particularly Comtean. Comte was an organicist but did not view nationalism in Croly's terms. Moreover, there was in Croly a concern for participatory democracy, individual liberty, and even social equality (especially evident in *Progressive Democracy*) that was clearly not derived from Comte. For example, just as Ward had developed Comte's educational ideas in a democratic direction, so Croly added Dewey to his positivism to stress education's democratizing role. On a higher philosophical level, Croly appeared to accept the sort of epistemological pluralism that most Victorian positivists could never entertain. Though apparently not a theist, Croly did not exclude unscientific beliefs in a rigid way, as had Ward or Wakeman.

Even with these important qualifications, the foregoing analysis confirms that the Comtean element best explains the peculiar texture of Croly's social thought. His system was certainly a hybrid—in some respects, a more complex and creative hybrid than Ward had produced—but an unmistakably Comtean amalgam nonetheless. Indeed, Croly's positivism represented the "arrival" of the American Comtean tradition. Freed from some of its now dated Victorianisms and explicitly utopian features, Herbert Croly's work was able to make a uniquely Comtean contribution to mainstream social and political thought in early twentieth-century America.

Conclusion

[T]he Narcissene self-worship of humanity was an inseparable part of Comte's philosophy: man must adore something, and, having denied God, he will find his deity somewhere much lower than the angels. And the planned state, dominated by the industrialist and the scientist, administered by a committee of bankers, supported by a vast uniform proletariat, leaving nothing to individual aspiration, repudiating democracy root and branch, liberty surrendered to the concept of control—this follows naturally from Auguste Comte's postulates. For men, having been instructed deliberately that there are no supernatural sanctions for moral conduct, must be made to conform and to labor either by naked force or by elaborate social machinery. The emancipated English admirers of Comte could not see that Positivism, as a social system, meant the very opposite of emancipation, the antithesis of liberalism.
—Russell Kirk, *The Conservative Mind*

THE PRECEDING CHAPTERS have concentrated on several representative figures in an attempt to construct a composite portrait of an American Comtean tradition. The picture that emerges is a complex one because few American Comtists remained long in the orthodox camp and because they are not all of the same generation or occupational milieu. Unique individuals in different contexts therefore employed Comte to articulate distinctive positions on the philosophical and social questions of their day. Comtean positivism bolstered the social conservatism of David Croly, fed the philosophical radicalism and social reformism of T. B. Wakeman, strengthened the interventionism of Lester Ward, helped to form the sociological vision of Albion Small and E. A. Ross and shaped the Progressivism of Herbert Croly. Yet there were important common currents that ran through the positivism of these very different individuals. The shared elements these Americans drew from Comte together formed a uniquely American Comtean language.

With regard to philosophical and religious thought, American Comtists clarify in a novel way several important features of the Victorian "crisis of faith."[1] For one, early social science's community of discourse was often driven by what were essentially religious questions.[2] New York intellectuals were involved in a search for a scientistic surrogate for traditional faith and some found Comte a satisfying substitute—satisfying because Comtean positivism addressed the needs of Victorian intellectuals frightened by the personal and social implications of irreligion. The Religion of Humanity furnished both emotional outlets and institutional structures to satisfy individual and communal needs. As Courtlandt Palmer expressed the perspective of his New York circle: "When people ask me why I have rejected Christianity, I always reply: 'It is because I wish to be a religious man.' "[3] Comte allowed these individuals to be pious in their heterodoxy in a way not envisaged by the era's other forms of scientific naturalism.[4] Besides enabling skeptics to remain religious in some sense, Comte also gave scientific sanction to the Victorian idolization of human progress. After all, many Gilded Age intellectuals had already placed "Humanity on the altar in place of God."[5] The Comtean system merely showed agnostics how to effect the apotheosis in a more explicit and self-conscious way.

Comtean positivism made an even greater contribution to the social and political thought of the late nineteenth century. Here, its most important role was the part it played in the transformation of American liberalism. American Comtists were key participants in the reform politics of the Gilded Age and in the reformism of the Progressive era. The former was a complex and contradictory hybrid of Jacksonian

1. See "American Intellectuals and the Victorian Crisis of Faith," in *Victorian America*, ed. Daniel Walker Howe (Philadelphia: University of Pennsylvania Press, 1976), 59–77. See also Paul A. Carter, *The Spiritual Crisis of the Gilded Age* (DeKalb: Northern Illinois University Press, 1971).

2. Arthur Vidich and Stanford M. Lyman make a similar point in their *American Sociology: Worldly Rejections of Religion and Their Directions* (New Haven: Yale University Press, 1985). This book contains some helpful insights but is marred by a careless use of (frequently undefined) terms and a host of unsubstantiated claims. Thomas Haskell's highly critical review in the *Journal of American History* strikes me as a fair assessment (*JAH* 72 [1985]: 665).

3. Courtlandt Palmer, *How Peace May Be Found Under the Faith of Science and Humanity* (New York: by the author, n.d.), 244.

4. Spencer's "Unknowable" appeared too abstract and remote to many, though some did turn it to serve theistic arguments.

5. James Turner, *Without God, Without Creed: The Origins of Unbelief in America* (Baltimore: Johns Hopkins University Press, 1985), 251.

principles and cooperative programs.[6] Its Comtean components were drawn from Bellamy and Ward, as well as from less prominent figures such as T. B. Wakeman. The departure of Gilded Age radicals from the negative-state liberalism of Jacksonian democracy can be attributed in part to the interventionist impulse of American Comtists like Ward and others. Antebellum Whigs had envisaged a positive liberal state but Comte provided compelling arguments cast in the new language of social science. The positivism of thinkers such as Lester Ward actually joined these two traditions, the native with the foreign.

Meanwhile, Comtean positivism also infused the reform liberalism being born at this time with potentially illiberal or antidemocratic elements. The cooperative commonwealth school of Gilded Age radicalism had its elitist, statist, and corporatist side, which included a strong Comtean component. American Comtists tended to be antipolitical and envisaged a government of publicly minded scientific elites that resembled Comte's "Positive priesthood." This Comtean element produced profound tensions within the systems of Wakeman, Bellamy, and Ward, yet the liberal, democratic emphasis of each usually prevailed.

It was mostly this elitist/organizational impulse that was taken up by Progressives at the turn of the century. As they left behind some of the now-dated features of Comte's philosophy, Albion Small and E. A. Ross retained in their sociology much of positivism's concern for social order and technocratic control. Herbert Croly, and others of less demonstrable Comtean lineage, placed singular stress upon scientific experts and their managerial role within the new liberal polity. Again, antebellum Whiggery constituted an indigenous source for this sort of paternalism; but Comte and the social science movement in general injected a new bureaucratic and scientific component into the Progressive mixture. Hence, liberals of the Progressive era were also able to draw upon Comte (mediated chiefly through Ward and Croly) for much of their distinctive reform ideology.

Another key element of the new liberalism that was being forged in the first years of the twentieth century was pluralist or corporatist. Many Progressives saw groups and not individuals as society's main building blocks. Here again, the Comtean contribution was critical. Abstract individual rights had been rejected by Comte (and by much of early sociology) in favor of duties that arose naturally from social groupings. Indeed, the social organism defined by a hierarchical division of labor

6. Dorothy Ross, "Liberalism," in *Encyclopedia of American Political History: Studies of the Principal Movements and Ideas*, ed. by Jack P. Greene (2 vols.; New York: Scribner, 1984), 756–61.

was derived primarily from the family, the basic social unit. Similarly, modern corporations were viewed as the necessary products of social evolution, with Comte and several of the early New York community even pressing corporate claims to political power. Meanwhile, other American Comtists such as Ward (perhaps because of their Whig background) saw the state, rather than the private corporation, as the prime political agent.[7]

The liberalism that emerged in the early twentieth century, then, clearly owed much to Comtean thought. This study shows that American intellectuals had access to Comte not only through English thinkers such as Mill or Spencer but through a diverse indigenous school. The preceding analysis should not, of course, obscure the crucial role of other related or competing discourses in the formation of a new liberalism. Liberal ideology has continued to evolve and develop in the decades since World War I, reacting to a changing socioeconomic order as it, in turn, shaped that new order. But, until quite recently, the Comtean contribution has been virtually ignored by scholars. The preceding chapters have tried to demonstrate, however, that Comtean thought represented an important resource for some of those involved in the reconstruction of American liberalism.

To what extent was the influence of this American school of positivists salutary? Perhaps the question has already been answered indirectly. Through the work of Ward and others, it did encourage Americans to have confidence in their ability to reform and improve their society, to construct a system that would better serve the common good. Certainly reformers of various kinds saw Comtean ideas as an effective antidote against the strictures of laissez-faire liberalism in its classical or Spencerian form. What modest state intervention the Progressive era witnessed did improve the material existence of most Americans. Insofar as it bolstered the best of the social reforms of the Progressive era, one can surely applaud its role.

However, it is difficult to conclude that the long-term influence of this cluster of ideas has been entirely benign. Again, because of its close relationship with the liberalism of the Progressives, the deficiencies of the Comtean school are intertwined with Progressivism's own failures. For most American positivists, the essential conservatism and statism of the Comtean system prevailed. Although a few (such as T. B. Wakeman) occasionally entertained a more radical approach, most of our Comtean connection never seriously questioned the relations of production that

7. Ibid., 757. See also in same volume, R. Jeffery Lustig, "Pluralism," esp. 911–12.

gave late nineteenth-century American capitalism its fundamental character. Here, Comte's conservatism, his reluctance to meddle with the system of private accumulation, reinforced the restricted vision of liberal political culture in America. Like most Progressives, American positivists excluded from the start the kind of foundational questions the socialist Left was asking.

The American positivists also followed Comte in assuming a far greater degree of social harmony than in fact existed.[8] To their credit, many understood that the contemporary crisis was, at its core, intellectual or spiritual, and that the solution had, therefore, to be grounded in a comprehensive religious or ethical system. As many in our own time are discovering, a socioeconomic system founded solely upon considerations of individual material gain does not satisfy the deepest human needs. But, though they decried the selfish ways of the robber barons, few moved beyond simple moral exhortation or educational ventures like Courtlandt Palmer's Nineteenth Century Club. Most failed to recognize how the narrow interests of the bureaucratic and industrial elites they looked to would undermine or redirect many of the reforms they envisaged. Although less spectacularly than Comte had done, American positivists indulged in a naive confidence in social perfectibility. Their dreams of a positivist republic remained unfulfilled because of their failure to come to terms with class divisions in American society and because of their unrealistic belief in the omnicompetence and neutrality of the state and its bureaucracy.

The troubling legacy of this sort of "Comtean liberalism" has been apparent in nearly all of the liberal reform movements of the twentieth century down to our own time. Without accepting the conclusions drawn by critics on the libertarian Right, one can agree that much of the failure of liberal reform in this century can be attributed to a credulous faith in technocratic elites and an unwarranted optimism about the malleability of human nature. From Theodore Roosevelt's New Nationalism, to the New Deal, to the Great Society, elite-led reform has invariably prevailed over alternative models that conceived of political or economic reformation as necessarily a grassroots affair.[9] Furthermore,

8. Arthur S. Link and Richard L. McCormick, *Progressivism* (Arlington Heights, Ill.: Harlan Davidson, 1983), 116.

9. Notably, Christopher Lasch portrays Croly as a champion of participatory democracy, though he appears to base this interpretation primarily upon Croly's more egalitarian *Progressive Democracy* (1914) and subsequent essays; see Lasch, *The True and Only Heaven: Progress and Its Critics* (New York: Norton, 1991), 340–48. Though his point is slightly overstated, I agree with Lasch that "[p]rogressives and social democrats were the founders of the modern welfare state—the negation of everything the old republican tradition stood for" (*True and Only Heaven*, 554).

reform-minded liberals understood that nineteenth-century individualism had been changed by the new corporate order but their revised
liberalism failed to promote the genuine community of a democratic
commonwealth, and built instead upon the solidarity of the private
corporation. Participatory or egalitarian alternatives to this sort of "corporate liberalism" have received little popular consideration in national
politics in recent decades. Given the fact that most American critics of
big government continue to evidence a peculiar blindness about the
threat to authentic community and to the commonweal represented by
its ally, big business, it seems unlikely that the misstep taken by
American liberalism at the turn of the century will be corrected very
soon.

All of the individuals mentioned herein were reported to have attended some meetings of the first two New York societies and several even held leadership positions. Prominent persons who visited meetings only once or twice are not included.

James D. Bell (b. 1845). New York–born and educated, Bell served in the Union cavalry during the Civil War. He served with Croly on the editorial staff of the *World*, and later on the *Graphic*. Bell edited the *Evolution*, and was probably second secretary of the New York Positivist Society. He was also judge advocate for the Department of New York in the Grand Army of the Republic (the main Union veterans organization). (See *Evolution* 1 [1877]: 31.)

Augusta Cooper Bristol (1835–1910). The tenth child of a large New Hampshire family, she graduated from Kimball Union Academy in 1850 and took up teaching. In 1868, she published a volume of poetry and soon became a popular speaker on social and moral subjects. Mrs. Bristol attended the International Convention of Freethinkers in Brussels in 1880. She was the author of several books on women's issues.

Stafford C. Cleveland (1822–85). A New York state assemblyman and editor of the upstate newspaper *Yates County Chronicle*.

Charles A. Codman (d. 1911). Previously a Brook Farm resident, Codman became a longtime inhabitant of Modern Times after moving there in 1857. A contributor to D. M. Bennett's Freethought journal, the *Truth Seeker*, Codman also manufactured paper boxes on a small scale.

David Goodman Croly (1829–89). A journalist, Croly was born in Ireland but grew up in New York. He became managing editor of the

New York World in 1863. A conservative Democrat, Croly edited and published a Comtist journal titled *Modern Thinker* and wrote at least two books. Croly was married to feminist Jane Cunningham ("Jenny June") and was the father of Progressive editor Herbert Croly.

John Elderkin (1841–1902?). Probably of Scottish Presbyterian stock, Elderkin was born in Setauket, New York. He was a journalist, author, and was affiliated with the *New York Ledger* for many years. Elderkin was a Civil War veteran and a lifelong Republican.

Henry Evans. Possibly the son of Jacksonian reformer George Henry Evans (1805–55) or that of his Shaker brother, Evans was secretary of the New York Positivist Society after William Owen. A Henry Evans is listed as a "printer" in one New York city directory.

H. H. Hall. Identity is uncertain. May have been Henry Hall (b. 1845) born in Auburn, New York. A journalist, Hall came to Manhattan and became business manager in 1875 of the *Tribune*.

Josiah Gilbert Holland (1819–81). An editor, novelist, poet, and lyceum speaker born in Massachusetts of Puritan ancestry. Though trained in medicine, Dr. Holland became co-editor with Samuel Bowles of the *Springfield Republican* and went on to become a very popular essayist and lecturer on moral topics. In 1870, Holland became editor of *Scribner's Monthly* and settled in New York City, where he lived until his death.

Mary Putnam Jacobi (1842–1906). Of Puritan ancestry, she was the daughter of publishing giant George Putnam. Studied medicine in New York and Philadelphia, and eventually traveled to Paris where she became the first female graduate of the Ecole de Medicine. Returning to New York City, she became a lecturer at the Medical College for Women of the New York Infirmary and married Dr. Abraham Jacobi. She was a noted author on women's subjects, especially those with medical themes.

Samuel Longfellow (1819–92). From a distinguished New England family, his father was a Federalist congressman from Maine and his brother was poet Henry Wadsworth Longfellow. Influenced by the transcendentalism of Theodore Parker and others at Harvard during the 1840s, Longfellow became a radical Unitarian clergyman and was pastor of churches in Brooklyn and Germantown, Pennsylvania, among others. Composed several collections of hymns and wrote religious poetry throughout his life.

Dyer Daniel Lum (1840–93). Radical polemicist, author of at least nine short books dealing with labor, anarchism, and Free Love.

Rutger Bleecker Miller (1805–77). Prominent Utica lawyer, state legislator, and briefly Democratic congressman in the late 1830s. Miller was born in Lewis City, New York, was involved in the construction business (as well as in railroads) and tended a farm in Oneida County.

Waterman Lilly Ormsby (1809–83). Born in Hampton, Connecticut, Ormsby was a skilled line engraver who designed several government bank notes in use during the Civil War. After coming to New York, Ormsby ran the New York Bank Note Company and helped found the famous Continental Bank Note Company. He was an accomplished artist and technician but a notoriously outspoken eccentric on most public issues.

William Owen. An English immigrant (in March 1867) and a friend of Henry Edger.

Courtlandt Palmer (1843–88). Son of a wealthy Connecticut merchant, Palmer graduated from Columbia Law School in 1869. Palmer was a prominent New York City lawyer and was founder and first president of the Nineteenth Century Club in 1880. His friend T. B. Wakeman encouraged Palmer to write several short books on positivist subjects.

Andrés Poëy y Aguirre (1826–1919). French meteorologist who published several scientific treatises in addition to his study *M. Littre et Auguste Comte* (1879).

John Swinton (1829–1901). Labor reformer and journalist was born in Edinburgh, Scotland. Swinton was editor of the *New York Times* between 1860 and 1870. After marrying in 1877, he settled permanently in Brooklyn. Though associated with radical causes, Swinton apparently retained his traditional Presbyterian faith.

Thaddeus Burr Wakeman (1834–1913). Wakeman was born in 1834 into an affluent Connecticut family of Puritan ancestry. His parents were Calvinists and soon directed their bright young son toward the ordained ministry. Accordingly, he was enrolled at Princeton, graduating second in his class in 1854. Arrangements had been made for Thaddeus to be placed in a Presbyterian church in New York City as an assistant upon graduation, but the introspective twenty-year-old had other plans. Wakeman had been reading widely in his final year and what he encountered led him to question Princeton orthodoxy. Thus, at about the time of his graduation, Wakeman approached his elder brother Abram and told him that he no longer felt called to the Christian ministry. Instead, he explained to his alarmed sibling, he would like to go to Germany to study philosophy. Abram, a prominent New York lawyer, quickly dismissed any plans to study abroad and informed the wayward Thaddeus that he would become an attorney under his tutelage. The younger Wakeman relented and worked in his brother's law office as he read for the bar exam. After being called to the bar, Thaddeus joined Abram's firm, though he later left to start his own practise on Nassau Street in Manhattan. Wakeman prospered as a lawyer and lived for many years in a fashionable residence on 116th Street in Harlem. It was as a freethinking young lawyer that Wakeman first encountered Comtean positivism through Henry Edger's lectures. See Chapter Four for other biographical details.

Charles F. Wreaks. Listed as an "adjuster" in one New York city directory.

Sources Consulted for Above Biographies

Biographical Directory of American Congress. Washington, D.C.: U.S. Government Printing Office, 1971.
Biographical Directory of the State of New York. New York: Biographical Directory Company, 1899.
Johnson, Allen, ed. *Dictionary of American Biography.* 10 vols. New York: Scribner, 1927.
Leach, William R. *True Love and Perfect Union: The Feminist Reform of Sex and Society.* New York: Basic Books, 1980.
Levy, David W. *Herbert Croly of the New Republic: The Life and Thought of an American Progressive.* Princeton: Princeton University Press, 1985.
National Cyclopedia of American Biography. New York: James White, 1898.
Walters, Ronald G. *American Reformers, 1815–1860.* New York: Hill and Wang, 1978.
Who Was Who in America, Vol. 1 *(1897–1942).* Chicago: A. N. Marquis, 1943.
Wilson, James G., and John Fiske, eds. *Appleton's Cyclopedia of American Biography.* New York: D. Appleton, 1887.

For T. B. Wakeman, I have consulted: Wakeman Hartley, personal interview at home, Norfolk, Conn., 30 July 1984; obituary, *Greenwich Graphic,* 25 April 1913, p. 1; *Encyclopedia of Connecticut Biography: Genealogical, Memorial* (New York: American Historical Society, n.d.), 9:20–21; Robert H. Down, *A History of Silverton Country* (Portland, Oreg.: Berncliff, 1926), 221–22; "Thaddeus B. Wakeman," *Social Science*

Review 2 (28 April 1888): 2. *Who Was Who in America,* 1 (Chicago: Marquis Publications, 1968), 1:1287; obituary, *The Nation* 96 (1 May 1913): 447. His brother Abram was elected to the thirty-fourth Congress as a Whig with Know-Nothing support, but failed reelection as a Republican in 1856. Abram was important in state Republican circles and was appointed postmaster of New York City by President Lincoln, a post he held during most of the Civil War. See *Biographical Directory of the American Congress, 1774–1971* (Washington, D.C.: U.S. Government Printing Office, 1971), 1866.

SELECT BIBLIOGRAPHY

Primary Sources

Interview

Hartley, Wakeman. Domicile, Norfolk, Connecticut. Interview. 30 July 1984.

Manuscripts

Bernard, L. L. Papers. Pennsylvania State University, Historical Collections and
    Labor Archives, Pattee Library. University Park, Pa.
Codman, Charles A. "History of the City of Modern Times." N.d. Suffolk
    County Historical Society. Riverhead, N.Y.
Marble, Manton. Papers. Library of Congress. Washington, D.C.
Wakeman, Thaddeus B. Papers. Home of Wakeman Hartley. Norfolk, Conn.
Ward, Lester F. Papers. Brown University. Providence, R.I.
————. Papers. Library of Congress. Washington, D.C.

Newspapers and Magazines

Commonwealth, 1893
Evolution: A Weekly Review of Politics, Religion, Science, Literature, and Art, 1877
Iconoclast, 1870–1871
Modern Thinker, 1870–1873
New York World, 1866–1876

Books and Articles

Adams, Charles Francis, Jr. "The Era of Change." In *Late Nineteenth-Century
    American Liberalism: Representative Selections, 1880–1900.* Edited by Louis
    Filler. New York: Bobbs-Merrill, 1962.
Allen, Joseph Henry. *Positive Religion: Essays, Fragments and Hints.* Boston: Robert
    Bros., 1891.

Annual Catalogue of the Liberal University. N.p.: Torch of Reason Printing Office, 1900.

Bell, James D. "Lewes on Life and Mind." *Evolution* 1 (July 1877): 234–36.

———. Review of *Modern Philosophy,* by Francis Brown. *Evolution* 1 (July 1877): 295–96.

———. "Spencer's Sociology." *Evolution* 1 (July 1877): 213–14.

Bellamy, Edward. *Looking Backward, 2000–1887.* With an Introduction by John L. Thomas. Cambridge: Belknap Press, Harvard University Press, 1967.

———. "Nationalism—Principles." *Commonwealth* 1 (14 January 1893): 3–4.

———. "A Positive Romance." *Century* (August 1889): 625–30.

Commager, Henry Steele., ed. *Lester Ward and the Welfare State.* New York: Bobbs-Merrill, 1967.

Comte, Auguste. *A General View of Positivism.* Translated by J. H. Bridges. London: Routledge, 1910.

———. *The Positive Philosophy of Auguste Comte.* Translated by Harriet Martineau. New York: William Gowans, 1868.

———. *System of Positive Polity.* Translated by Richard Congreve. New York: Burt Franklin, 1966.

Courtlandt Palmer: Tributes Offered by Members of the Nineteenth Century Club to Its Founder and First President. New York: F. W. Christern, 1889.

Croly, David G. "Creation, God, Soul, Hereafter: The Four Fruitless Problems." *Modern Thinker* 2 (1873).

———. [D. Goodman, pseud.]. "King Wealth Coming." *Modern Thinker* 1 (1870): 45–47.

———. "Personal Representation." *Galaxy* 4 (July 1867): 307–14.

———. "Religion Reconstructed." *Modern Thinker* 1 (1870).

———. "Remarks by Editor." *Modern Thinker* 1 (1870).

———. "Stewart–Astor–Vanderbilt: Letters Addressed to Three Millionaires on the Social Function of Wealth." *Modern Thinker* 2 (1873).

———. "What the Matter Is." *Modern Thinker* 2 (1873).

Croly, Herbert D. Introduction to *Social Discovery: An Approach to the Study of Functional Groups,* by Eduard C. Lindeman. New York: Republic, 1924.

———. "The Memoirs of Herbert Croly: An Unpublished Document." Edited by Charles Hirschfeld. *New York History* 58 (July 1977): 313–29.

———. *Progressive Democracy.* New York: Macmillan, 1914.

———. *The Promise of American Life.* New York: Macmillan, 1909.

———. "A School of Social Research." *New Republic* (8 June 1918): 167–71.

"The Death and Funeral of Hugh Byron Brown." *Truth Seeker* 25 (6 August 1898): 504.

DeGrange, McQuilkin. *The Curve of Societal Movement.* Hanover, N.H.: The Sociological Press, 1930.

———. *The Nature and Elements of Sociology.* New Haven: Yale University Press, 1953.

Dudley, Elizabeth. "The New York Positivists." *Old and New* 3 (1873): 299–304.

Edger, Henry. *Auguste Comte and the Middle Ages.* Pozsony, Hungary: H. Edger, 1885.

———. *The Positive Community: Glimpse of the Regenerated Future of the Human Race.* Modern Times, N.Y.: Positive Typographical Fund, 1863.

———. *The Positivist Calendar: Or, Transitional System of Public Commemoration Instituted by Auguste Comte.* Modern Times, N.Y.: H. Edger, 1856.

Etienne, Louis. "Le Positivisme dans l'histoire." *Revue des deux mondes* 74 (1868): 375–408.

Fisk, Ethel F., ed. *The Letters of John Fiske.* New York: Macmillan, 1940.

Hall, G. Stanley. *Life and Confessions of a Psychologist.* New York: D. Appleton, 1924.

Harrison, Frederic. "Auguste Comte in America." *Positivist Review* 102 (1 June 1901): 121–25.

———. "Mr. Lewes' Problems of Life and Mind." *Fortnightly Review* 16 (July–December 1874): 89–101.

Henderson, G. L. *The Positive Catechism: A Text Book on Religion, Philosophy and Morals.* New York: New York Liberal Publishing, 1878. Published in two parts.

"In Memoriam David Goodman Croly. Estimates of His Life and Work." *Real Estate Record and Builder's Guide* 43 (18 May 1889): 3–11.

Lenzer, Gertrud, ed. *Auguste Comte and Positivism: The Essential Writings.* New York: Harper and Row, 1975.

Lonchampt, Joseph. *Positivist Prayer.* Translated by John G. Mills. Goshen, N.Y.: Independent Republican Job Office, 1877.

Memories of Jane Cunningham Croly—"Jenny June." New York: Putnam, 1904.

Mill, John Stuart. *Auguste Comte and Positivism.* London, 1865. Ann Arbor: University of Michigan Press, 1961.

Officers, Members and Constitution of the Nineteenth Century Club . . . 1899–1900. New York: n.p., n.d.

Palmer, Courtlandt. *Aims, Objects and Methods of the Nineteenth Century Club of New York.* New York: n.p., 1886.

———. *The Cause of Humanity, Or, the Waning and Rising Faith: An Essay from the Standpoint of the Positive Philosophy.* New York: New York Liberal Publishing, 1879.

———. "European Aristocracy: Its Responsibilities and Opportunities." *Westminster Review* 128 (August 1887): 620–26.

———. *How Peace May Be Found Under the Faith of Science and Humanity.* New York: by the author, n.d.

———. *The Nineteenth Century Club of New York, Shall Similar Associations Become General?* London: William Reeves, 1887.

———. *The Spiritual Life.* New York: n.p. (1883?)

Real Estate Record and Builder's Guide 43 (13 May 1889): 3–11.

Ross, Edward Alsworth. *Foundations of Sociology.* New York: MacMillan, 1905.

———. *Seventy Years of It: An Autobiography.* New York: Arno, 1977. [Originally published 1936]

———. *Social Control: A Survey of the Foundations of Order.* Edited and with an Introduction by J. Weinberg, G. J. Hinkle, and R. C. Hinkle. Cleveland: Case Western Reserve University Press, 1969. [Originally published 1901]

Small, Albion W. "A Comtean Centenary." *American Journal of Sociology* 27 (1921–1922): 510–13.

———. "The Era of Sociology." *American Journal of Sociology* 1 (1895): 1–15.

———. "The Evolution of a Social Standard." *American Journal of Sociology* 20 (1914–1915): 10–17.

———. "Fifty Years of Sociology in the United States, 1865–1915." *American Journal of Sociology* 21 (1916): 721–864.

———. *General Sociology.* Chicago: University of Chicago Press, 1905.

————. "Lester Frank Ward." *American Journal of Sociology* 19 (1913–1914): 61–78.

————. "The Letters of Albion W. Small to Lester F. Ward. I–IV." *Social Forces* 12, 13, 15 (1933, 1935, 1936, 1937).

————. *The Meaning of Social Science.* Chicago: University of Chicago Press, 1910.

————. *Origins of Sociology.* New York: Russell and Russell, 1967. [Originally published 1924]

————. "Scholarship and Social Agitation." *American Journal of Sociology* 1 (1895): 564–82.

————. "Static and Dynamic Sociology." *American Journal of Sociology* 1 (1895): 195–209.

Small, Albion, and George E. Vincent. *An Introduction to the Study of Society.* New York: American Book, 1894.

"The Society of Humanity." *Commonwealth: A Monthly Magazine and Library of Sociology* 1 (1894): 3.

Somerby, C. P. "Aims and Objects." *Commonwealth* 1 (14 January 1893): 2.

Stern, Bernhard J., ed. *Young Ward's Diary.* New York: Putnam, 1935.

Thompson, Kenneth, ed. *Auguste Comte: The Foundations of Sociology.* New York: John Wiley and Sons, 1975.

Wakeman, Thaddeus Burr. *Addresses of Thaddeus Burr Wakeman at and in Reference to the First Monist Congress.* Cos Cob, Conn: by the author, 1913.

————. "Auguste Comte and Philosophy in America." *Open Court* 3 (24 October 1889): 1902–4.

————. "Emancipation by Nationalism." *Arena* 4 (October 1891): 591–603.

————. *An Epitome of the Positive Philosophy and Religion.* New York: Society of Humanity, 1877.

————. *Ernst Haeckel.* New York: D. Appleton, 1891.

————. *Evolution or Creation?* New York: National Liberal League, 1883.

————. *An Extension and Enlargement of the Positive Classification of the Sciences.* New York: New York Liberal Publishing, 1881.

————. *Free Thought: Past, Present and Future.* Chicago: H. L. Green, 1899?

————. "The Latest Phase of Herbert Spencer's Philosophy." *Open Court* 5 (13 August 1891): 2907–9.

————. "The Nature of the Soul." *Open Court* 5 (7 December 1891): 3057–59.

————. "A New Nation." *Commonwealth* 1 (February 1893): 3–5.

————. "The New York–Manhattan Liberal Club: The Story of Its Past and Present, and a Prophecy of Its Future." *Truth Seeker* 1 (23 January 1909): 50–51.

————. "Only One World After All! But That Infinite." *Open Court* 3 (7 November 1889): 1925–28.

————. "Our Future Polity." *Open Court* 5 (30 April 1891): 2790–91.

————. "Our Unchurched Millions." *Arena* 2 (October 1890): 604–13.

————. "Politics and the People." *Nationalist* 2 (December 1889): 11–17.

————. *The Religion of Humanity.* New York: New York Liberal Publishing, 1878.

————. "Science and Prayer." *North American Review* 137 (July 1883): 193–203.

————. *Science Is Religion: The Monist Religion.* Los Angeles: Singleton W. Davis, 1905.

————. "Shall We Have a New Calendar?" *Man: A Monthly Journal of Progress and Reform* 2 (April 1882): 1.

————. "The Sociology of Free Trade and Protection." *Social Science Review* 2 (28 April 1888): 3–6.

————. *Thomas Paine: The Father of Republics.* New York: Truth Seeker, 1899.

————. "The Universal Faith: A Memorial Address Upon Mr. Courtlandt Palmer." *Open Court* 2 (3 January 1889): 1391–94.

———— . "The Universal Faith: A Monistic, Positive, Human, Constructive Religion." *Open Court* 3 (25 April 1889): 1583–86.

Ward, Lester F. *Applied Sociology: A Treatise on the Conscious Improvement of Society by Society.* Boston: Ginn, 1906.

————. "Book Reviews." *Open Court* 9 (22 August 1895).

————. "Collective Telesis." *American Journal of Sociology* 2 (1897): 801–22.

————. "Contemporary Sociology." *American Journal of Sociology* 7 (1902): 475–500.

————. *Dynamic Sociology or Applied Social Sciences as Based Upon Statistical Sociology and the Less Complex Sciences.* 2 vols. New York: D. Appleton, 1883.

————. "Economics—General." *Commonwealth* 1 (14 January 1893): 5.

————. "Evolution of Social Structures." *American Journal of Sociology* 10 (1905): 589–605.

————. *Glimpses of the Cosmos.* 6 vols. New York: Putnam, 1913–1918.

————. "The Place of Sociology." *American Journal of Sociology* 1 (July 1895): 16–27.

————. "The Proper Functions of Government." *Commonwealth* 1 (11 March 1893): 3–4.

————. *Psychic Factors of Civilization.* Boston: Ginn, 1897.

————. *Pure Sociology: A Treatise on the Origin and Spontaneous Development of Society.* New York: Macmillan, 1903.

————. "Religion and Progress." *Iconoclast* 1 (September, 1870): 2.

————. "A Religion Without a God." *Iconoclast* 2 (June 1871): 1.

————. "Religious Influence of Science." *Iconoclast* 1 (15 November 1870): 1.

————. "Revealed Religion vs. Human Progress." *Iconoclast* 1 (November 1870): 2.

————. "The Rising School." *Iconoclast* 1 (December 1870): 2.

————. "The Situation." *Iconoclast* 1 (March 1870): 1.

————. "Social Genesis." *American Journal of Sociology* 2 (1897): 532–46.

————. "The Sociology of Political Parties." *American Journal of Sociology* 13 (January 1908): 439–54.

Youmans, Edward L., ed. *Herbert Spencer on the Americans and the Americans on Herbert Spencer.* New York: D. Appleton, 1883.

Secondary Sources

Books and Articles

Ahlstrom, Sydney E. *A Religious History of the American People.* New Haven: Yale University Press, 1972.

Bannister, Robert. *Social Darwinism: Science and Myth in Anglo-American Social Thought.* Philadelphia: Temple University Press, 1979.

————. *Sociology and Scientism: The American Quest for Objectivity, 1880–1940.* Chapel Hill: University of North Carolina Press, 1987.

Becker, Ernest. *The Lost Science of Man.* New York: George Braziller, 1971.

————. *The Structure of Evil: An Essay on the Unification the Science of Man.* New York: George Braziller, 1968.

Bender, Thomas. *New York Intellect: A History of Intellectual Life in New York City, From 1750 to the Beginnings of Our Own Time.* New York: Knopf, 1987.

Benton, Ted. *Philosophical Foundations of the Three Sociologies.* London: Routledge and Kegan Paul, 1977.

Bernard, L. L., and Jessie Bernard. *Origins of American Sociology: The Social Science Movement in the United States.* New York: Crowell, 1943.

Bertier de Sauvigny, Guillaume de. *The Bourbon Restoration.* Translated by Lynn M. Case. Philadelphia: University of Pennsylvania Press, 1966.

Bierstedt, Robert. *American Sociological Theory: A Critical History.* New York: Academic Press, 1981.

Bloch, J. M. "The Rise of the New York World." Ph.D. dissertation, Harvard University, 1941.

Boelsche, Wilhelm. *Haeckel: His Life and Work.* Translated by Joseph McCabe. Philadelphia: G. W. Jacobs, 1906.

Boller, Paul F., Jr. *American Thought in Transition: The Impact of Evolutionary Naturalism, 1865–1900.* Chicago: Rand McNally, 1969. Reprint, New York: University Press of America, 1981.

Bowman, Sylvia E. *The Year 2000: A Critical Biography of Edward Bellamy.* New York: Bookman, 1958.

Bozeman, Theodore D. *Protestants in an Age of Science: The Baconian Ideal and Antebellum American Religious Thought.* Chapel Hill: University of North Carolina Press, 1977.

Bramson, Leon. *The Political Context of Sociology.* Princeton: Princeton University Press, 1961.

Cape, Emily. *Lester F. Ward: A Personal Sketch.* New York: Putnam, 1922.

Carter, Paul A. *The Spiritual Crisis of the Gilded Age.* DeKalb: Northern Illinois University Press, 1971.

Cashdollar, Charles D. "European Positivism and the American Unitarians." *Church History* 45 (1976): 490–506.

————. *The Transformation of Theology, 1830–1890: Positivism and Protestant Thought in Britain and America.* Princeton: Princeton University Press, 1989.

Chamberlain, John. *Farewell to Reform: The Rise, Life and Decay of the Progressive Mind in America.* New York: John Day, 1933.

Charlton, D. G. *Positivist Thought in France During the Second Empire, 1852–1870.* New York: Oxford University Press, 1959.

Chugerman, Samuel. *Lester F. Ward: The American Aristotle—A Summary and Interpretation of His Sociology.* Durham: Duke University Press, 1939.

Cohen, Morris. "Later Philosophy." In *Cambridge History of American Literature,* edited by William P. Trent et al., 3:226–65. Cambridge: Cambridge University Press, 1943.

Coser, Lewis. *Masters of Sociological Thought.* New York: Harcourt Brace Jovanovich, 1971.

Cravens, Hamilton. "The Abandonment of Evolutionary Social Theory in America: The Impact of Academic Professionalization Upon American Sociological Theory, 1890–1920." *American Studies* 12 (1971): 5–20.

Daniels, George H. *American Science in the Age of Jackson*. New York: Columbia University Press, 1968.

Destler, Chester M. *American Radicalism, 1865–1901*. Chicago: Quadrangle, 1966. [Originally published 1946]

Dexter, Byron. "Herbert Croly and the Promise of American Life." *Political Science Quarterly* 70 (1955): 197–218.

Dibble, Vernon K. *The Legacy of Albion Small*. Chicago: University of Chicago Press, 1975.

Down, Robert H. *A History of the Silverton Country*. Portland, Oreg.: Berncliff, 1926.

Filler, Louis, ed. *Late Nineteenth-Century American Liberalism: Representative Selections, 1880–1900*. New York: Bobbs-Merrill, 1962.

Fine, Sidney. *Laissez-Faire and the General-Welfare State: A Study of Conflict in American Thought, 1865–1901*. Ann Arbor: University of Michigan Press, 1956.

Fine, William F. *Progressive Evolutionism and American Sociology, 1890–1920*. N.p.: UMI Research Press, 1979.

Flack, J. Kirkpatrick. *Desideratum in Washington: The Intellectual Community in the Capital City, 1870–1900*. Cambridge, Mass.: Schenkman, 1975.

Fleming, Donald. *John William Draper and the Religion of Science*. Philadelphia: University of Pennsylvania Press, 1950.

Flower, Elizabeth, and Murray G. Murphey. *A History of Philosophy in America*. New York: Capricorn, 1977.

Forcey, Charles. *The Crossroads of Liberalism: Croly, Weyl, Lippman and the Progressive Era, 1900–1925*. New York: Oxford University Press, 1961.

Fredrickson, George M. *The Inner Civil War: Northern Intellectuals and the Crisis of the Union*. New York: Harper and Row, 1965.

———. "Intellectuals and the Labor Question in Late Nineteenth-Century America." Paper delivered at the annual meeting of the American Historical Association, New York, December 1985 (in author's possession).

Furner, Mary. *Advocacy and Objectivity: A Crisis in the Professionalization of American Social Science, 1865–1905*. Lexington: University of Kentucky Press, 1975.

Gabriel, Ralph H. *The Course of American Democratic Thought: An Intellectual History Since 1815*. New York. Ronald Press, 1956 (2d ed.).

Garraty, John A. *The New Commonwealth, 1877–1890*. New York: Harper and Row, 1968.

Gasman, Daniel. *The Scientific Origins of National Socialism: Social Darwinism in Ernst Haeckel and the German Monist League*. New York: American Elsevier, 1971.

Goldman, Eric F. *Rendezvous With Destiny: A History of Modern American Reform*. New York: Knopf, 1963.

Goodwyn, Lawrence. *The Populist Moment: A Short History of the Agrarian Revolt in America*. New York: Oxford University Press, 1978.

Graebner, William. "The Unstable World of Benjamin Spock: Social Engineering in a Democratic Culture, 1917–1950." *Journal of American History* 67 (1980): 612–29.

Halfpenny, Peter. *Positivism and Sociology: Explaining Social Life*. London: Allen and Unwin; 1982.

Hall, David D. "The Victorian Connection." In *Victorian America*. Edited by Daniel W. Howe. Philadelphia: University of Pennsylvania Press, 1976.

SELECT BIBLIOGRAPHY

Harp, Gillis J. " 'The Church of Humanity': New York's Worshipping Positivists." *Church History* 60 (1991): 508–23.

Hartz, Louis. *The Liberal Tradition in America: An Interpretation of American Political Thought Since the Revolution.* New York: Harcourt, Brace and World, 1955.

Haskell, Thomas L. *The Emergence of Professional Social Science: The American Social Science Association and the Nineteenth-Century Crisis of Authority.* Urbana: University of Illinois Press, 1977.

Hawkins, Richmond L. *Auguste Comte and the United States, 1816–1853.* Cambridge: Harvard University Press, 1936.

———. *Positivism in the United States, 1853–1861.* Cambridge: Harvard University Press, 1938.

Hays, Samuel P. *The Response to Industrialism, 1885–1914.* Chicago: University of Chicago Press, 1957.

Hinkle, Roscoe C. *Founding Theory of American Sociology, 1881– 1915.* London: Routledge and Kegan Paul, 1980.

Hirschfeld, Charles, ed., "The Memoirs of Herbert Croly: An Unpublished Document." *New York History* 58 (July 1977): 313–29.

Hofstadter, Richard. "Abraham Lincoln and the Self-Made Myth." In his *The American Political Tradition and the Men Who Made It.* New York: Random House, 1973.

———. *Social Darwinism in American Thought.* Boston: Beacon, 1955.

Hollinger, David A. "Historians and the Discourse of Intellectuals." In *New Directions in American Intellectual History.* Edited by John Higham and Paul K. Conkin. Baltimore: Johns Hopkins University Press, 1979.

House, Floyd N. *The Development of Sociology.* Chicago: University of Chicago Press, 1936.

Howe, Daniel Walker. "European Sources of Political Ideas in Jeffersonian America." *Reviews in American History* 10 (1982): 28–44.

———. *The Political Culture of the American Whigs.* Chicago: University of Chicago Press, 1979.

———, ed. *Victorian America.* Philadelphia: University of Pennsylvania Press, 1976.

Hughes, H. Stuart. *Consciousness and Society: The Reorientation of European Social Thought, 1890–1930.* New York: Random House, 1958.

Huston, James L. "A Political Response to Industrialism: The Republican Embrace of Protectionist Labor Doctrine." *Journal of American History* 70 (June 1983): 35–57.

Kaplan, Sidney. "The Miscegenation Issue in the Election of 1874." *Journal of Negro History* 34 (July 1949): 274–343.

Keller, Morton. *Affairs of State: Public Life in Late Nineteenth Century America.* Cambridge: Harvard University Press, 1977.

Kent, Christopher. *Brains and Numbers: Elitism, Comtism, and Democracy in Mid-Victorian England.* Toronto: University of Toronto Press, 1978.

Kloppenberg, James T. *Uncertain Victory: Social Democracy and Progressivism in European and American Thought, 1870–1920.* New York: Oxford University Press, 1986.

Kolakowski, Leszek. *The Alienation of Reason: A History of Positivist Thought.* Translated by Norman Guterman. Garden City, N.Y.: Doubleday, 1968.

Kuklick, Bruce. *The Rise of American Philosophy, 1860–1930.* Cambridge: Harvard University Press, 1977.

Lacey, Michael. "The National Seminary of Learning: Washington Scientists and the Rise of the Modern State in the Late Nineteenth Century." Paper delivered at the annual meeting of the American Historical Association, Washington, D.C., December 1982 (in author's possession).

Lasch, Christopher. *The True and Only Heaven: Progress and Its Critics*. New York: Norton, 1991.

Leach, William. *True Love and Perfect Union: The Feminist Reform of Sex and Society*. New York: Basic Books, 1980.

Lears, T. J. Jackson. *No Place of Grace: Antimodernism and the Transformation of American Culture, 1880–1920*. New York: Parthenon, 1981.

Levy, David W. *Herbert Croly of the New Republic: The Life and Thought of an American Progressive*. Princeton, N.J.: Princeton University Press, 1985.

———. "The Life and Thought of Herbert Croly, 1869–1914." Ph.D. dissertation, University of Wisconsin, 1967.

Levy-Bruhl, Lucien. *The Philosophy of Auguste Comte*. Translated by Kathleen de Beaumont-Klein. New York: Putnam, 1903.

Link, Arthur S., and Richard L. McCormick. *Progressivism*. Arlington Heights, Ill.: Harlan Davidson, 1983.

Lipow, Arthur. *Authoritarian Socialism in America: Edward Bellamy and the Nationalist Movement*. Berkeley and Los Angeles: University of California Press, 1982.

Lustig, R. Jeffery. *Corporate Liberalism: The Origins of Modern American Political Theory, 1890–1920*. Berkeley and Los Angeles: University of California Press, 1982.

MacDonald, George E. *Fifty Years of Freethought—Being the Story of the Truth Seeker, with the Natural History of its Third Editor*. New York: Truth Seeker, 1929.

Mandelbaum, Maurice. *History, Man and Reason: A Study in Nineteenth-Century Thought*. Baltimore: Johns Hopkins University Press, 1971.

Marsden, George M. *Fundamentalism and American Culture: The Shaping of Twentieth-Century Evangelicalism, 1870–1925*. New York: Oxford University Press, 1980.

Martindale, Donald. *The Nature and Types of Sociological Theory*. Boston: Houghton Mifflin, 1960.

———. "The Roles of Humanism and Scientism in the Evolution of Sociology." In *Social Change: Explorations, Diagnoses, and Conjectures*. Edited by G. Zollschan and W. Hirsch. New York: Wiley, 1976.

Marvin, F. S. *Comte: The Founder of Sociology*. New York: John Wiley, 1937.

Matthews, Frederick. *Quest for an American Sociology: Robert E. Park and the Chicago School*. Montreal: McGill-Queen's University Press, 1977.

May, Henry F. *End of American Innocence: Study of the First Years of Our Own Time, 1912–1917*. New York: Knopf, 1959.

McGee, John Edwin. *A Crusade for Humanity: The History of Organized Positivism in England*. London: Watt, 1931.

McJimsey, George T. *Genteel Partisan: Manton Marble, 1834–1917*. Ames: Iowa State University Press, 1971.

Meyer, D. H. "American Intellectuals and the Victorian Crisis of Faith." In *Victorian America*. Edited by Daniel W. Howe. Philadelphia: University of Pennsylvania Press, 1976.

Meyers, Marvin. *The Jacksonian Persuasion: Politics and Belief*. New York: Random House, 1960.

Nelson, Alvin F. "Lester Ward's Conception of the Nature of Science." *Journal of the History of Ideas* 33 (1972): 633–38.

Noble, Daniel W. *The Paradox of Progressive Thought.* Minneapolis: University of Minnesota Press, 1958.

Oleson, Alexander, and John Voss, eds. *The Organization of Knowledge in Modern America, 1860–1920.* Baltimore: Johns Hopkins University Press, 1979.

Palmer, Bruce. *"Man Over Money": The Southern Populist Critique of American Capitalism.* Chapel Hill: University of North Carolina Press, 1980.

Parrington, Veron L. *Main Currents in American Thought.* Vol. 3. New York: Harcourt, Brace and World, 1958.

Peardon, Thomas P. Introduction to *The Second Treatise on Government,* by John Locke. Indianapolis: Bobbs-Merrill, 1952.

Peel, J. D. Y., ed. *Herbert Spencer on Social Evolution.* Chicago: University of Chicago Press, 1972.

Persons, Stow. *Free Religion: An American Faith.* New Haven: Yale University Press, 1947.

Quint, Howard. *The Forging of American Socialism: Origins of the Modern Movement* Columbia: University of South Carolina Press, 1953.

Riley, Woodbridge. "La Philosophie française en Amérique." *Revue philosophique de la France et de l'étranger* 87 (1919): 369–423.

Ross, Dorothy R. "Liberalism." In *Encyclopedia of American Political History: Studies of the Principal Movements and Ideas.* 2 vols. Edited by Jack P. Greene. New York: Scribner, 1984, 1:750–63.

———. *The Origins of American Social Science.* Cambridge: Cambridge University Press, 1991.

———. "Socialism and American Liberalism: Academic Social Thought in the 1880s." *Perspectives in American History* 11 (1977–1978): 5–80.

Russett, Cynthia Eagle. *Darwin in America: The Intellectual Response, 1865–1912.* San Francisco: Freeman, 1976.

Schiffman, Joseph, ed. *Edward Bellamy: Selected Writings on Religion and Society.* New York: Liberal Arts, 1955.

Schlesinger, Arthur M., Jr. Introduction to *The Promise of American Life,* by Herbert Croly. Edited by Arthur M. Schlesinger, Jr. Cambridge: Belknap Press, Harvard University Press, 1965.

Schlesinger, Arthur M., Jr., and Morton White, eds. *Paths of American Thought.* Boston: Houghton Mifflin, 1963.

Schneider, Robert E. *Positivism in the United States: The Apostleship of Henry Edger.* Argentina: Rosario, 1946

Scott, Clifford H. *Lester Frank Ward.* Boston: G. K. Hall, 1976.

Seideman, David. *The New Republic: A Voice of Modern Liberalism.* New York: Praeger, 1986.

Shearer, Benjamin Francis. "The Positivist Ideal in the United States: The Origins and Reform of the New Machine." Ph.D. dissertation, Saint Louis University, 1978.

Simon, W. M. *European Positivism in the Nineteenth Century: An Essay in Intellectual History.* Ithaca, N.Y.: Cornell University Press, 1963.

Sklar, Katherine Kish. *Catherine Beecher: A Study in American Domesticity.* New Haven: Yale University Press, 1973.

Sklar, Martin J. *The Corporate Reconstruction of American Capitalism, 1890–1916.* Cambridge: Cambridge University Press, 1988.

Somkin, Fred. *Unquiet Eagle: Memory and Desire in the Idea of American Freedom, 1815–1860.* Ithaca: Cornell University Press, 1967.

Spann, Edward K. *The New Metropolis: New York City, 1840–1857.* New York: Columbia University Press, 1981.

Still, Bayrd. *Mirror For Gotham: New York As Seen by Contemporaries From Dutch Days to the Present.* New York: New York University Press, 1956.

Thomas, John L. *Alternative America.* Cambridge: Harvard University Press, 1983.

———. Introduction to *Looking Backward, 2000–1887,* by Edward Bellamy. Cambridge: Belknap Press, Harvard University Press, 1967.

Trachtenberg, Alan. *The Incorporation of America: Culture and Society in the Gilded Age.* New York: Hill and Wang, 1982.

Turner, James. *Without God, Without Creed: The Origins of Unbelief in America.* Baltimore: Johns Hopkins University Press, 1985.

Vernon, Richard. "Auguste Comte and the Withering Away of the State." *Journal of the History of Ideas* 45 (1984): 549–66.

Vidich, Arthur J., and Stanford M. Lyman. *American Sociology: Worldly Rejections of Religion and Their Directions.* New Haven: Yale University Press, 1985.

Walters, Ronald G. *American Reformers, 1815–1860.* New York: Hill and Wang, 1978.

Warren, Sidney. *American Freethought, 1860–1914.* New York: Columbia University Press, 1943.

Weinberg, J., G. J. Hinkle, and R. C. Hinkle. Introduction to *Social Control: A Survey of the Foundations of Order,* by Edward A. Ross. Cleveland: Case Western Reserve University Press, 1969. [Originally published 1901]

Welter, Rush. *The Mind of America, 1820–1860.* New York: Columbia University Press, 1975.

White, Morton. *Social Thought in America: The Revolt Against Formalism.* Boston: Beacon, 1957.

Wiebe, Robert H. *The Search for Order, 1877–1920.* New York: Hill and Wang, 1967.

Wilentz, Sean. *Chants Democratic: New York City and the Rise of the American Working Class, 1788–1850.* New York: Oxford University Press, 1984.

Wilson, Edmund. "H.C." *New Republic* (16 July 1930): 266–68.

Wilson, R. Jackson. *In Quest of Community: Social Philosophy in the United States, 1860–1920.* New York: Wiley, 1968.

Wunderlich, Roger. *Low Living and High Thinking at Modern Times, New York.* Syracuse: Syracuse University Press, 1992.

INDEX